Script Culture
and the
American Screenplay

                    BRIGID:
          [. . .] I told him . . . Yea . . . But please
          believe me, Sam. I wouldn't have told him if I
          had thought Floyd would kill him. I wouldn't for
          a minute . . .

                    SPADE:
                    (interrupting)
          If you thought he wouldn't kill Miles, you were
          right, Angel.

                    BRIGID:
                    (her upraised face holds utter astonishment)
          Didn't he?

                    SPADE:
          Miles hadn't many brains but he had too many
          years experience as a detective to be caught like
          that - by a man he was shadowing - up a blind
          alley with his gun tucked away in his hip and his
          overcoat buttoned.
                    (he takes his hand away from her shoulder,
          looks at her for a long moment smiling, then:)
          But he would have gone up there with you, Angel.
          He was just dumb enough for that. He'd have
          looked you up and down and licked his lips and
          gone grinning from ear to ear. And then you could
          have stood as close to him as you liked in the
          dark and put a hole through him with the gun you
          had gotten from Thursby that evening.

          Brigid shrinks back from him until the edge of the
          table stops her.

                    BRIGID:
                    (staring with terrified eyes)
          Don't - don't talk to me like that, Sam. You know
          I didn't . . . you know -

                    SPADE:
          Stop it!
                    (he glances at the clock)
          The police will be blowing in any minute now.
          Talk!

Script Culture
and the
American Screenplay

Kevin Alexander Boon

Wayne State University Press
DETROIT

© 2008 by Wayne State University Press, Detroit, Michigan 48201.
All rights reserved.
No part of this book may be reproduced without formal permission.
Manufactured in the United States of America.
12 11 10 09 08   5 4 3 2 1

Library of Congress Cataloging-in-Publication Data
Boon, Kevin A.
Script culture and the American screenplay / Kevin Alexander Boon.
p. cm. — (Contemporary approaches to film and television series)
Includes bibliographical references and index.
ISBN-13: 978-0-8143-3263-4 (pbk. : alk. paper)
ISBN-10: 0-8143-3263-3 (pbk. : alk. paper)
1. Motion picture authorship. I. Title.
PN1996.B665 2008
812'.0309—dc22
2007029907

Some of the material in this book appeared in a different form
in *Creative Screenwriting* between 1994 and 2001.

∞ The paper used in this publication meets the minimum requirements
of the American National Standard for Information Sciences—
Permanence of Paper for Printed Library Materials, ANSI Z39.48-1984.

Designed and typeset by Maya Rhodes
Composed in Courier Std and Dante MT

Contents

Preface

I spent part of my youth among the community theater crowd, performing in amateur stage productions of plays such as *1984* and *You Can't Take It with You,* and auditioning for minor, walk-on parts whenever some rogue film company found its way into central Florida. Only occasionally did I find myself in front of the camera, and when I did my efforts usually wound up carpeting the floor of the cutting room. Nevertheless, those auditions were my first introduction to screenplays, which seemed to me at the time to differ only slightly from theatrical stage plays.

When I began to write, I considered the screenplay just as viable a literary form as the novel, the short story, and the stage play, and I approached screenplays with the same interest that I approached other narratives. It was not until I began my graduate studies in English that I discovered how much the screenplay and screenwriter were marginalized by the film industry, the academy, and the literati. Literary scholarship, while fully absorbed with drama, ignored the screenplay, and film studies, though aware of the screenplay as an interstitial cog in the filmmaking process, only occasionally cast a critical eye toward the written text, which had been the controlling narrative voice in most contemporary American film production for nearly a century. Even Peter Brunette and David Wills's engaging *Screen/Play* (Princeton University Press, 1989), which effectively argues that film is a "type of writing" (61), avoids discussion of the writing that prescribes film. In light of the screenplay's pervasive influence over the twentieth century, the limited mention of the screenplay in both film and literary studies struck me as curious.

In the absence of adequate critical scholarship, screenplay analysis has fallen primarily under the auspices of vocational instruction. Much of what has been written about the screenplay over the last twenty-five years can be classified into three general types: books on the business of screenwriting, how-to books on screenwriting, and books on the structure of storytelling. There are exceptions, such as Kristen Thompson's *Storytelling in the New Hollywood*, which critiques storytelling and its relationship to Hollywood films, Lance Lee's *A Poetics for Screenwriters*, which attempts to establish aesthetic principles for screenwriting, Marsha McCreadie's *The Women Who Write the Movies*, which chronicles the shifting role of women screenwriters in the film industry, and Andrew Horton's *Screenwriting for a Global Market*[1] (perhaps the closest example of screenplay scholarship to date), but most screenwriting books are instructional. Books such as Jennifer Lerch's *500 Ways to Beat the Hollywood Script Reader* and Carlos de Abreu and Howard Jay Smith's *Opening the Doors to Hollywood* focus on the business of screenwriting, the how and where of selling a screenplay. Books such as Syd Field's influential *Screenplay*, Linda J. Cowgill's *Secrets of Screenplay Structure*, Alan A. Armer's *Writing the Screenplay*, Robin U. Russin and William Missouri Downs's *Screenplay: Writing the Picture*, and Tudor Gates's *Scenario: The Craft of Screenwriting*, among myriad others, focus on practical methods for writing a screenplay. Books such as Mark Axelrod's *Aspects of the Screenplay* and Lajos Egri's *The Art of Dramatic Writing* focus on the craft of storytelling. These three categories denote general trends in the works; however, inevitable overlap occurs within works as books that focus on storytelling also offer some practical writing advice and technical books necessarily touch on storytelling. Books, such as Christopher Keane's *How to Write a Selling Screenplay* and David Trottier's *The Screenwriter's Bible*, intentionally combine categories.

The lack of critical attention paid to screenplays has not been lost on screenwriters, many of whom expected screenwriters to achieve more status than they actually have. Jeanie Macpherson, who enjoyed a forty-year collaboration with Cecil B. DeMille in the early days of film, predicted in 1917 that "photo-dramatists" would become "as well known and as distinguished as the dramatists of the speaking stage . . . [and that] photodramatic writers . . . [would] be given their proper place and . . . be remembered for their contributions toward this new art" (qtd. in Francke 18). Ninety years later, we still find screenwriters, such as Guillermo Arriaga, author of *Babel* (2006) and *21 Grams*

---

1. See also Horton's *Laughing Out Loud: Writing the Comedy-Centered Screenplay*, which, despite its title, offers more than mere writing tips.

(2003), struggling for adequate recognition. Arriaga aggravated director Alejandro González Iñárritu by claiming that he, as the writer of
21 Grams, deserved much of the credit for that film's success. Arriaga
explains, "When they say it's an auteur film, I say auteurs film. I have
always been against the 'film by' credit on a movie. It's a collaborative
process and it deserves several authors" (Rafferty 13). Actors frequently
acknowledge the overarching significance of the screenplay and its critical contribution to film. William H. Macy, in an interview for *The Cooler*
(2003), credits the screenplay for the establishment of character, claiming, "as an actor you need to go out and learn some skills, but in terms
of preparation for understanding the character, it's all on the page, and
if it's not on the page, you're in trouble. If it ain't on the page, the audience isn't going to understand it" (Mitchell n.p.). Directors, too, often
acknowledge the indispensable importance of the screenplay. Director
Brett Ratner admits, "If it's not on the page, then I'm not going to do
it. I can't create it" (Stack n.p.). Macy's and Ratner's comments echo a
belief that can be traced back to the early days of film: *If it's not on the
page, it's not on the stage.*

Screenplays occupy a space somewhere between literary studies
and film studies. Because they are written texts, they share an affinity
with other written forms. The dramatic principles at work in screenplays are the same as those in fiction and stage plays, thus they share a
common literary heritage tracing back to Hellenistic theater, and are
amenable to the earliest literary criticism—Aristotle's *Poetics.* Because
they are an integral part of the filmmaking process, screenplays are important to our understanding of the complex dynamic that embodies
film production.

Three characteristics distinguish screenplay studies from traditional film studies. First and foremost, the primary object under examination in screenplay studies should be the written text. This does not
preclude reference or discussion of the film. A screenplay and its resul-
tant film are intimately linked, which often makes reference to the film
unavoidable in the same way the film studies scholars are sometimes
compelled to make reference to a film's screenplay. Second, screenplay
studies posit the writer (or writers) as the author of the work (i.e., the
screenplay), and, at least, *an* author of the film, as Arriaga argues. The
dynamic interplay between a screenwriter's vision and a director's vision are ultimately what we see on a screen, and the interaction be-

tween writing and filming are worthy of critical inquiry. This is no less true when directors author their own screenplays, as a director's vision as a writer may differ from his or her vision as a director. Third, screenplay studies, like literary studies, should illuminate a reader's understanding of a text, and thereby differentiate itself from pedagogy. The primary objective of screenplay studies should not be to help readers write screenplays any more than the primary objective of Hemingway scholarship is to help the reader write novels and short stories.

Script Culture and the American Screenplay is an attempt to partially redress the dearth of scholarship involving the screenplay and argue for the importance of the screenplay as worthy of critical examination in both literary and film studies. The book is divided into two sections. Part 1 (Foundations) offers three foundational discussions of the screenplay, tracing its evolution and emergence, examining its relationship to performance, and viewing it in light of Aristotle's *Poetics*. Part 2 (Critiques) examines specific screenplays in its discussions of rhetoric, gender, and race. Chapters 6 and 7 look at screenplay adaptation and screenplays originally written for the screen.

I have chosen to work with mainstream American screenplays, excluding, for the most part, screenplays for foreign, independent, and experimental films. I have done so for a number of reasons, not the least of which are the difficulties inherent in obtaining and translating foreign screenplays and the fact that mainstream American films dominate the worldwide film industry. I am working under the assumption that most, if not all, of the screenplays I discuss in *Script Culture and the American Screenplay* are either widely known or readily accessible to readers. My hope is that this will make what follows accessible to a broad readership.

1 Foundations

1

Form and Function

The Evolution of the Screenplay

Prehistory

The history of the screenplay begins about sixteen years after the birth of film, in the 1910s, around the time Thomas Harper Ince began making films.[1] Jean-Pierre Geuens credits Ince as the one who first "successfully managed to codify and standardize the entire practice of filmmaking" (82). Under Ince's guidance, "writing for film became truly efficient for the first time . . . and developed into the indispensable core" (82) of the filmmaking system. The written text that guided a film's production became a literary form. The text rendered the shots that the director later realized. Geuens points out that "screenplays . . . became detailed shooting scripts that were given to the director for implementation" (83). As with all shifts in power, when creative control increased in the screenplay, it decreased for production personnel, most significantly, the director. Directors were forced to surrender much of their domain to writers. Some directors resisted the loss of control and Ince's focus on the written word. Barry Salt argues that Ince's influence may have temporarily stunted film technique, deducing from the absence of multiple-angle cuts in *An Apache Father's Vengeance* (1912)—

----

1. Ince began writing and directing shorts in 1911, but it is perhaps best to mark the beginning of the screenplay around the middle of the decade when Ince moved into producing, around 1916 when he directed *Civilization*.

3

a technique found in director Reginald Barker's earlier films for Reliance[2]—that "when Ince took over the Reliance company at the end of 1912 he also took over the director who knew how to" piece together shots from different angles (293). Nevertheless, many directors adopted the "Ince style" of filmmaking and Ince avoided conflicts with directors who were reluctant to adapt by employing directors "willing to work into his scheme of production" (Geuens 143).

Screenplay form, which is bound by function and intimately linked to the film performance, evolved quickly from the mid-1910s until sound and the introduction of dialogue around the end of the 1920s, when it settled into a format similar to the one still found in contemporary screenplays. The formation of the screenplay and its increasing significance to film during the silent era is the result of film's early transformation from an arcade novelty into a narrative medium. Complex storylines, multiple-shot scenes, and budget concerns forced filmmakers to plan the shape and structure of a film before the start of principal photography. As Lewis Jacobs notes, "stories ended the production of the trifling 'report' or 'incident' films" and reframed the motion picture as a complex narrative construction (67). Cameramen could no longer wander cities and scenic countrysides merely looking for something to capture on film. They needed narratives on which to hang their visual images, and they needed a method for planning, recording, and recalling these narratives. Early producers, spurred by the popularity of narrative film, scrambled for ideas, filming "half-remembered anecdotes, newspaper headlines, cartoons, jokes, domestic affairs, social issues, economic tribulations—all sorts of everyday American ideas and activities" (67), any shred of narrative that could be adapted to film. Text, which was the primary repository of story at the turn of the century, became an attractive source of inspiration.

Early predecessors of the screenplay did little more than frame the narrative context for a scene. One of the first major infusions of story into filmmaking was Georges Méliès's A Trip to the Moon (Le voyage dans la lune, 1902), which astounded American audiences and film producers and involved a great deal of preparation from Méliès. One part of this preparation was the writing of a sparse scenario, which provided the

----

2. Cf. Wheels of Destiny (1911).

backbone for the finished film. No more than a primitive list, Méliès's scenario represents one of the earliest predecessors to the modern screenplay. The following is the complete text of Méliès's original scenario for *A Trip to the Moon*.

1. The scientific congress at the Astronomic Club.
2. Planning the trip. Appointing the explorers and servants. Farewell.
3. The workshops. Constructing the projectile.
4. The foundries. The chimney-stacks. The casting of the monster gun.
5. The astronomers enter the shell.
6. Loading the gun.
7. The monster gun. March past the gunners. Fire!!! Saluting the flag.
8. The flight through space. Approaching the moon.
9. Landed right in the eye!!!
10. Flight of the shell into the moon. Appearance of the earth from the moon.
11. The plain of craters. Volcanic eruption.
12. The dream (the Solies, the Great Bear, Phoebus, the Twin Sisters, Saturna).
13. The snowstorm.
14. 40 degreees below zero. Descending a lunar crater.
15. Into the interior of the moon. The giant mushroom grotto.
16. Encounter with the Selenites. Homeric flight.
17. Prisoners!!!
18. The kingdom of the moon. The Selenite army.
19. The flight.
20. Wild pursuit.
21. The astronomers find the shell again. Departure from the moon.
22. Vertical drop into space.
23. Splashing into the open sea.
24. At the bottom of the ocean.
25. The rescue. Return to port.
26. The great fete. Triumphal march past.
27. Crowning and decorating the heroes of the trip.
28. Procession of Marines and the Fire Brigade.
29. Inauguration of the commemorative statue by the manager and the council.
30. Public rejoicings. (Jacobs 27-28)

Méliès's list is simply an enumeration of scenes, but as filmmakers, such as Edwin S. Porter and D. W. Griffith, began to concentrate more on individual shots, more narrative detail was added to each item. Scenes acquired headings, which marked location, and descriptive passages were placed beneath each heading, as seen in the following excerpt from Edwin S. Porter's scenario for *The Great Train Robbery* (1903) as it appeared in the Edison Catalogue in 1904.

Scene 1: *Interior of railroad telegraph office.* Two masked robbers enter and compel the operator to get the "signal block" to stop the approaching train, and make him write a fictitious order to the engineer to take water at this station, instead of "Red Lodge," the regular watering stop. The train comes to a standstill (seen through window of office); the conductor comes to the window, and the frightened operator delivers the order while the bandits crouch out of sight, at the same time keeping him covered with their revolvers. As soon as the conductor leaves, they fall upon the operator, bind and gag him, and hastily depart to catch the moving train.

Scene 2: *Railroad water tower.* The bandits are hiding behind the tank as the train, under the false order, stops to take water. Just before she pulls out they stealthily board the train between the express car and the tender.

Scene 3: *Interior of express car.* Messenger is busily engaged. An unusual sound alarms him. He goes to the door, peeps through the keyhole and discovers two men trying to break in. He starts back bewildered, but, quickly recovering, he hastily locks the strong box containing the valuables and throws the key through the open side door. Drawing his revolver, he crouches behind a desk. In the meantime, the two robbers have succeeded in breaking in the door and enter cautiously. The messenger opens fire, and a desperate pistol duel takes place in which the messenger is killed. One of the robbers stands watch while the other tries to open the treasure box. Finding it locked, he vainly searches the messenger for the key, and blows the safe open with dynamite. Securing the valuables and mail bags they leave the car.
(rpt. Jacobs 43-44)

Technical details were added to the scene headings and descriptions, as needed, to identify interior and exterior scenes, close-ups, long shots, titles, and such. Eventually, most information about the proposed film found its way into the scenario, and the scenario became a centralized guide to the proposed film performance.

Scenario to Screenplay: The Silent Era

A silent film scenario consists of four main parts: a synopsis, a cast of characters, a scene plot, and the continuity (or the plot of the action). All four are still in use today in slightly different forms. The synopsis is comparable to a contemporary film treatment; the cast of characters and the scene plot are similar to documents used to facilitate production; and the continuity is much like the contemporary screenplay.

The Synopsis

The synopsis is straight narrative, although greatly condensed from what we would find in novels or short stories. As with contemporary treatments, synopses were used to pitch film ideas to producers, but they also served as an overview of the story. It is common to find one writer credited for the synopsis and another for the story, but the writer credited for the scenario usually wrote the synopsis, as is the case in the following synopsis for Metro Pictures' *Her Inspiration* (1918), story and scenario by George D. Baker and Thomas J. Geraghty.

```
              "Her Inspiration"
                  Synopsis

Harold Montague, a young playwright, is told by the man-
ager that his latest opus lacks proper atmosphere and as
it is a moonshine story, Harold takes himself off to the
Kentucky mountains, there to meet the originals of the
counterparts of his play. He becomes acquainted with such
denizens of the mountains as Curt Moots, Big Hank and
Loony Lige—at last, but not by any manner of means least,
with Kate Kendall—a wild mountain crew all of them—just
the right people to contribute to Harold that atmosphere
he needs to put his play over.
     Of course, the moonshiners regard him suspiciously,
particularly Big Hank, who sees him making progress in a
romance with Kate and doesn't like it at all. Big Hank
tries to interpret every move made by Harold as that of
```

a revenue officer. The others, however, accept him for
what he is. Loony Lige, a half-witted and self-constituted
guardian of Kate, nurses a hatred for Big Hank that is
augmented into a fury when he sees him trying to kiss the
girl. He threatens to go for the revenue officers and give
away the secrets of the illicit still.

Soon after, twelve revenue officers arrive. Harold,
not knowing who they are, directs them to the hiding place
of the moonshines. Big Hank sees him and decides that he
must hang. He is only prevented by the arrival of Looney
Lige at the head of the band of officers. After this, Harold decides that he has atmosphere enough and that he must
return to the city, because it would never do to marry an
uncouth girl of the mountains, no matter how much he loves
her. As he is watching the rehearsal of his play the manager requests that he meet the leading lady—Kate Kendall,
who strange enough, was also seeking atmosphere.

(Palmer and Howard 99–100)

Despite its abbreviated nature, the synopsis adheres to principles of
storytelling, employing dramatic techniques such as conflict, irony, and
resolution, and is historically significant and important as a source for
the film performance. But the film synopsis is too limited by its focus
on plot to be read as a fully realized literary piece. It subserves the
filmed work and offers little of critical significance when viewed as an
autonomous work.

A Cast of Characters

The cast of characters in a scenario is seldom more than a list of the
characters involved in the photoplay. Similar in function to a cast listing
in a theatrical play (although sometimes the cast of characters would
include a list of scenes in which each character appeared), the cast of
characters fulfilled the same need as a cast list (and sometimes, call
sheets) in use today. It provided an overview of the number of actors
needed for a production. Although a cast of characters was commonly
included in a scenario, it was eventually separated from the script and
became a preproduction document. This change parallels the evolution of the screenplay and reflects the screenplay's increased literary
status. The more cohesive and complete the scenario became, the less
it was marked as a preliminary document by its inclusion of other production-related documents.

A Scene Plot

The scene plot, like the cast of characters, is another production-related document that was originally included in the script, but that is now separate. The scene plot is a list of interior and exterior locations that chronicles the scenes taking place at each location. Like all production documents, the scene plot aids in the scheduling of principle photography, making it possible to schedule together all scenes taking place in a particular location regardless of their position in the photoplay.

```
                    "Witchcraft"
                    SCENE PLOT
                     Interiors
STRUBLE'S OFFICE
1-20-61-102-104-107-108-109-110-111-129
NOKOMIS' HUT
3-35-101-123-127-139-145-147-154
[. . . and so on]

             Exteriors and Locations
SUZETTE'S COTTAGE
8-9-10-12-14-16-19-32-58-76-78
DOOR-SUZETTE'S COTTAGE
4-70-72-80-87-91-95
[. . . and so on] (Turnbull and Reed 197-98)
```

As with the cast of characters, the scene plot became a separate document as the screenplay became more unified and literary.

The Continuity

The continuity is where story elements are arranged in cinematic form. It is the section of the scenario that most parallels contemporary screenplay format, and it is where the script enters the realm of art.[3] Frances Taylor Patterson, in her 1928 book on the scenario, claims that it is the continuity that "lifts the script out of the category of mere mechanical hack work" (*Scenario* 36). Patterson goes on to say,

---

3. The term "script," although interchangeable with the term "screenplay" in contemporary jargon and implicative of the continuity in the late 1920s, was originally synonymous with "scenario."

The continuity writer should really have a vivid imagination and an ingenious mind; in fact, it is not too exalted a notion of his calling to say he must be half poet and half musician. Continuity writing is not by any means merely a matter of reproducing other people's ideas. It is a matter of improvising pictures which will render these ideas visible. It must make mental processes graphic. It must give tangibility to the abstract. . . . In the continuity writer, as in the director, there should be combined the artist, the dramatist, the actor, and the mechanic. (*Scenario* 36)

The continuity shapes the story, complete with characters, settings, and emotional context. It is the first film document to fully articulate what is to be performed and the earliest literary form of the screenplay.[4]

Various forms were used for the continuity in the early days of film as filmmakers wrestled with the young industry. The hand-drawn continuities used by the Douglas Fairbanks Company, for example, served as production schedules, listing the settings and the days the sets would be needed on the left of the page and the characters and the action they would perform on the right (fig. 1).

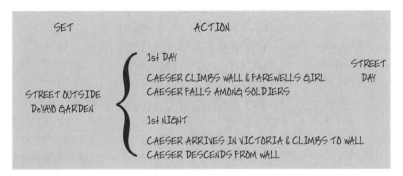

Fig. 1. Example of one bracketed segment from the continuity for the Douglas Fairbanks Company's 1925 production of *Don Q Son of Zorro* (Rpt. Patterson *Scenario* 52).

----

4. Whether or not a screenplay is ultimately produced (read: *performed*) is a matter of consequence, not necessity.

The Evolution of the Screenplay

Eventually, it became necessary to standardize the form of the continuity in order to assure consistency. As film grew away from its primitive beginning, during which time cameramen, directors, actors, and even "office staff" (Hampton 30) would extemporaneously compose the content of film, power shifted to the screenwriter. Studios developed scenario departments to craft stories prior to filming. The continuities in these early works left quite a bit of interpretive and creative power in the hands of the production team. As a result, "critics at the time complained a lot about sloppy continuity" (Geuens 82). Objects would unintentionally disappear and reappear from scene to scene. Wardrobe and sets would change. People would jump positions on the screen. To solve this problem, writers and studios refined screenplay format to accommodate the increased function a screenplay was expected to perform. As a result, more power shifted to the screenplay and more creative control flowed to the screenwriter.

By the end of the silent era, the form of the continuity had become highly literary. Ole Storm, in his introduction to the 1970 publication of Carl Theodor Dreyer's *Four Screenplays,* says of Dreyer's scripts:

> Comprehensively, the scripts reflect the integral nature of Carl Dreyer's vision. He commits to paper not only pictorial effects, but even the most transient moods and impalpable atmospheres. All those elements which coalesce into an artistic whole only on the shooting-floor and in the cutting-room, he finds it natural to epitomize in the novelistic form that best enables him to abide by his primary intentions: the development of the plot, the atmosphere, and the feelings that each shot is intended to evoke in the spectator. Of the practical details of procedure the scripts say next to nothing. (Storm 10)

By the mid-1920s the screenplay had risen from the simplicity of practical necessity to a literary form in its own right. Note the literary quality of the following excerpt from Dreyer's *The Passion of Joan of Arc.*

    At the Bibliothèque Nationale in Paris it is possible
    to see one of the most famous documents in the history
    of the world—the official record of the trial of Joan
    of Arc.

    The Bibliothèque Nationale's original record of the

trial of Joan of Arc is shown on the screen. An invisible hand turns over the manuscript pages.

If you turn over the pages, yellow with age, which contain the account of her martyrdom . . .

Page after page is shown of this unique document with its lines as straight as arrows, its marginal annotations, and the naïve miniature drawings for which the notaries have found time and space.

. . . you will find Joan herself . . . not the military genius who inflicted on the enemy defeat after defeat, but a simple and natural young girl . . . who died for her country.

The last pages are turned. Then the picture disappears and gives way to the first scene of the film, which shows

1 The prison, where Joan is sitting, praying. The flagstones, the floor in Joan's cell. We see two straws and a hand, Joan's hand, which lays the straws on the floor in the form of a cross.

2 Scenes from the church are shown: the chalice is brought out.

3 In the prison we see Joan kneeling before her straw cross—this most fragile and exalted of crosses. She prays in ecstatic joy, at one moment bending right forward so that her forehead touches the flagstones, the next moment kneeling with her hands folded and her eyes raised to heaven as if she saw beings visible only to her. From time to time she mutters a short prayer.

4 THE CHURCH
A young monk makes his way through rows of kneeling priests. He is the Usher Massieu, who is on his way to summon Joan and conduct her to her first examination.

5 THE PRISON
Joan in front of her little cross. Suddenly the two straws spin round in a mysterious gust of wind. What is it? Joan sits for a moment, overcome with astonishment, then puts the straws back in the form of a cross. Again a hostile power attacks this cross and scatters it over the flagstones. Joan doesn't know what to believe. Can

it be one of her voices? A divine intervention? Once
again she replaces the cross. Then there is a roar of
laughter from the door behind her. Joan turns and sees
three soldiers, who have been standing in the half-open
door, blowing at her straw cross through a long tube.
  Enter the soldiers. They are tormentors and bullies
of the worst kind. They continue to jeer at her.

6 Now the jailer appears, an elderly man, followed by a
blacksmith. Joan turns in terror and looks up at them.
When she sees the chains in the blacksmith's hands, her
eyes fill with tears, and she shrinks back a step. The
jailer seizes her by the foot, and the blacksmith puts
the ankle-chains on her.

7 While he is thus occupied, Massieu enters. He is an
engaging young man of twenty-five, healthy, vivacious
and open; he radiates youth, health and life. He remains standing by the door until the others have left
the cell. The jailer, who goes out last, certifies that
the prisoner is the Maid. The door closes behind the
jailer. And now that Massieu is alone with this woman,
whom he has heard described as a dangerous witch and
an object of fear-he is afraid. He prays inaudibly
and crosses himself. He has brought with him a small
stoup and aspergillum, and as he stands by the door he
sprinkles Joan eagerly with holy water. Joan, who has
dragged herself over to the boards which serve as her
bed, looks at him in gay surprise, and with a slight
smile says:
Come a little nearer, I shan't fly away!
Massieu, astonished, approaches her, asks if she is
Joan, the Maid, and when she confirms this begins to
read the summons:
*. . . that you summon the aforesaid Joan, commonly
called the Maid, to appear before us . . .*
Joan declares herself ready to follow him. Massieu
calls for the jailer. They lead Joan out.

8 THE CHAPEL
Bishop Cauchon takes the chair for the trial. To
either side of him sit the Inquisitor, Lemaître, and
Jean d'Estivet, who is to present the case against
Joan. These three men are surrounded by the other
forty-one clerics, all men of learning, thoroughly
versed in the art of dragging confessions out of
accused persons. A special table is reserved for the
notaries. Cauchon gives orders for the accused to be
brought in.

9 Every face turns towards the entrance. They all see
   Joan for the first time. It is so quiet in the chapel
   that you can hear the grating noise of the chains round
   Joan's ankles.

10 Joan comes forward. Through the pointed, colored windows the sunlight falls obliquely into the room in long
   shafts. Suddenly Joan finds herself in the middle of
   one of these shafts and stops for a moment. She becomes
   aware that every eye is turned towards her; she sees
   that they are hard, cold and uncomprehending. For a few
   seconds it seems as if she is going to collapse, overcome by the cold, remorseless atmosphere. On one side
   a completely human, simple, young country girl; on the
   other the flower of this century's talents, learned
   doctors, the fine fruits of the university, every prod-
   igy in Christendom . . . the instruments of reason—and
   of death. The personification on one side of innocence,
   on the other of magnificence. The terrible, relentless
   way in which they look at this girl in man's clothes,
   all these bishops, all these ascetics and members of
   orders with their newly cropped tonsures! These learned
   gentlemen regard her man's shoes and short hair as
   something loathsome and indecent. They believe as one
   man that it will be all easy matter to get the upper
   hand over this child. (Dreyer 27-30)

Storm notes that Dreyer's "original scripts are annotated on the blank left-hand pages with manuscript jottings about properties, lighting, sound effects, panning shots, plot and similar practical manners" (10). This bifurcation of content implies distinctions between the literary and the practical, exposing the presence of literary content in a form that was born of practical necessity. What had begun for Méliès as a mnemonic device had grown into a literary form. Dreyer recognized the importance of the script, realized the significant creative contribution the script represented, and so advocated that directors write their own continuities. As is clear in the opening from Dreyer's script for *The Passion of Joan of Arc,* the engendering of the cinematic is already present within the text. When Joan sits in prison watching bits of straw disrupted by the wind, Dreyer fulfills Patterson's mandate and renders ideas visible. The scene is complete with emotional content for the reader. We do not need the camera to realize the visual. In fact, the first seven scenes of Dreyer's script were cut just prior to shooting, so these scenes exist only as literature and would be lost if the literary value of Dreyer's writing were discarded in presumed appreciation of his art as a director.

With the introduction of sound (thus spoken dialogue) at the end of the 1920s, screenplay format stabilized, but dialogue was present in the continuity prior to sound, in the form of titles. Titles, which were indented in the scenario, shifted away from mere descriptions of actions or explanatory textual inserts and "became substitutes for the missing voices of the players, telling us in effect what the characters were saying to each other" (Geuens 84). They presented dialogue that was not yet technically possible, but was nonetheless presumed to be necessary. Note the dominance of dialogue in the following excerpt from Alfred A. Cohn's scenario for *The Jazz Singer*.

```
270. CLOSE-UP       LEE AND DILLINGS
     Dillings has finished saying something to him as
     Lee's jaw drops. He looks at him in surprise and
     blurts out:

TITLE 108:   "You don't mean you'd take your money out of
             the show the last minute?"

     Back to scene. Dillings nods firmly. Lee demands to
     know the reason for this sudden determination. Dill-
     ings points in the direction of Mary's room and then
     to Jack. He says:

TITLE 109:   "Just the idea of Mary's interest in this
             jazz singer of yours."

     Back to scene. Lee starts to argue with Dillings,
     telling him that it is nothing serious. Dillings,
     however, has guessed the true state of affairs. He
     adds:

TITLE 110:   "I have no further interest in her career.
             Just mail me a check today."

     He starts to leave. (Cohn and Raphaelson 107)
```

The form of the continuity was obliged to accommodate dialogue, a logical result of the increasing narrative demands placed on film in the first three decades of the twentieth century. Wordless films may have been the ideal for Sergei Eisenstein and others, including Patterson (who lectured on film at Columbia University in the 1920s), who claimed, "The motion picture should be a story told without words" (*Cinema* 102). But even Patterson admitted in 1920 that the form had not yet achieved that objective, as it was "almost impossible to construct a photoplay without calling in the assistance of words" (102), but envisioned wordless films as the ultimate realization of the art form. But film did not evolve as Patterson imagined it would. Instead of shaking its dependence on words, film embraced them. As it turned out, film's evolution was more than the advancement of the visual image; it was also the incorporation of sound (nonvisual language) and thus the photoplay did not evolve into a story told through a series of juxtaposed moving images; it evolved into a story told through visual *and* auditory modes. Film, which was often touted as a medium under the exclusive providence of the eye, ultimately fell under the providence of the eye and the ear. Aesthetic philosophies touting the visual purity of the art suffered beneath the weight of popular opinion. Once sound became possible, it quickly became inevitable, and dialogue moved from the title cards to the soundtrack.

According to Geuens, Ince's system had "located the essence of the movies inside the screenplays" and divided film into "two distinct movements, two discrete labors, the writing and the execution" (85). Cinema was "essentially . . . dominated by the story" and "the visualization process remained entirely subservient to the drama described by the script" (85). Although some (Geuens included) complained that Ince's system, in disempowering the director, resulted in dull, commercial productions, which were rescued midcentury from banality by the artistic brilliance of New Wave directors (e.g., François Truffaut, Jean-Luc Godard, Eric Rohmer, Jacques Rivette, Claude Chabrol), these arguments are more attempts at privilege than assessments of aesthetic content, as they overlook the work of directors such as Preston Sturges, John Ford, Ernst Lubitsch, Howard Hawks, Orson Welles, and many others. The battle to attribute authorship waged by the *Cahiers du Cinéma* critics presumes an exclusivity that does not in fact exist.[5] To credit a director is not to discredit a screenwriter; and to credit

----

5. This debate is discussed in more detail in Harvard Film Studies' *Cahiers du Cinéma: 1960–1968*, edited by Jim Hillier.

a screenwriter is not to dismiss the vision of a director, anymore than praising a stage production of *Macbeth* diminishes Shakespeare's literary art. Despite paradoxical attacks on the artistic value of scripts, the screenplay in the 1930s assumed the basic form it has maintained (with only minor changes) throughout the remainder of the twentieth and into the twenty-first century.

The Screenplay after Sound

Screenplays after sound are similar in form to theatrical plays. Dialogue is pervasive, although often more terse than theatrical dialogue. Narrative sections between passages of dialogue describe movement and setting much in the way stage directions do for theatrical plays. The entire screenplay is divided into scenes, which can often be subdivided into shots or visual sequences. The language throughout is concise and connotative. All of these elements are evident in the following excerpt from Noel Langley, Florence Ryerson, and Edgar Allen Woolf's 1939 screenplay for *The Wizard of Oz*.

```
FADE IN—Title:

For nearly forty years this story has given faithful
service to the Young in Heart; and Time has been power-
less to put its kindly philosophy out of fashion.

To those of you who have been faithful to it in return

. . . and to the Young at Heart—we dedicate this pic-
ture.

                                              FADE OUT:

MS [medium shot⁶]—Dorothy stoops down to Toto—speaks to
```

----

6. Specific camera shots were prevalent in early screenplays. Over time writers began to imply particular shots rather than explicitly state them. By the 1970s it was common practice to leave out specific references to the camera (although screenplays written by directors often include them). By the end of the twentieth century, scene transitions (e.g., DISSOLVE TO:, CUT TO:) began to disappear, but the staccato narrative style, the visual focus, and the unadorned dialogue have remained. I contend that over time fewer technical terms were needed because the screenplay became increasingly more literary and more able to shape visual imagery for readers.

him—then runs down road to b.g.—Toto following—

> DOROTHY
> She isn't coming yet, Toto. Did she hurt
> you? She tried to, didn't she? Come on—we'll
> go tell Uncle Henry and Auntie Em. Come on,
> Toto.

LS [long shot]—Farm yard—Dorothy enters left b.g. along
road—Toto following her—CAMERA PANS right—she comes
thru gate—runs forward to Aunt Em and Uncle Henry working at Incubator—

> DOROTHY
> Aunt Em! Aunt Em!

MS—Aunt Em and Uncle Henry working with baby chicks in
incubator—Dorothy runs in—speaks to them—Dorothy picks
up baby chick—CAMERA TRUCKS back as Aunt Em and Dorothy
come forward—Aunt Em puts chick in coop with hen—then
TRUCKS forward as they go to b.g. to incubator—Dorothy
reacts—Uncle Henry looks at her—CAMERA PANS her to left
across yard—

> DOROTHY
> Aunt Em!

> AUNT EM
> Fifty-seven, fifty-eight—

> DOROTHY
> Just listen to what Miss Gulch did to Toto!
> She—

> AUNT EM
> Dorothy, please! We're trying to count!
> Fifty-eight—

> DOROTHY
> Oh, but Aunt Em, she hit him over the—

> UNCLE HENRY
> Don't bother us now, honey—this old incuba-
> tor's gone bad, and we're likely to lose a
> lot of our chicks.

```
                     DOROTHY
     Oh—oh, the poor little things. Oh, but Aunt
     Em, Miss Gultch hit Toto right over the back
     with a rake just because she says he gets in
     her garden and chases her nasty old cat ev-
     ery day. (Langley et al. 1)
```

More contemporary examples, such as Jim Uhls's highly stylized 1999 screenplay for *Fight Club*, resemble the form of Langley and collaborators' 1939 screenplay for *The Wizard of Oz*.

```
                     TYLER
     This is our world now. Two minutes.

                     JACK (V.O.)
     Two minutes to go and I'm wondering how I
     got here.

MOVE IN ON JACK'S FACE.

SLOWLY PULL BACK from Jack's face. It's pressed against
TWO LARGE BREASTS that belong to . . . BOB, a big
moose of a man, around 35 years old. Jack is engulfed
by Bob's arms in an embrace. Bob weeps openly. His
shoulders inhale themselves up in a long draw, then
drop, drop, drop in jerking sobs. Jack gives Bob some
squeezes in return, but his face is stone.

                     JACK (V.O.)
     Bob had bitch tits.

PULL BACK TO WIDE ON

INT. HIGH SCHOOL GYMNASIUM-NIGHT

All the men are paired off, hugging each other, talk-
ing in emotional tones. Some pairs lean forward, heads
pressed ear-to-ear, the way wrestlers stand, locked.
Near the door a temporary sign on a stand: "REMAINING
MEN TOGETHER."

                     JACK (V.O.)
     This was a support group for men with tes-
     ticular cancer. The big moosie slobbering
     all over me was Bob.
```

```
                    BOB
    I owned my own gym. I did product endorse-
    ments.


                    JACK
    You were a six-time champion.


                    JACK (V.O.)
    Bob, the big cheesebread. Always told me his
    life story.


                    BOB
    We're still men.


                    JACK
    Yes. We're men. Men is what we are.
    (Uhls 2-3)
```

Since the introduction of sound, the American screenplay's form has remained relatively constant. Its function, at a superficial level, has also remained the same: to inform its own performance and guide the execution of a motion picture.

Film has undergone more changes to its form since the introduction of sound than the screenplay, new technologies and cinematic innovations being responsible for the majority of the changes. While the Steadicam, computer-generated imagery (CGI), improved audio recording and tracking, 24P video, increased camera mobility, and other innovations have greatly altered the visual/auditory experience of film, the screenplay has experienced only a few changes to its form. Among these are fewer direct camera references, less cinema-graphic marginalia, and more concise scene descriptions. For example, note the prevalence of camera directions in the opening of Peter Stone's 1 October 1962 draft for *Charade* (1963).

```
    FADE IN (BEFORE TITLES)


1.  EXT. FRENCH COUNTRYSIDE—DUSK
    Silence—complete silence for the urbanite, though
    the oncoming darkness is punctuated by the sounds of
    farm country—a few birds, a distant rumble of thun-
    der from some heavy clouds on the horizon, a dog's
    barking.

    CAMERA PANS the green, squared-off flatland, lit
```

only by a fine sunset in its final throes. Then, gradually, starting from nothing, a rumble is heard, quickly growing louder and louder until the sound of a train can be recognized.

CAMERA PANS quickly, discovering the railroad line atop a man-made rise of land, and the speeding passenger train is upon us, flashing by with a roar.

Then, as if from nowhere, the figure of a man hits the embankment and rolls crazily down to the bottom into the thick underbrush alongside the tracks.

2. CLOSE SHOT—BODY
   It lies in the bushes, still, unmoving—dead. CAMERA PANS AWAY to the quiet peaceful countryside as the sound of the train fades off until there is silence once more.

   TITLE MUSIC begins with a crash.

                    (MAIN TITLES)
3.)
4.) DELETED
5.)

6. FADE IN
   EXT. MEGEVE—DAY
   A handsome and elegant hotel perched on the mountain-side overlooking the French resort town. A large, open sun deck—tables, gaily colored parasols, sun bathers.

   One of the latter is REGINA LAMPERT, a lovely young girl. She is, besides taking in the sun, involved in her favorite activity—eating.

   Then—a dark, ominous shape intrudes in the f.g. FOCUS CHANGES to bring into sharp relief a revolver—shining, black and ugly in the sunlight.

   REGGIE, unaware of her danger, continues to eat.

   The finger tightens around the trigger and finally the gun shoots—a stream of water arcs, with unerring aim, straight into REGGIE's face.

7. ANOTHER ANGLE

CHAPTER I

Including JEAN-LOUIS, a French boy of six or so.
REGGIE looks at him sternly.

                    JEAN-LOUIS (in for trouble)
        Oh, la.

                    REGGIE
        Don't tell me you didn't know it was loaded.
        (calling) Sylvie!

8. WIDER ANGLE
    SYLVIE GAUDET, French, attractive, blonde, in her
    early thirties, comes from the railing of the sun
    deck to join REGGIE and JEAN-LOUIS.

                    REGGIE
        Isn't there something constructive he can
        do—like start an avalanche?

                    SYLVIE (to JEAN-LOUIS)
        Va jouer, mon ange. (Stone n.p.)

Reference to the camera is common throughout Stone's screenplay, yet
when we compare Stone's writing in 1962 to the opening of Robert
Towne's third draft (9 October 1973) for *Chinatown*, written only eleven
years later, we find that pervasive references to the camera have begun
to disappear.

1   FULL SCREEN PHOTOGRAPH

    grainy but unmistakably a man and woman making love.
    Photograph shakes. SOUND of a man MOANING in an-
    guish. The photograph is dropped, REVEALING ANOTHER,
    MORE compromising one. Then another, and another.
    More moans.

                    CURLY'S VOICE
                (crying out)
        Oh, no.

2   INT. GITTES' OFFICE

    CURLY drops the photos on Gittes' desk. Curly towers
    over GITTES and sweats heavily through his workman's
    clothes, his breathing progressively more labored. A
    drop plunks on Gittes' shiny desk top.

Gittes notes it. A fan whiffs overhead. Gittes glances up at it. He looks cool and brisk in a white linen suit despite the heat. Never taking his eyes off Curly, he lights a cigarette using a lighter with a "nail" on his desk.

Curly, with another anguished sob, turns and rams his fist into the wall, kicking the wastebasket as he does. He starts to sob again, slides along the wall where his fist has left a noticeable dent and its impact has sent the signed photos of several movie stars askew.

Curly slides on into the blinds and sinks to his knees. He is weeping heavily now, and is in such pain that he actually bites into the blinds.

Gittes doesn't move from his chair.

> GITTES
> All right, enough is enough—you can't
> eat the Venetian blinds, Curly. I just
> had 'em installed on Wednesday.

Curly responds slowly, rising to his feet, crying. Gittes reaches into his desk and pulls out a shot glass, quickly selects a cheaper bottle of bourbon from several fifths of more expensive whiskeys.

3   Gittes pours a large shot. He shoves the glass across his desk toward Curly.

> GITTES
> —Down the hatch.

Curly stares dumbly at it. Then picks it up, and drains it. He sinks back into the chair opposite Gittes, begins to cry quietly.

> CURLY
> (drinking, relaxing a little)
> She's just no good.

> GITTES
> What can I tell you, Kid? You're
> right. When you're right, you're
> right, and you're right. (Towne n.p.)

23

The camera, which is explicitly referenced in Stone's writing, is adequately implied in Towne's. We may attribute many of the structural changes, such as this, that we find in screenplays during the last thirty years to the screenplay's shaking off of the influences of staged theater that shaped the early days of film, and the establishment of the screenplay as a more autonomous literary form. Screenwriting, as it turned out, could sufficiently convey directions to filmmakers that were previously—and wrongly—considered necessary. The result was the more refined style we find in contemporary screenplays.

2

Parallel Forms
The Architecture of Performance

I appeal to all film critics . . . to remember
that a film begins with a screenplay.
—Ernest Lehman

When Ernest Lehman accepted an honorary Oscar in 2001 for his impressive body of work as a screenwriter, producer, and director, he stressed the importance of the screenplay to film, restating what directors, producers, actors, writers, and other professionals have been saying for the last century—that the screenplay is of central importance in the film industry. What is surprising about Lehman's comment is that it still needed to be said. In 1935 screenwriter Dudley Nichols, who won a Best Writer award for his screenplay *The Informer,* became the first person to boycott the Academy Awards in his efforts to draw more attention to screenwriters.[1] Throughout the history of the American screenplay, screenwriters have been fighting for recognition as the screenplay's merits have been undervalued.

One difficulty lies in the fact that screenplays are written for filmmakers and have no other intended audience; therefore, they adhere to a rigid form that presumes its own performance, and their audience is substantially smaller than a film's audience. Millions of people have seen Sidney Lumet's *Network* (1976), but only a few hundred students

----

1. Nichols's primary objective in boycotting the event was to garner support for the Writers Guild.

of film and film industry professionals (actors, directors, cinematographers, set designers, and so on; and professionals involved in the business of filmmaking: agents, entertainment lawyers, managers, accountants, etc.) have read Paddy Chayefsky's screenplay.

The primary function of a screenplay is to facilitate production of the film in the same way that a stage play's primary function is to facilitate the stage production.[2] The only people who read a screenplay are those who have an interest in its production and those who intentionally track down a copy. The latter group has grown in the last three decades to include a large number of would-be screenwriters, students of the screenplay, professors teaching screenwriting courses for film, communication and English departments, and entrepreneurs marketing screenwriting courses and related services. Kristen Thompson credits this increase to the "rise in package production since the 1970s" and a resurgence of "freelance scriptwriting" that resulted in a "flood of manuals . . . cater[ing] to aspiring authors" (11).

Interest in screenwriting among the general population continued to blossom through the 1980s. In 1990 screenwriter Shane Black sold his spec script called *The Last Boy Scout* for $1.75 million, an unprecedented amount for an unsolicited screenplay bought on speculation and a substantially larger amount than studios paid in the early days of film when studios such as Edison, Vitagraph, Imperial, and Biograph paid screenwriters $20 per reel for their work. Black's sale drew national attention and set off another flurry of interest among nonprofessionals wanting to become screenwriters. This broad-based interest in screenwriting stimulated a thriving screenwriting culture. Syd Field, one of the first to write a popular book on the craft of screenwriting (*Screenplay: The Foundations of Screenwriting*, 1982), became a central figure in the emergent field of screenplay training materials. Numerous books appeared, such as Robert McKee's *Story: Substance, Structure, Style, and the Principles of Screenwriting* (1997), David Trottier's *The Screenwriter's Bible* (originally published in 1994, published as a general trade book in 1995, and revised in 2005), Linda Seger's *Making a Good Script Great*

----

2. To a lesser degree, the screenplay can, and often does, function as a sales piece used to acquire funding for a project or to attract important talent to a project, thus improving its chances of being produced.

(1994), and myriad others. Periodicals dealing with screenwriting and the screenplay appeared, among them *Creative Screenwriting, Script, Screentalk, Screenwriter's Monthly,* and *Written By.* In 2001 Matt Damon and Ben Affleck participated in the formation of Project Greenlight, a Web site that offered unknown screenwriters entry into a contest that could result in the production of their screenplays. Thousands of amateur writers entered screenplays into Project Greenlight's screenwriting contests.[3]

Despite a booming script culture, the screenplay and the screenwriter remain undervalued, a point *Washington Post* film critic Desson Thomson stressed in a 2004 live online discussion: "How on earth would Anthony Hopkins be effective in *Silence of the Lambs* without words in his mouth? Without the situation set up which makes him the only person who can help Clarice Starling? Hollywood has always had a hate-hate relationship with the writer. Baffling. People like Joe Eszterhas and Shane Black broke the impasse, luckily, with million dollar-plus salaries for their scripts. But let's face it, compared to the lowest star in Hollywood it's still nothing" (n.p.). The screenplay has received far less attention in scholarly circles than in popular culture. Some mention of the screenplay occasionally makes its way into film scholarship, but this inclusion is frequently sparse and overpowered by examinations of the film or a preceding work, such as a novel or a play that the screenplay has adapted for film. For example, Rick Worland's 2002 examination of Hitchcock's *Suspicion* considers the screenplay,[4] but focuses primarily on Anthony Berkeley's novel, *Before the Fact,* on which the screenplay is based, and Hitchcock's film, with the screenplay functioning as a link between the two, rather than a creative work of equivalent value. Worland is not to be faulted for this, as his primary objective in the article is to redress the critical reception of the film; however, it is a measure of

----

3. Project Greenlight's first contest received 7,000 entries and resulted in the film *Stolen Summer* (2002), which was written and directed by Pete Jones. Its second contest produced *The Battle for Shaker Heights* (2003), written by Erica Beeney and codirected by Efram Potelle and Kyle Rankin. The third contest paired the screenplay *Feast* (2005), co-written by Marcus Dunstan and Patrick Melton, with first-time director John Gulager.

4. Cf. Rick Worland, "Before and after the Fact: Writing and Reading Hitchcock's *Suspicion," Cinema Journal* 41 (Summer 2002).

the limited coverage screenplays receive on those rare occasions when they are addressed at all.

It would be fallacious to argue that the screenplay as a literary form has been wholly ignored. On occasion, the screenplay has been recognized in scholarly and popular discourses. One of the earliest acknowledgments of the screenplay as a viable literary form was Otto Rank's use of *The Student of Prague* (1913) as the narrative source for his book on the double in literature (*Der Doppelgänger* [*The Double*]). Rank's argument privileges Hanns Heinz Ewers's screenplay over the Edgar Allan Poe story ("William Wilson") that inspired the screenplay and the film that resulted from the screenplay. Rank claims that in *The Student of Prague* "we can . . . trace back the developmental and semantic history of an old, traditional folk-concept which has stimulated imaginative and thoughtful writers to use it in their works" (3). He further argues that "those whose concern is with literature may be reassured by the fact that the scenarist of this film, *The Student of Prague*, is an author currently in vogue and that he has adhered to prominent patterns, the effectiveness of which has been tested by time" (3–4).

Rank's comments are significant for two reasons. First, Rank, in a work specifically focused on literature, identifies Ewers, the scenarist, as the author of the work—not Poe, whose story preceded Ewers's work, or Stellan Rye and Paul Wegener who directed the film. Second, Rank wrote *The Double* in 1914 (though the work was first published in 1925), one year after Ewers wrote *The Student of Prague*. More recent acknowledgments of the importance of screenplays also exist. The January 2005 issue of *Vanity Fair* includes a twelve-page excerpt from John Logan's screenplay for *The Aviator*. The introduction to the piece states: "In *Vanity Fair*'s continuing endeavor to celebrate the craft of superb screenwriting, we offer an extended excerpt from Logan's *The Aviator*, a spirited, sumptuous, and psychologically astute portrait of one of the titanic characters in the annals of 20th-century wealth and power" (Logan 3).

One reason for the scant critical attention to the screenplay as a literary form involves how we define "film" as it is used in terms such as "film studies," and in how critics and scholars have presumed the term required little or no definition. Most criticism up until the 1970s focused on the film tableau—the projected rectangle with its accouterments: sound and story. Since the 1970s, an increased interest in film's relationship to the representation and construction of culture, gender, ethnicity, and social class stretched the boundaries of the discipline but retained the object of its original focus. We should not be surprised that film studies focuses primarily on the screen text instead of the screenplay text; however, when we consider the extent to which that film text has been expanded to include the spectator, as in Jean-Luis Baudry's work in the 1970s on the ideological effect of the cinematic apparatus, and the application of Jacques Lacan to film studies in the works of Laura Mulvey, Christian Metz, and Slavoj Žižek, we realize that critical film studies have extended the discussion of film proper beyond the borders of the reel into its broader cultural context. Why then has the screenplay failed to become an integral part of the mix? One likely explanation is a privileging of performance over text. In a similar manner to the way speech was long privileged over writing (until Jacques Derrida in *Of Grammatology* demonstrated that such privilege was untenable), the articulation of the screenplay is privileged over the written document. At the core of this problem is the metaphysical notion of presence. The film proper—the light and sound show experience—creates an illusion of presence that the screenplay does not. Jean-Louis Baudry, in "Ideological Effects of the Basic Cinematographic Apparatus," for example, points out that "the image is not reducible to language" (40). However, signifying production is no less present in written text. Just as image is text, text is image. Text is more symbolic than film, but no less capable of signification and no less dependent on a viewer for meaning. What varies between the two is the level of subjectivity. Film is one imaginary remove from the screenplay. Ingmar Bergman begins *The Seventh Seal:*

```
The night had brought little relief from the heat,
and at dawn a hot gust of wind blows across the
colorless sea. The KNIGHT, Antonius Block, lies
prostrate on some spruce branches spread over the
fine sand. His eyes are wide-open and bloodshot
from lack of sleep.
```

This text, when interpreted, is mutated into imaginary representations; a reader must imagine a dawn preceded by a hot night, how a "hot gust of wind" looks when it "blows across a colorless sea." Even more necessary to the narrative, a reader must imagine the prostrate knight.

However, these textual details, once filmed, shift the locus of subjective creation from the reader to the filmmakers (and not to the film audience). The opening shots of the film remove the necessity for an audience to imagine these particular details (though, as Baudry, among others, points out, the audience is still engaged in the imaginary by the film apparatus). The knight looks like Max von Sydow and cannot be imagined any other way because von Sydow was cast in the role. The ocean is the ocean Bergman chose to shoot, not the ocean that a reader would have necessarily imagined from the text. Thus, the imaginary is rendered more rigid and less subjective by the translation of text to film. This increased rigidity engenders the illusion of presence that to some degree accounts for film's predominance over text.

Interestingly, this relationship is often inverted for drama. Scholars generally approach Shakespeare's plays as written documents, not performances. That is, the written play is privileged over its performance. The issue of privilege we may attribute to the notion of permanence. The most seemingly permanent manifestation of a work is often the one that is privileged. A dramatic staging of a play is transient and mutable, while the written text, though subject to interpretation, is unchanging. In film, however, the performance of the screenplay—the film proper—is permanent (relatively), and the screenplay, which often involves numerous drafts and revisions, is seemingly impermanent, in that it is difficult to arrive at an authoritative version. The film proper usually offers a single, consistent film text (excepting remakes).

But just as theater includes more than a staged production, film encompasses more than a cinematic performance. Film as a medium involves many elements, including lighting, set design, blocking, sound effects, storyboards, costume design, marketing, and writing. Of all of these, which contribute in varying degrees to the film performance, the screenplay contributes the most, as Alan A. Armer points out when he claims that "a well-written screenplay is the single most important ingredient in the making of a successful motion picture" (xvi).

Even the screenplays of literary luminaries such as William Faulkner, F. Scott Fitzgerald, and Vladimir Nabokov are ranked somewhere below their personal correspondence, and are often mentioned only out of historical curiosity. Those who wrote almost exclusively for film found their works marginalized almost as soon as the corresponding films were complete. While some writers, such as Preston Sturges and Paddy Chayefsky, have received attention, many writers, such as Frances Marion (whom Mary Pickford called "the pillar of my career" [Beauchamp 9]), Ben Hecht, Charles MacArthur, Jules Furthman, Sidney Joseph Perelman, Nedrick Young, Wendell Mayes (among many others) and their works have yet to receive the scholarly attention their literary accomplishments warrant, despite their contributions to the history, art, and evolution of film. As William Froug aptly puts it: "The screenwriter is beaten, battered, and belittled by film esthetes, critics, scholars, and historians whose unshakeable adherence to the auteur theory goes against all logic and verifiable fact, particularly when applied to the American motion picture" (vii). The denigration of the screenplay and the devaluation of the screenwriter persist today more out of habit than any critical judgment. Froug is right to point out the damaging effects of auteur theory. By supplanting the author of the screenplay with the film director, auteur theory has contributed (albeit unintentionally) more to the continued dismissal of the screenplay's merit than any other factor. The irony is unmistakable. In employing the literary term "author," advocates of auteur theory inadvertently privilege the literary while paradoxically diminishing the contributions of the literary to the film text.

As Donald E. Staples points out in his 1966 reexamination of François Truffaut's article, "Une certaine tendance du cinéma français," the foundational article was not intended to establish a "framework of criticism" (Staples 1), although auteur theory in many circles has become just that. Truffaut's article was "more of an anti-screen-writers article" (2). Truffaut objected to the stranglehold that psychological realism exercised over the work of French screenwriters. Truffaut viewed these works as too literary and argued that they enclosed "beings in a closed world, barricaded by formulas, plays on words, [and] maxims instead of letting us see them for ourselves with our own eyes" (Truffaut 24). But it was not writing, per se, to which Truffaut raised objection, it was the particular writing of French screenwriters of the time. His privileging of directors, such as Jean Renoir, Jean Cocteau, Abel Gance, Robert Bresson, Max Ophüls, Roger Leenhardt, and Jacques Tati, acknowledges that "these are auteurs who often write their dialogue and some of them invent themselves the stories that they direct" (26).

Thus, auteur theory as outlined by Truffaut and André Bazin's "De la politique des auteurs" does not, de facto, dismiss screenwriting or the significance of the writing of the screenplay; although, as Graham Petrie notes, the *Cahiers* double issue of December 1963–January 1964 classifies directors "with not a scriptwriter . . . being deemed worthy of mention" (61). Robert Self points out that "the success of auteur theory, which presupposes a unity of meaning and of authorial style and theme, is everywhere apparent—in the public media, in the university classroom, in academic publishing, in film festival retrospectives, in professional film conferences" ("Theory of Authorship" 3). The theory's proliferation (in all various forms) has diminished both screenwriter and screenplay. Despite critical attempts to lesson the import of auteur theory, its influence continues to dominate the general aesthetics of film culture. Michael Patrick Allen and Anne E. Lincoln's recent study of 1,277 revered films concludes that "the retrospective consecration of films is affected by the discourse produced by film critics and scholars who function, in effect, as reputational entrepreneurs. However, this discourse is influence by the availability of certain cultural schemas. Specifically, the ascendancy of 'auteur theory' as a discourse of value within film studies serves to privilege the director as the primary creative agent in film production. It also serves to privilege certain directors over others" (871).

Despite these aftereffects, we must acknowledge that Truffaut's work on auteur theory was printed fifty-nine years after the Lumière brothers debuted their first films to a paying audience in Paris, and that criticizing auteur theory does nothing to explain the screenplay's nearly sixty years of diminished status prior to the theory's critical arrival.

A number of dynamically interactive factors have helped to marginalize the screenplay among film scholars. First among these is the nature of early film. During its emergent days at the end of the nineteenth century, film did not adhere to the oft-chimed saw about being a story told with pictures. The early films of Thomas Edison and Lumière were not stories at all, but moving pictures—literally, pictures that moved. This was not only their function but also the way they were perceived. The process of capturing still images with wet-plate photography had led to Eadweard Muybridge's serial photographs, which in turn led to William Dickson and Edison's Kinetograph. The Kinetograph was an extension of photography, a device designed to make pictures move. It was not originally conceived of or employed as a medium for storytelling, which joined film later. Prior to the inclusion of stories, no writing was needed. The handful of cameramen who produced the earliest films lugged their cameras around cities and across the countryside with the single aim to get the shot, whatever that might be: Madison Avenue, New York Harbor, people dancing, and so on, anything that might amuse audiences. The early work of American cameramen, such as Edwin S. Porter with Edison Studios, J. Stuart Blackton with Vitagraph, and Billy Bitzer with Biograph, was about the image of motion and paralleled still photography more than theater. All they needed for their one-shot productions were interesting visuals. It was only a matter of months before Lumière's *L'arroseur arrose* (1895) demonstrated the effect story could have on an audience, but those few months were enough to establish the primacy of film.

The issue of the screenplay was further complicated by the genre's slow birth.[5] The connection between film and writing evolved slowly, out of necessity. Written predecessors to the screenplay drew scant attention because they were little more than notes, often merely a list of scenes jotted down to remind a filmmaker of what needed to be shot. However, when films grew in length and became more complex, writing gained in importance: existing first as a simple mnemonic device, then as a preproduction list of the film's imagined structure, and finally as the guiding force in the film's execution. The screenplay (or *script*) became the accumulation site of much of the information surrounding the production of a film, including technical details—lighting, wardrobe, and so on—all of which made it difficult to see the screenplay as an artistic form.

Part of the cold reception the screenplay has received from critical circles over the past century is a result of the ancillary nature of writing's early role in film production. Early film commentary focuses primarily on establishing film's autonomy, particularly distinguishing it from vaudeville and the theatrical stage. Hugo Münsterberg's claim that film is incomparable to drama because the "view of dramatic events" it gives us is "completely shaped by the mind" (401) and similar claims by others, such as Béla Balázs who argues in *Theory of the Film*

---

5. I use the term "genre" here, and throughout, out of convenience, as a placeholder for an ignored segment of literature, and do not intend to imply that the boundaries traditionally presumed between works are unproblematical.

that film differs from theater in the way it manipulates an audience's point of view, represent attempts to define film by articulating how it differs from other artistic mediums (passim). This agenda is obvious in V. I. Pudovkin's later claim that the "path to a real art will be found only when it has been freed from the dictates of an art-form foreign to it—that is, the Theatre" (27). This goal in early film criticism served practical ends. The medium was new and needed to establish itself first as a creative enterprise and then as an art form on a par with theater and the novel. It may very well be that the later tendency to aggressively deny the screenplay's literary merit is linked to attempts at establishing the artistic legitimacy of film. Film was for many critics, as Vachel Lindsay claimed, "the new universal alphabet" (203), and much effort was invested in characterizing its grammar and syntax. Lev Kuleshov, for example, compared it to poetry: "A poet places one word after another, in a definite rhythm, as one brick after another. Cemented by him, the word-images produce a complex conception as a result. So it is that shots, like conventionalized meanings, like the ideograms in Chinese writings, produce images and concepts" (91). These attempts to posit film as visual literature were largely successful and led to claims, such as André Bazin's, that "the director writes in film" (39), and also led to the establishment of auteur theory and the dominance of semiotics in film studies. Auteur theory did much to elevate the stature of film by promoting the perception of film as text and the director as author, but further supplanted the literary significance of the screenplay.

The problem is largely semantic. If the film proper is defined as the text of the film, how are we to define the screenplay? No one would deny that a screenplay is text, but when the same term is applied to the stream of images in a film, "text" connotes an irreconcilable ambiguity. Instead of addressing this issue, scholarship appears to have sidestepped it by ignoring the screenplay altogether, enabling theorists to apply linguistic terms to images without equivocating. Stuart M. Kaminsky, in his 1974 study of film genres, admits that "authorship studies are of great value in understanding film," but claims that "it may be of even more importance at the present state of film study to encourage additional descriptive generic studies" (10). Kaminsky's point is valid, but he fails in his call for a broader understanding of film to mention the possibility that the screenplay might be worthy of examination. Peter Brunette and David Wills, in their well-conceived 1989 work on Derrida and film theory, ironically titled *Screen/Play*, discuss at length the applicability of Derrida's theories about writing to studies of film, extending the boundaries of previous studies. They articulate clear distinctions between speech and writing, as Derrida does, yet eschew mention of the screenplay—the written text of nearly every film since the start of the twentieth century. This is particularly disappointing since much of their discussion could have added a great deal to our understanding of the screenplay and its function in film. Derrida's concept of invagination,[6] for example, which Brunette and Wills use to illuminate genre, could have been used to denote the interaction between the screenplay and the film proper—to show how the screenplay is both external and internal to the film.

Some scholars might argue that the screenplay falls outside the parameters of their particular study. This would be an adequate defense if not for the dearth of scholarship on the screenplay in film studies and the fact that less significant factors, such as on-set antics and the private lives of actors, have received more critical attention than screenplays and screenwriters. Despite observations, such as Andrew Sarris's, that "writing and directing are fundamentally the same function" (Corliss xv), auteur advocacy (even Sarris's) continues to valorize the director at the expense of the screenwriter (even if the director also wrote the screenplay). The essential core of film is the image in motion; thus the image is the essential core of film studies (though not its limit)—but films, although they can, rarely do exist without other factors. Even during the silent era, films were often accompanied by music, and dialogue was supplied by title cards. Purely visual storytelling in film was rare even in films such as Buster Keaton's *Sherlock, Jr.* (1924). Keaton's masterpiece is mainly visual storytelling; however, note the following title card from the film:

```
By the next day the
master mind had
completely solved the
```

----

6. Brunette and Wills offer the following summation of Derrida's term: "Briefly, invagination destroys the notion of a clearly identifiable and intact inside easily distinguishable from an outside, since the vagina (or the mouth or the anus or the ear, for that matter) can be seen in a sense as exterior tissue that has been folded inside, and thus as exterior and interior at the same time" (46).

```
mystery—with the
exception of locating
the pearls and finding
the thief.⁷
```

This title card functions as a transitional device to move the story to the next day (which could have been handled visually), but it also contains a joke wholly unavailable anywhere else in the film; it is purely literary.

Even in silent film, images and sound signified together. The fact that Charlie Chaplin composed music for his films acknowledges that he recognized the joint signification of image and sound. We may rightly call Chaplin an *auteur* filmmaker, because he directed and also wrote, performed in, edited, produced, and scored his films. The creation of his works and the performance of his works are inextricably bound. But few directors were directly responsible for as many facets of their films as Chaplin. Hitchcock's films are marked by his unique cinematic presence, but Hitchcock did not write *Vertigo* or *The Birds*. The same is true for John Ford's *Stagecoach*, Martin Scorsese's *Taxi Driver*, Clint Eastwood's *Unforgiven*,⁸ and scores of other films.

Acknowledging writers and their works does not diminish the contributions of directors. Writers and directors are both integral to a film. The contributions of a writer and a director to a performance of a work should be recognized in a manner similar to theater. A writer writes a play; a director guides its performance. A screenwriter writes a screenplay; a director guides its performance.

Ironically, playwrights garner more attention than screenwriters. When *Barefoot in the Park* opened at the Biltmore Theatre in New York City in 1963, Mike Nichols directed the production, but the work was attributed to its author, Neil Simon. When *Hud* opened in movie theaters that same year, it was attributed to its director Martin Ritt, not the writers, Harriet Frank Jr. and Irving Ravetch.

---

7. Transcribed from the film (line breaks are original to the title card).

8. *Vertigo* was written by Samuel A. Taylor and Alec Coppel, who adapted Pierre Boileau and Thomas Narcejac's novel *D'entre les morts* for the screen. Daphne du Maurier wrote the source for *The Birds* and Evan Hunter wrote the screenplay adaptation. Dudley Nichols and Ernest Haycox wrote *Stagecoach*. Paul Schrader wrote *Taxi Driver*. David Webb Peoples wrote *Unforgiven*.

The writer and the director are collaborators, and the writer's contributions are already inseparable from the director's production. Attending to the screenplay does not diminish the status of the director or undermine existing trends in film criticism (even auteur theory is useful when applied appropriately). Published or unpublished, produced or unproduced, the screenplay's importance to the film is second only to the importance of photography, and a rich cache of works worthy of critical examination are waiting to be brought into the light of intellectual critique.

Story and Montage

We may with some confidence parallel the beginning of the screenplay to the introduction of dramatic elements into film, although we can find earlier snippets of writing that foreshadow the screenplay. Entries in Edison's catalogues, for instance, strongly resemble scene descriptions we find in modern screenplays:

> New York in a Blizzard . . . Our camera is revolved from right to left and takes in Madison Square, Madison Square Garden, looks up Broadway from South to North, passes the Fifth Avenue Hotel and ends looking down 23rd Street West. (Jacobs 10)

This passage from the 1901–2 Edison Catalogue shares several characteristics with contemporary scene descriptions: It is written in the present tense. It tracks the action. It implies mood. Yet descriptions such as this hardly qualify as screenplays.

Story made screenwriting necessary, and the work of Georges Méliès, more than any other single filmmaker, helped transform film into a storytelling medium. When Méliès's works were imported to America, American film producers saw the "theatrical potential of the new medium" (Jacobs 11), and turned to narrative as a means of regaining audiences' waning interest in the novelty of moving pictures. This shift altered the medium's potential by transforming each image into a contextually driven signifier with an unlimited potential for reference. Prior to the introduction of story, film was little more than a descendent of Muybridge's serial photography. After the introduction of story, film images could be applied in an infinite number of ways, their meaning determined by the narrative context into which they were placed rather than merely the content of the shot. Edwin S. Porter glimpsed this potential—D. W. Griffith even more so—but of the early silent filmmakers, it was Pudovkin, Dziga Vertov, Sergei Eisenstein, and other students of the Kuleshov Workshop who most experimented with the placement of image within narrative context and the effect that placement had on signification.

Méliès's work made possible the work of those who followed: Porter, Griffith, Eisenstein, Chaplin, Mack Sennett, and so on. The shot, which previously had been primarily about *what* was being shot, became about *why* it was being shot; it came under the controlling influence of narrative. The arrangement of these shots made up what Méliès labeled artificially arranged scenes. The artificially arranged scene was the predecessor to montage. With the juxtaposition of two shots, interpretation becomes not only possible, but necessary. This is what Eisenstein refers to when he claims "montage is not an idea composed of successive shots stuck together but an idea that DERIVES from the collision between two shots that are independent of one another" ("Dramaturgy" 28).[9] As Eisenstein was aware, the dialectic between two diverse shots inspires interpretive thought. Audiences attempt to discern significance in the collision of signifying images by questioning their relationship to the story. The shot is the smallest unit of film (and competent filmmakers weigh each shot against the story), but montage requires a minimum of two shots, which prompt the reader to engage abstract thought, and moves film further into the realm of art. Eisenstein pointed out that "a constant evolution from the interaction between two contradictory opposites" creates a "dynamic conception of objects" ("Dramaturgy" 25), and that "in the realm of art this dialectical principle of the dynamic is embodied in CONFLICT as the essential basic principle of existence of every work of art and every form" (26). Since the story controls how images are sequenced in narrative film, the construction of filmic signs is at least partly a performance of the written word. Even the purely visual elements of films, such as those found in Stanley Kubrick's *2001: A Space Odyssey* (1968), George Dunning's *Yellow*

---

9. Eisenstein takes issue with Pudovkin and others who claim that "montage is a means of *unrolling* an idea through single shots" ("Dramaturgy" 28).

Submarine (1968), or Adrian Lyne's *Jacob's Ladder* (1990), serve the narrative. Eisenstein was aware of the relationships between film and narrative when he said, "There is no doubt that the treatment of an event is primarily determined by the author's attitude to the content. But [film] composition, as we understand it, is the means of expressing the author's attitude and influencing the spectators" (*Potemkin* 13). Eisenstein, for all his formalistic validations, recognized that the treatment of the story must be part and parcel of any "exhaustive analysis of all the film's aspects" (*Potemkin* 7). Most films are not manifestations of, but translations of, literary works.[10] Visual narrative is not autonomous of literary narrative.

When we date the emergence of the screenplay as a literary object—that is, a literary form in its own right—depends greatly on how we define "literary." Formalism might look to early screenplays that defamiliarize conventions. Poststructuralists might consider the nascent forms as marginal texts within the form. Historicists might look to the first screenplay to reflect (and possibly contribute to) its social milieu. No definitive determination is likely; however, within the motion picture industry, the nature of a screenplay remained in question until sometime after the introduction of sound. In a 1929 lecture, Benjamin Glazer (supervisor of sound for Pathé and F.B.O. Studios) articulates the difficulty in early definitions of the form:

> In the old days, a director was rather the master of the situation. If what he had down on the paper did not seem to suit the needs of the situation, he could improvise something that did seem to fit. But even a motion picture director hesitates to improvise dialogue. Some tried it, and the results were lamentable. Others were wiser. "If it is dialogue we need," they said, "let's get some playwrights, and have dialogue written." But even that did not work out so well, because, boiled down, a mere factual statement, like the old printed movie title, is not convincing in talk because it is not life-like.

----

10. My discussion and claims here and throughout are exclusive of experimental, improvised films without story. This is not an attempt to diminish their significance to film studies, but as my argument focuses on the screenplay, I am restricting my discussion to *mainstream* films, including independent and experimental films that begin as text.

On the other hand, picture audiences are not interested in common-places, such as "Good Morning," and "How do you do?" and "Won't you please sit down?" and such like. They are accustomed to the bare essentials of scene and story. And so we producers are forced back on the conclusion that we have got to have picture and dialogue that go together, that contribute each to the telling of the story, that together make a complete artistic unity. (Glazer 46)

Glazer goes on to point out that in 1929 New York had "a whole army . . . trained to write silent pictures, but . . . none trained to write talking pictures," and though playwrights and screen-writers were writing screenplays, they were "fumbling in the dark" (46). Glazer admits that "if the talking picture is to be a true art form, its form is yet to be invented" (46).

Inherent Difficulties in the Study and Perception of the Screenplay

Several factors make the screenplay a difficult object for literary study. For one, screenplays usually pass through many hands and many revisions before reaching the screen. This results in a boggling number of versions, often by a number of different writers, some credited and some not. The screenplay for Pierre Boulle's novel *La planète des singes* was written by Rod Serling and revised several times by Michael Wilson, with input from the director Franklin J. Schaffner. The Franklin J. Schaffner Collection housed at the Franklin and Marshall College Library in Lancaster, Pennsylvania, includes all of the following manuscripts:

> *Planet of the Apes* screenplay by Rod Serling, dated March 1, 1965
>
> Revision of *Planet of the Apes* screenplay, by Michael Wilson, dated January 17, 1967
>
> Revision of *Planet of the Apes* screenplay, by Michael Wilson, dated March 23, 1967
>
> Final Draft (1st half) of further revision of *Planet of the Apes* screenplay by Michael Wilson, dated March 31, 1967
>
> Final Revised Screenplay for *Planet of the Apes,* by Michael Wilson, dated April 18, 1967

Shooting Script for *Planet of the Apes*, by Michael Wilson, dated May 5, 1967 (photoreproduction with later revisions)

Shooting Script for *Planet of the Apes*, by Michael Wilson, dated May 5, 1967 (photoreproduction of copy with Schaffner's notes)

Which is the authoritative text? Which should we study? Identifying the most authoritative text for a screenplay is more difficult than identifying the most authoritative text for a novel or a play. Unlike novels, for which the published final draft is usually considered authoritative, and plays, for which the version performed at the play's debut is usually privileged, screenplays are seldom published, resulting in a daunting number of versions. Even when screenplays are published, the published versions often merely transcribe the films (*tran*-scripts rather than scripts), and bear only a passing resemblance to the shooting script used in production. Determining which version to examine may appear daunting until we recognize that the notion of an authoritative text for any written work is a matter of critical consensus. An individual screenplay may have more extant versions than a novel or a play, in part because of the lengthy production process and in part because the various drafts of a novel or play are often discarded. But the ease with which authoritative versions of a novel or play can be identified is a function of the works being published and studied by large numbers of scholars and lay readers. One possibility is that, if screenplays were analyzed to the extent that novels and plays have been for hundreds of years, consensus would develop about them as it has for the others. Another more likely possibility is that critics and scholars might reevaluate critical approaches that privilege an individual text, acknowledging and sometimes incorporating the multiplicity of texts into their analyses.

The numerous incarnations and transformations of a screenplay make the process of textual construction more obvious, but they do not roadblock analysis; they merely expose a truth about text that has long been obscured by wishful thinking. Which version of a screenplay we examine depends on which version seems most suited to our examination. More often than not, that will be the shooting script or the continuity script, which are usually the closest versions to what is filmed. But there are plenty of exceptions to that general guideline. For example, we might prefer to examine Quentin Tarantino's screenplay for *Natural Born Killers* over Oliver Stone's revision (or, as I do in this book, compare both), or Rod Serling's version of *Planet of the Apes* before Michael Wilson began revisions. The only version of any screenplay that begs to be discounted is the version that is transcribed from the film, because these are too far removed from the screenwriter and, other than dialogue, carry none of his or her language.

Another inherent difficulty is the relative inaccessibility of screenplays. Screenplays for recent, popular films are plentiful. You can download them off the Internet and purchase them from bookstores specializing in the sale of screenplays. Screenplays from early films and independent, experimental, foreign, and other marginalized films are much more difficult to locate. The largest collection is housed at the Fairbanks Center for Motion Picture Study in Beverly Hills, California, which includes the Margaret Herrick Library and the Academy Film Archive. The center contains over 6,000 early screenplays from the silent and sound era. The American Film Institute's Louis B. Mayer Library, the Frances Howard Goldwyn Hollywood Regional Library, UCLA's special collections, University of Southern California's Cinema and Television Library, and the Writers Guild–West all maintain screenplay collections. In 1998, the Margaret Herrick Library began publication of *Motion Picture Scripts: A Union List,* which contains location information for over 23,000 screenplays housed in various collections around Southern California. The Union List is the most concentrated source of screenplays, treatments, drafts, and so on, though screenplays can be found in special collections throughout the country. For example, the University of Iowa Libraries has ten screenplays by Louis Buñuel, which are located in the special collections of the University of Iowa Libraries, including copies of the scripts for *Un chien andalou* and *L'age d'or.*

Many of the screenplays from American movies still exist, but their copies are held in private collections and libraries. It is particularly difficult to locate photoplays from the silent era.[11] Specialized works are scattered all across the country and locating a copy of a particular

----

11. The most extensive collections of screenplays in English are housed in libraries at the American Film Institute (AFI); the Academy of Motion Pictures and Sciences (AMPAS); the Frances Howard Goldwyn Hollywood Regional Library; the University of California, Los Angeles; the University of Southern California; and the Writers Guild of America, West.

screenplay (or a particular copy of a screenplay) often involves travel and a great deal of effort.

A third factor, and perhaps the most difficult for literary scholars to overcome, is the formulaic nature of the screenplay. Screenplay format has evolved from its primitive beginnings, but even contemporary screenplays are written for an audience of filmmakers. Nearly all screenplays are laid out with scene headings, setting markers, dialogue markers, transitions, and other technical production information, which might lead some to dismiss their literary merit, but these notations are not substantially different from the stage directions we find in stage plays. In fact, the screenplay has much in common with the stage play. Both are written to be performed. Both employ dramatic elements: conflict, resolution, irony, paradox, and so on. For both, the story and the dialogue are the central focus of the writer's art. Both imply the direction a production should take. Both include technical information about sets, costumes, props, sound effects, visual effects, and movement. Other than the fact that stage plays have existed much longer than screenplays, it is difficult to come up with objective criteria that would enable us to embrace one and eschew the other.

Writing about the Screenplay

Most of what is written in praise of screenplays exists in publications oriented toward future screenwriters. Aimed at students of the craft, these articles are more instructional than critical. A few qualify as scholarly works, but most suffer from a vocational slant. Frances Taylor Patterson, who taught photoplay composition at Columbia University during the silent era, wrote the first books on screenwriting in the 1920s. Patterson admits that a screenplay (then called a "scenario") is "composed upon the typewriter, and its merit, or lack of merit, is judged while the idea is still clothed in words, not in celluloid" (*Scenario* 8) and that "writing for the screen is an art" (*Cinema* 2); nevertheless, he makes depreciatory comments about the screenplay's place in literature:

A photoplay has no objective reality until it reaches the screen. Closet drama may exist, if you will—the plays of Tennyson and Swinburne may be read with the deepest enjoyment in the library—but there can be no closet photodrama. A stage play in manuscript form may be literature, although not necessarily so. The dialogue exists exactly as it is to be upon the stage with only the voices and mannerisms of the actors and actresses lacking. The action is usually written in. The plays of Shaw, Galsworthy, Barrie, Pinero, Jones, are almost as popular as reading matter in the libraries as are novels and short stories of a like literary flavor. Not so with the photoplay. A photoplay does not actually become one until it exists in film. (*Cinema* 2)

Patterson's dismissal of the screenplay's literary merit foreshadows contemporary opinion. He, like those who follow, confuses popular apprehension with literary merit. Whether or not a screenplay is popular as reading matter is irrelevant to its value as a written work. Employing that criterion to judge the value of written works would result in the decanonization of many masterpieces (*Finnegans Wake,* for example), which also are not popular parlor reading.

Although dismissals like Patterson's can be unearthed well into the twentieth century, most scholars do not actively deny the screenplay's literary merit; they simply don't consider it, which is far more damaging than critical dismissal. As William Horne notes, "There will be no substantive study of the script, until and unless it is afforded its own legitimate aesthetic existence—not merely as a set of interim production notes or as a substitute film—but as a separate work . . . it is crucially important that the screenplay be viewed not only as a shooting script but as an independent *text*" (53).

To judge works as unworthy of critical attention requires some critical attention, at least enough to make a reasoned judgment. But the screenplay has been, for the most part, ignored, making critical redemption difficult. The lack of scholarship on the screenplay is more oversight than verdict. Wherever one chooses to situate the analysis of the screenplay (e.g., film studies, literary studies, cultural studies), it merits serious inquiry. The screenplay is of historical and literary significance to studies in film, literature, and culture, and it is amenable to the same critical approaches.

3

Aristotle, Aesthetics, and Critical Approaches to the Screenplay

> In constructing the plot and working it out with the proper diction, the poet should place the scene, as far as possible, before his eyes. In this way, seeing everything with the utmost vividness, as if he were a spectator of the action, he will discover what is in keeping with it, and be most unlikely to overlook inconsistencies.
>
> —**Aristotle,** *Poetics* (87)

Critical examinations of screenplays summon the longer critical histories of drama and literary studies, the earliest being those of Plato and Aristotle, that are founded on the view of art as reproduction. Both Plato and Aristotle equate fidelity to ideal forms with aesthetic value and argue that the further a work of art is removed from its ideal, the more its aesthetic qualities diminish. This raises some interesting questions. How, for example, do we judge the aesthetic merits of a screenplay if the film is always to be privileged? To a strictly Platonic sensibility, in situations where a film is made based on a screenplay, the film must be seen as a copy of the screenplay, since a copy cannot precede that which it copies just as a painting of a pot cannot predate the throwing of the pot. A film would always be one remove further from the ideal than the screenplay upon which the film is based. This somewhat absurd notion exposes the difficulties inherent in applying linear thinking to the screenplay. In the case of a novel adaptation, for instance, it is just as misleading to approach the film as a reproduction

45

of the screenplay as it is to approach the screenplay as a reproduction of the novel. We would hardly consider Woody Allen's screenplay for *Everything You Always Wanted to Know about Sex but Were Afraid to Ask* (1972) as further from an aesthetic ideal than David Reuben's self-help book by the same title any more than we would judge Shakespeare's *Hamlet* to be a knockoff of Thomas Kyd's *The Spanish Tragedy*.[1] Historically, screenplay adaptations, despite their prevalence, have been doubly condemned; often considered to fall short of the works they are adapting and inferior to the films they inspire. Platonic and Aristotelian aesthetics at least point out the absurdity of such judgments.

Most popular script-writing/screenplay texts take a formalistic approach to the aesthetics of the screenplay, referring and alluding almost exclusively to Aristotle's *Poetics*. Lajos Egri, in *The Art of Dramatic Writing*, for example, uses Aristotle to contrast his approach to drama.[2] Egri refers to Aristotle's privileging of action over character as a "basic error" (90), agreeing with John Galsworthy that "character creates plot" (91). Robert McKee agrees with Aristotle on this point, claiming that "why a man does a thing is of little interest once we see the thing he does" (377). Egri's chicken-and-the-egg argument with Aristotle does little to dethrone Aristotle's dominance over the craft of the writing of drama.[3] Critics who argue, as Warren Buckland notes, that in the New Hollywood films "narrative complexity is sacrificed on the alter of spectacle" (167)[4] recall Aristotle's claim that "the production of spectacular effect depends more on the art of the stage machinist than on that of the poet" (*Poetics* 64).

----

1. Thomas Kyd's *The Spanish Tragedy* is the most often cited source for Shakespeare's *Hamlet*, but as David Bevington points out, there are possibly other sources, such as a "lost *Hamlet* play" (1073) by Kyd in existence around 1589.

2. Although Lajos Egri's *The Art of Dramatic Writing* is written as a guide for the writing of stage plays, it is often used in screenwriting classes and therefore is relevant to our discussion here.

3. Egri argues that "character creates plot, not vice versa" (95) without ever dealing with the fact that the actions an audience witnesses a character make are the primary basis for how they judge that character. For example, does Oedipus seek the murderer who has brought a plague to Thebes because he is a good king or is he perceived as a good king because he seeks the murderer? This unresolvable paradox is at the heart of every character/plot argument.

4. Buckland considers this position to be overstated.

Aristotle, Aesthetics, and Critical Approaches

Excerpts from Plato's *Ion* and *The Republic* make useful tools for critiquing the dramatic elements of screenplays; however, because Aristotle's *Poetics* offers the earliest, fully realized paradigm for drama, I will focus most of my discussion on the *Poetics*. The *Poetics* can partially explain why many great screenplays are great and why many failed screenplays fail, but after the bodies are counted and the gold is divided, there are a number of screenplays that, although they fail to satisfy Aristotle's guidelines, still manage greatness. It would be negligent to end this discussion without some mention of those works and how they challenge Aristotelian aesthetic principles.

The argument could be made that applying what Aristotle said in the *Poetics* to anything other than tragedy represents a misapplication of those ideas. However, if we closely examine the screenplays being written, most of them (excluding comedies) are close enough in dramatic form to be examined under Aristotle's lamp. Nevertheless, we should keep in mind that Aristotle's focus in the *Poetics* is staged tragedy, and we are stretching his argument whenever we apply it to other forms, such as black comedy, action adventure, parody, dramatic comedy, and so on.

That caution in mind, it is difficult to imagine any mainstream contemporary American screenplay that is not knowingly or unknowingly influenced by Aristotle, either in the adoption or abeyance of Aristotelian principles. Aristotle is doubly apt, as the *Poetics* has been read as both descriptive and prescriptive (Adams 218). Francis Fergusson points to the prescriptive function of the *Poetics* in his introduction to the S. H. Butcher translation of the *Poetics* when he says that Aristotle's "whole discussion of plot-making is interspersed with practical suggestions for the playwright" (20). Fergusson is referring to suggestions such as, "As for the story, whether the poet takes it ready made or constructs it for himself, he should first sketch its general outline, and then fill in the episodes and amplify in detail" (88). These suggestions, although written about Greek theater more than 2,300 years ago, are stunningly relevant to the contemporary screenplay, both in the insight they provide into the basic structure of drama and the guidance they offer screenwriters.

Aristotle knew that "a play must, by definition, hold and please an audience in the theater" (Fergusson 20), and claimed that the tragedy was a superior form to the epic, because he believed that ideal storytelling focused on a single action, and epics were burdened with multiple storylines. Not surprisingly, most of the *Poetics* discusses the different parts of tragedy, particularly plot. Although Aristotle touches on comedy and makes occasional references to other forms (e.g., music, epic poetry) in the *Poetics,* his primary focus is on what he considers to be the foremost dramatic form, and in his discussion of tragedy we find the closest parallels to screenwriting.

Aristotle's Box

Aristotle's mimetic aesthetic contains none of the complications later raised by figures such as George Berkeley and Immanuel Kant, and it is not roadblocked by the radical indeterminacy that many poststructuralist thinkers have demonstrated in the last thirty years. Aristotle believed in absolutes, and he believed in the accessibility (or "approachability") of those absolutes. He differs from other thinkers of his day primarily in his approach. It is the way a writer[5] manages to offer access to the "truth" that concerns Aristotle in the *Poetics*.

In a frequently quoted passage, Aristotle says tragedy "is an imitation of an action that is serious, complete, and of a certain magnitude" (*Poetics* 61).[6] At first glance, this definition seems simple enough, but we need to closely examine what Aristotle specifically meant by his definition before we can define its relevance to the screenplay.

According to Aristotle, the writer's job is to accurately represent the world according to rules of probability and necessity, rules that Aristotle considered available to any thinking person. A writer could present the world two ways: through narrative, as novelists do (and in ancient Athens, epic poets did) or by writing a script for actors to act out on stage, that is, a writer could "present all of his characters as

----

5. Here and throughout I use "writer" instead of "poet," which is the term Aristotle uses throughout the *Poetics*.

6. The full definition, as it is often quoted, is: "Tragedy, then, is an imitation of an action that is serious, complete, and of a certain magnitude; in language embellished with each kind of artistic ornament, the several kinds being found in separate parts of the play; in the form of action, not of narrative; through pity and fear effecting the proper purgation of these emotions."

living and moving before us" (*Poetics* 53). Screenwriters are engaged in virtually the same enterprise as the ancient Athenian dramatists: They are attempting to present their stories through characters that live and move on the screen. The actions of characters propel the story, and it is the actions of characters that most concern Aristotle. This is why Aristotle privileges plot over character, because "most important of all is the structure of the incidents [i.e., plot]. For Tragedy is an imitation, not of men, but of an action and of life, and life consists in action, and its end is a mode of action, not a quality" (62). No doubt, this statement will raise a harumph or two from those who relish films eschewing or subduing plot for in-depth character analysis (e.g., Peter Greenaway's *Prospero's Books* or David Cronenberg's *Naked Lunch*) or visual experimentation (e.g., Buñuel and Dali's *Un chien andalou*), but for those who focus on traditional mainstream cinema, the statement is somewhat self-evident.

To understand Aristotle's position, we need to understand what Aristotle means by action. Action for Aristotle is not mere movement, as the term is often used in contemporary parlance. Action in Aristotle's philosophy implies the underlying psychic forces that drive a particular character to move in a particular way. It is *motivated* action, movement driven by the psychological and moral predisposition of the character. It is an action that is probable and necessary for a particular character because of the nature of that character's psyche. Tragedy imitates "men in action" (*Poetics* 52), and the actions of these men are made necessary and probable by underlying moral dispositions.

We find this principle in the character of Jerry Lundegaard from the Coen brothers' *Fargo*. Jerry's plan to buy himself out of trouble with ransom money from the arranged kidnapping of his wife fails because Jerry is unable to stand up to his father-in-law. At a crucial moment in the story, Jerry is incapable of exerting any influence over Wade:

```
KITCHEN OF LUNDEGAARD HOUSE

Jerry, Wade, and Stan Grossman sit around the kitchen
table. It is night. The scene is harshly toplit by a
hanging fixture. On the table are the remains of coffee
and a cinammon [sic] filbert ring.

                      WADE
         Dammit! I wanna be a part of this thing!
```

CHAPTER 3

                    JERRY
No, Wade! They were real clear! They said
they'd call tomorrow, with instructions, and
it's gonna be delivered by me alone!

                    WADE
It's my money, I'll deliver it—what do they
care?

                    STAN
Wade's got a point there. I'll handle the
call if you want, Jerry.

                    JERRY
No, no. See—they, no, we, they only deal
with me. Ya feel this, this nervousness on
the phone there, they're very—these guys're
dangerous—

                    WADE
All the more reason! I don't want you—with
all due respect, Jerry—I don't want you
mucking this up.

                    JERRY
The heck d'ya mean?

                    WADE
They want my money, they can deal with me.
Otherwise I'm going to a professional.

He points to a briefcase.

                    WADE
. . . There's a million dollars here!

                    JERRY
No, see—

                    WADE
Look, Jerry, you're not sellin' me a damn
car. It's my show here. That's that.

                    STAN
It's the way we prefer to handle it, Jerry.
(52-53)

Jerry cannot wield any influence with his father-in-law, because his character is flawed. He is weak and ineffectual. As a result, his rhetoric is uncertain and unbalanced. The Coen brothers reveal this weakness in Jerry at the beginning of the script.

```
                ANDERSON [Jerry]
      I'm, uh, Jerry Lundegaard—

                YOUNGER MAN [Carl]
      You're Jerry Lundegaard?

                JERRY
      Yah, Shep Proudfoot said—

                YOUNGER MAN
      Shep said you'd be here at 7:30. What gives,
      man?

                JERRY
      Shep said 8:30.

                YOUNGER MAN
      We been sitting here an hour. I've peed
      three times already.

                JERRY
      I'm sure sorry. I—Shep told me 8:30. It was
      a mix-up, I guess.
```

Then, later in the conversation . . .

```
                JERRY
      . . . So I guess that's it, then. Here's the
      keys—

                CARL
      No, that's not it, Jerry.

                JERRY
      Huh?

                CARL
      The new vehicle, plus forty thousand
      dollars.

                JERRY
      Yah, but the deal was, the car first, see,
      then the forty thousand, like as if it was
```

```
                    the ransom. I thought Shep told you—

                            CARL
                    Shep didn't tell us much, Jerry.

                            JERRY
                    Well, okay, it's—

                            CARL
                    Except that you were gonna be here at 7:30.

                            JERRY
                    Yah, well, that was a mix-up, then.

                            CARL
                    Yeah, you already said that.

                            JERRY
                    Yah. But it's not a whole pay-in-advance
                    deal. I give you a brand-new vehicle in
                    advance and—

                            CARL
                    I'm not gonna debate you, Jerry.

                            JERRY
                    Okay.  (4-5)
```

Jerry cannot exert any authority over the two hoods he hires to kidnap his wife. His inability to form authoritative statements, his tendency toward redundancy, and his easily bent will reflect an underlying moral weakness that renders his actions probable and necessary, as Jerry's weakness will not allow him to take any direct action to rectify his situation. His inability to face his troubles head-on prompts him to pass responsibility onto Shep in the above exchange. The mix-up over the meeting time was Shep's fault, according to Jerry, just as all of his problems are as a result of other people. Jerry's inability to take responsibility engenders Wade's distrust. It is the reason Jerry is in need of money in the first place, and it is the reason he hires Carl and Grimsrud to kidnap his wife. Jerry's character renders his actions necessary, and as a result of those necessary actions, his wife dies and he is arrested. Thus, the botched kidnapping is directly traceable to Jerry's flawed moral character.

Fig. 2. Jerry Lundegaard (William H. Macy) framed behind blinds as if behind bars in the Coen brothers' *Fargo* (1996).

This exposition of Jerry, its complications to the plot, and its revelations about character are literary; they are rendered in the text of the screenplay. The dialogue and events that shape the core thrust of the story exist fully in text. The film recasts these elements into visual representations, but it does not add complexity or complication. Just as Hamlet exists as a textual construction outside performance, Jerry Lundegaard exists outside the film proper. He is made of words, first and foremost, and is merely performed in the film.

Despite the well-constructed characters in *Fargo*, the screenplay does not meet Aristotle's criteria for the best type of tragedy, because Jerry is too ineffectual to qualify as a worthy opponent to Marge's strong moral character. Judged by Aristotelian standards, the screenplay fails to satisfy the moral sense of an audience. In the *Poetics*, Aristotle praises the poet Agathon for his "marvelous skill in the effort to hit the popular taste—to produce a tragic effect that satisfies the moral sense" (91). This is achieved, according to Aristotle, when a "clever rogue . . . is outwitted, or the brave villain defeated" (91–92). But Jerry is neither. Therefore, Marge's victory over him has less impact than it would if Jerry had been more sharp-witted and less cowardly. In inverting the Aristotelian hero, Joel and Ethan Coen parody tragedy, creating a mock tragedy. What Alexander Pope's *The Rape of the Lock* does for the epic, the Coen brothers' screenplay does for tragedy. This is one of the sources of the screenplay's black humor.

The character of Brigid in John Huston's *The Maltese Falcon,* on the other hand, does fit Aristotle's criteria. Brigid is clever and manages to outwit nearly everyone in the screenplay. When Spade cuts through her act at the end, the dramatic effect satisfies Aristotelian standards for a well-crafted tragedy:

```
                    BRIGID:
[. . .] I told him . . . Yea . . . But
please believe me, Sam. I wouldn't have told
him if I had thought Floyd would kill him. I
wouldn't for a minute . . .

                    SPADE:
          (interrupting)
If you thought he wouldn't kill Miles, you
were right, Angel.

                    BRIGID:
          (her upraised face holds utter
          astonishment)
Didn't he?

                    SPADE:
Miles hadn't many brains but he had too many
years experience as a detective to be caught
like that—by a man he was shadowing—up a
blind alley with his gun tucked away in his
hip and his overcoat buttoned.
          (he takes his hand away from her
          shoulder, looks at her for a long
          moment smiling, then:)
But he would have gone up there with you,
Angel. He was just dumb enough for that.
He'd have looked you up and down and licked
his lips and gone grinning from ear to ear.
And then you could have stood as close to
him as you liked in the dark and put a hole
through him with the gun you had gotten from
Thursby that evening.
```

Brigid shrinks back from him until the edge of the table stops her.

                    BRIGID:
               (staring with terrified eyes)
          Don't—don't talk to me like that, Sam. You
          know I didn't . . . you know—

                    SPADE:
          Stop it!
               (he glances at the clock)
          The police will be blowing in any minute
          now. Talk!

                    BRIGID:
               (puts the back of her hand to her
               forehead)
          Oh, why do you accuse me of such a terrible
          . . . ?

                    SPADE:
               (very low—impatient)
          This isn't the spot for the school-girl act.
          The pair of us are sitting under the
          gallows.

He grasps her wrists forcing her to stand up straight
in front of him. Her face becomes suddenly haggard.

                    SPADE:
          Why did you shoot him?

                    BRIGID:
               (voice hushes [sic] and troubled)
          I didn't mean to at first. I didn't really
          but when I saw that Floyd couldn't be
          frightened, I—I can't look at you and tell
          you this, Sam.
               (she starts to sob, clings to him)

                    SPADE:
          You thought Thursby would tackle him and one
          or the other of them would go down. If
          Thursby was the one, then you were rid of
          him. It if was Miles, then you could see
          that Thursby was caught and you'd be rid of
          him. That it?

                    BRIGID:
          S—something—like—that.

CHAPTER 3

>   SPADE:
> And when you found that Thursby didn't mean
> to tackle him, you borrowed the gun and did
> it yourself. Right?

She nods mutely.

>   SPADE:
> You didn't know then that Gutman was here
> hunting for you . . . You didn't suspect
> that or you wouldn't have been trying to
> shake your protector. But you knew Gutman
> was here when you heard Thursby had been
> shot and you knew you needed another protec-
> tor—So you came back to me.

She puts her hands up around the back of his neck push-
ing his head down until his mouth all but touches hers.

>   BRIGID:
> Yes, but—Oh, sweetheart, it wasn't only
> that. I would have come back to you sooner
> or later. From the very first instant I you
> I knew. . . .

He puts his arms around her holding her tight to him.

>   SPADE:
>   (tenderly)
> You Angel! Well, if you get a good break,
> you'll be out of San Quentin in twenty years
> and you can come back to me then.

She draws away from him slightly, throws her head far
back to stare up at him, uncomprehending.

>   SPADE:
>   (tenderly)
> I hope they don't hang you, Precious, by
> that sweet neck.

He puts his hand up and caresses her throat. In an instant she is out of his arms back against the table
crouching, both hands spread over her throat. Her face
is wild-eyed, haggard. Her mouth opens and closes.

>   BRIGID:
>   (in a small parched voice)

You're not . . . ?
                (she can get no other words out)

Spade's face is damp with sweat now. His mouth smiles
and there are smile wrinkles around his glittering
eyes.

                    SPADE:
                (gently)
        I'm going to send you over. The chances are
        you'll get off with life. That means you'll
        be out again in twenty years. You're an
        angel! I'll wait for you.
                (he clears his throat)
        If they hang you, I'll always remember you.

Brigid drops her hands, stands erect. Her face become's
smooth and untroubled except for the faintest of dubi-
ous glints in her eyes. She smiles back at him.

                    BRIGID:
        Don't Sam. Don't say that—even in fun. Oh,
        you frightened me for a moment. I really
        thought—you do such wild and unpredictable
        things. . . .

She breaks off, thrusts her head forward and stares
deep into his eyes. The flesh around her mouth shivers
and fear comes back into her eyes. She puts her hands
to her throat again. Spade laughs—His laugh is a croak.

                    SPADE:
        Don't be silly. You're taking the fall.
        (138-41)

Then, toward the end of the scene, we see into Spade's character:

                    SPADE:
                (hoarsely)
        Listen. . . . This won't do any good. You'll
        never understand me but I'll try once and
        then give it up. Listen . . . when a man's
        partner is killed, he's supposed to do some
        thing about it. It doesn't make any differ
        ence what you thought of him. He was your
        partner and you're supposed to do something
        about it. Then it happens we're in the

```
detective business. Well, when one of your
organization gets killed, it's bad business
to let the killer get away with it—bad all
around—bad for every detective everywhere.
(142-43)
```

This key scene at the end of *The Maltese Falcon* is a good example of what Aristotle meant by *Peripeteia,* or Reversal of the Situation. Aristotle considers Reversal of the Situation and Recognition to be "the two most powerful elements of emotional interest" in a plot (*Poetics* 63). He defines Reversal of the Situation as "a change by which the action veers round to its opposite, subject always to our rule of probability or necessity" (72). He defines Recognition as "a change from ignorance to knowledge, producing love or hate between the persons destined by the poet for good or bad fortune" (72). In Spade's final encounter with Brigid, Spade's suspicions about her are confirmed by the confession he pries from her. Although Aristotle would not consider this recognition on the level of Oedipus's recognition when the messenger delivers his ironic message about Oedipus's lineage, it does exemplify Recognition.

Spade's moment of Recognition is coupled with a Reversal of the Situation, a combination that Aristotle praises. Spade and Brigid's situation is completely reversed. They go from accomplices to adversaries. More to the screenplay's credit, the Recognition and the Reversal of the Situation are coupled with the revelation of Spade's ethical nature. In turning Brigid over to the police, Spade does not only outwit a clever opponent, thereby demonstrating a superior mental faculty, he does the *right* thing by his partner. Unlike Jerry Lundegaard, Spade is ethical, and the moral nature of his character determines his actions. Furthermore, the tragic event in *Fargo* does not happen to the hero, Marge, whereas the tragic event in *The Maltese Falcon* does happen to Spade (although, not to the level of an Oedipus or Macbeth)—Spade must sacrifice Brigid to the police, thus he must give up money and love in order to keep his ethical nature consistent.

The Maltese Falcon meets Aristotle's definition of a "complex" tragedy, the best of four kinds. A complex tragedy in Aristotle's view is one wherein the tragic turn depends wholly on Reversal of the Situation and Recognition. The line of action (i.e., plot) leading to tragic events is rendered inevitable by the character of the tragic hero, who is com-

Fig. 3. Ilsa (Ingrid Bergman) and Rick (Humphrey Bogart) experience
an Aristotelian reversal of the situation in *Casablanca* (1942).

pelled by his nature to act as he does, which engenders irony. Oedipus,
for example, must seek the killer of the previous king because Oedipus
is a good king, and avenging the previous king's death is the only way
to rescue his people from the plague. But it is from this single action
that the tragedy proceeds. Thus, to avoid tragedy, Oedipus would have
to be less of a king and ignore the needs of his people. What makes
Oedipus a great tragedy in Aristotelian terms is that the line of action
renders Oedipus's actions inevitable. Furthermore, it is through the
Oedipus's actions that his character is revealed. Thus, action precedes
character.

In "pathetic" tragedy, Aristotle claims the hero is driven by his
passion. Desire fuels the precipitant event leading to tragedy. We find
examples of this type of drama in David Mamet's script for *The Post-
man Always Rings Twice* (1981), Billy Wilder's *Double Indemnity*, James
Dearden and Nicholas Meyer's *Fatal Attraction* (1987), Joe Eszterhas's

Basic Instinct (1992), and Scott B. Smith's *A Simple Plan* (1998). Consider the following exchange between Clarence and Alabama from Quentin Tarantino's *True Romance:*

```
                      ALABAMA
          [. . .] and I feel really goofy saying this
          after only knowing you one night and me
          being a call girl and all. But I think I
          love you.

                      CLARENCE
          Now don't bullshit me. I've been trying to
          keep perspective on this whole situation.
          If you say you love me, and I say I love you
          and then I throw caution to the wind and let
          the chips falls [sic] where they may and
          you're lying to me, I'm gonna fuckin' die.

                      ALABAMA
                 (holding up palm)
          I'm not lying to you. And I swear right now,
          from this moment forth, I will never lie to
          you again.

                      CLARENCE
                 (as if he can't say it fast enough)
          Okay, I love you too I fell in love with you
          last night. (28)
```

Clarence's motivation is his desire for Alabama, his desire for love. This is what drives him and renders inevitable everything that happens from this scene forward. If Clarence's passion had not influenced him, no misfortune would have ensued, but Clarence would do anything (literally) for love.

Fergusson explains that "in Aristotle's philosophy . . . the concepts 'action' and 'passion' (or *praxis* and *pathos*), are sharply contrasted. Action is active: the psyche perceives something it wants, and 'moves' toward it. Passion is passive: the psyche suffers something it cannot control or understand, and 'is moved' thereby" ("Introduction" 11). The two are in opposition. Sam Spade decides what he will do based on his ethical nature; Clarence is compelled to action by his desire. In pairing up with Alabama, Clarence surrenders control to other forces; as Tarantino puts it, he "throw[s] caution to the wind" and must deal with the consequences, whatever they may be—wherever the chips may fall. He is at the mercy of other forces; therefore, he does not control the events (although he may appear to).

Aristotle distinguishes moral conscience from emotional motivation, and privileges moral conscience as the more intellectual of the two, the one ruled by the mind—a superior motivating force in Aristotle's thought. Emotions are less noble. When human passions motivate action, it is baser, more primal, more ephemeral, and less effective in the construction of an enduring tragedy. Emotions are fickle; truth is constant. A story driven by truth would necessarily reveal more about the universe as it is, and therefore it carries more import.

The third kind of tragedy is one for which "the motives are ethical" (*Poetics* 90). This type is distinguishable from complex tragedy in that ethical principles drive actions in ethical tragedy, whereas the actions in complex Tragedy are inevitably linked to Reversal of the Situation and Recognition. In an ethical tragedy, Reversal of the Situation and Recognition are not necessarily present (if they are, the tragedy may actually be complex). Aristotle's third type of tragic drama is didactic and tends to moralize. Ron Nyswaner's *Philadelphia*, for example, shapes the unethical treatment of homosexual men into tragedy. Andrew Beckett (Tom Hanks) is not a particularly remarkable man aside from the injustice he suffers from antigay sentiment. Beckett is everyman, and it is precisely this status that helps an audience identify with him and perceive his misfortune as tragic. Note the ideological slant in the following excerpt:

```
SPECTATORS STREAM OUT OF CITY HALL INTO THE HUBBUB OF
TWO DISTINCT GROUPS SHOUTING AT EACH OTHER (EXT/DAY):
GAY RIGHTS ACTIVISTS in T-shirts with pink triangles,
denouncing discrimination; BORN AGAIN ACTIVISTS wav-
ing placards citing AIDS as God's punishment for homo-
sexuality; POLICEMEN keeping them apart; A MEDIA CIRCUS
getting it on videotape.

Joe and Miguel FLANK Andrew, who walks weakly. with a
cane. Sarah and Jill follow close behind, running the
gauntlet of ACTIVISTS and REPORTERS.

Andrew's POV on a placard: "We Die-They Do Nothing!"

Jill's POV on a placard: "AIDS Cures Homosexuality!"
```

```
A TV CREW shines HOT LIGHTS on Andrew.

               TV REPORTER (ANGELA MEDINA)
          Do you see this as a gay rights issue?

                    ANDREW
          I'm not political. I just want compensation
          for being fired.

                    REPORTER MEDINA
          But you are gay, aren't you?

IMAGE: ANDREW SEEN ON A TV SCREEN (INT./NIGHT):

                    ANDREW
          "I don't see how that's any of your business
          . . . (a smile) But yes, I am."
          (n.p.)
```

Philadelphia is not a particularly good or effective tragedy when judged by Aristotelian principles, because inevitable elements of the plot do not control the action; rather, ethical issues control it. Events happen the way they do because they must happen that way in order to put forth an ethical message. Compare this to Larry McMurtry and Diana Ossana's screenplay adaptation of E. Annie Proulx's *Brokeback Mountain* (2005), which is fueled by desire (thus, a "pathetic" tragedy in Aristotelian terms) and avoids didacticism. Homosexuality in *Brokeback Mountain* is relevant to the action, but not essential. *Brokeback Mountain* is a love story, whereas *Philadelphia* is a message film.

The fourth kind of tragedy is one that lacks Recognition and Reversal of the Situation; it lacks the characteristics normally present in a complex tragedy. "Simple" tragedies often rely on spectacle and lack what we might conventionally refer to as well-structured plot. Barré Lyndon's screenplay for the 1953 adaptation of *War of the Worlds* and Josh Friedman and David Koepp's 2005 screenplay for the Stephen Spielberg version are both faithful adaptations of H. G. Wells's novel, and both can be seen as examples of Aristotle's fourth kind of tragedy. The 1953 and 2005 versions retain the deus ex machina ending, which necessitates neither recognition nor reversal of the situation, and reduces the principle characters to backdrop for the spectacular alien invasion. Both screenplays resort to subplots to mask the fact that the principle characters are mere bystanders: Lyndon crafts a behind-the-scenes look at science and government working together to find a way of combating the invasion. Friedman and Koepp focus on Ray Ferrier's (Tom Cruise) struggle to assume his role as father for his children. But neither is instrumental in the resolution of the principle conflict; neither contributes to the defeat of the aliens. The aliens' lack of immunity to earthbound diseases, something none of the characters foresees or commands, foils the invasion.

Ethics are important in Aristotelian philosophy, but in the *Poetics* they are inferior to the line of action and subservient to the plot. Character does not determine what happens, *what happens* determines character. Nevertheless, character is still significant,[7] and ethics define character: "Character is that which reveals moral purpose, showing the kind of things a man chooses or avoids. Speeches, therefore, which do not make this manifest, or in which the speaker does not choose or avoid anything whatever, are not expressive of character" (*Poetics* 64). Aristotle claims that four things should be aimed at in respect to character. A character must be: good, appropriate, true to life, and consistent. Of these four, the most important is that a character "must be good" (81). By "good," Aristotle means ethical. Furthermore, Aristotle points out that *"any* speech or action that manifests moral purpose of any kind will be expressive of character: the character will be good if the purpose is good" (81). This principle is particularly evident in the opening of the Coen brothers' script for *Miller's Crossing:*

```
FADE IN:
CLOSE SHOT        A WHISKY TUMBLER

That sits on an oak side bar under a glowing green
bankers lamp, as two ice cubes are dropped in. From
elsewhere in the room:

                    Man (off)
          I'm talkin' about friendship. I'm talkin'
          about character. I'm talkin' about—hell,
          Leo, I ain't embarrassed to use the word—I'm
          talkin' about ethics.
```

----

7. Aristotle divides tragedy into six parts, all of which are used to determine its quality. They are, in order of importance: Plot, Character, Diction, Thought, Spectacle, and Song (*Poetics* 62).

CHAPTER 3

Whisky is poured into the tumbler, filling it almost to the rim, as the offscreen man continues.

> . . . You know I'm a sporting man. I like to make the occasional bet. But I ain't <u>that</u> sporting.

THE SPEAKER

A balding middle-aged man with a round, open face. He still wears his overcoat and sits in a leather chair in the dark room, Illuminated by the offscreen glow of a desk lamp. This is Johnny Caspar.

Behind him stands another man, harder looking, wearing an overcoat and hat and holding another hat—presumably Caspar's. This is Bluepoint Vance.

> Caspar (cont'd)
> When I fix a fight, say—if I pay a three-to-one favorite to throw a goddamn fight—I figure I got a right to expect that fight to go off at three-to-one. But every time I lay a bet with this sonofabitch Bernie Bernheim, Before I know it the odds is even up—or worse, I'm betting the short money . . .

Behind Caspar we hear the clink of ice in the tumbler and a figure emerges from the shadows, walking away from the glowing bar in the background.

> . . . The sheeny knows I like sure things. He's selling the information I fixed the fight. Out-of-town money comes pourin' in. The odds go straight to hell. I don't know who he's sellin' it to, maybe the Los Angeles combine, I don't know. The point is, Bernie ain't satisfied with the honest dollar he can make off the vig. He ain't satisfied with the business I do on his book. He's sellin' tips on how I bet, and that means part of the payoff that should be ridin' on my hip is ridin' on someone else's. So back we go to these questions—friendship, character, ethics.

The man with the whiskey glass has just passed the camera and we cut to the:

```
REVERSE

Another well dressed, middle aged man, behind a large
polished oak desk, listening intently. This is Leo. He
is short but powerfully built, with the face of a man
who has seen things.

The man with the whiskey enters frame and passes Leo to
lean against the wall behind him, where he listens qui-
etly.

                    Caspar
       . . . So its clear what I'm sayin'?

                    Leo
          Clear as mud.

Caspar purses his lips but continues unfazed.

                    Caspar
          It's a wrong situation. It's getting' so a
          businessman can't expect no return from a
          fixed fight. Now if you can't trust a fix,
          what can you trust? For a good return you
          gotta go bettin' on chance, and then you're
          right back with anarchy. Right back inna
          jungle. On account of the breakdown of
          ethics. That's why ethics is important. It's
          the grease makes us get along, what seper-
          ates us from the animals, beasts a burden,
          beasts a prey. Ethics. Wheras Bernie Bern-
          heim is a horse of a different color ethics-
          wise. As in, he ain't got any. He's stealin'
          from me plain and simple.
          (1-2)
```

And later, when Leo questions Caspar about other people who know about the fix, Caspar replies:

```
                    Caspar
          I guess you ain't been listening. Sure other
          people know. That's why we gotta go to this
          question of character, determine just who
          exactly is chiseling in on my fix. And
          that's how we know it's Bernie Bernheim. The
          Motzah Kid. 'Cause ethically, he's kinda
          shaky. (4)
```

This opening demonstrates the complexity of Aristotelian principles. Caspar's speech manifests moral purpose. Caspar is upset because Bernie Bernheim is interfering with Caspar's honest fix. Caspar wants justice. He wants Leo to let him right the wrong. The very fact that Caspar is asking Leo's permission to kill Bernie demonstrates that Caspar understands propriety. He takes actions that are appropriate for the universe in which he lives. Caspar's character is defined by this articulation of moral purpose. Because we recognize that his purposes are not "good," we recognize that he is not a good man. He is, however, a man of high standing—not in ancient Athens, but in the universe that the Coen brothers create—and therefore makes for a worthy adversary. Caspar is not inept like Jerry Lundegaard; he is powerful and capable of taking action, when that action is appropriate to his moral understanding. Only his moral understanding is flawed, and that is precisely what qualifies him as a bad man.

The "good" man in *Miller's Crossing* is, understandably, the screenplay's hero: Tom Reagan. Like Caspar, Tom has moral purpose, but unlike Caspar, Tom's moral purpose is based on "good" ethics: loyalty, fairness, responsibility, and so on.[8] Tom makes the actions he must make based on his character, and those actions lead inevitably to the tragic loss of Verna and his career with Leo. However, like Oedipus, Tom finds himself in the situation he is in because he is a good man. Tom's recognition comes when Bernie returns to town, figuring to outmaneuver Tom:

    He [Tom] crosses to the chair facing Bernie's.

                       Tom
         . . . What's on your mind, Bernie?

                      Bernie
         Things. . . I guess you must be kind of
         angry. I'm supposed to be gone, far away. I
         guess it seems sort of irresponsible, my
         being here . . .

----

8. Tom is loyal to Leo throughout the screenplay. He refuses to kill Bernie (the first time) because he judges that it is unfair for him to die—letting him go at risk to his own life—and he exhibits responsibility by refusing to let Leo buy him out of his gambling debts.

```
Bernie leaves room for a response but Tom is only lis-
tening.

            . . . And I was gonna leave. Honest I was.
            But then I started thinking. If I stuck
            around, that would not be good for you. And
            then I started thinking that . . . that
            might not be bad for me.

Tom still doesn't answer.

            . . . I guess you didn't see the play you
            gave me. I mean what'm I gonna do? If I
            leave . . . I got nothing—no money, no
            friends, nothing. If I stay, I got you. Any
            one finds out I'm alive—you're dead, so
            . . . I got you, Tommy.

Tom is silent.

            . . . What's the matter, you got nothin' to
            crack wise about? Bernie ain't so funny any
            more? (94-95)
```

Just as Oedipus immediately recognizes the trouble he has gotten himself into by doing what he was ethically bound to do, Tom realizes that in letting Bernie live he has put himself in a deadly predicament.

The fact that Bernie is Verna's brother echoes another Aristotelian principle. Aristotle's explanation for the appeal of tragedy is that wellcrafted tragedy results in a purgation of pity and fear; in addition to complete action, a tragedy presents incidents that arouse pity and fear in an audience, thus resulting in a cathartic purging of these emotions. How a narrative is structured to arouse pity and fear is a factor in determining the quality of the storytelling. Aristotle notes that these emotions can be stimulated by "spectacular means," but that this method is "less artistic"—because of its dependence on "extraneous aids" (read: special effects, explosions, gore, and so on)—than when pity and fear "result from the inner structure of the piece" (*Poetics* 78). Because Bernie is related to the woman Tom loves, we experience pity and fear when Tom is forced to kill Bernie. As Aristotle explains: "If an enemy kills an enemy, there is nothing to excite pity either in the act or the intention—except so far as the suffering in itself is pitiful. So again with indifferent persons. But when the tragic incident occurs between those who are near or dear to one another—if, for example, a brother kills, or intends to kill, a brother, a son his father, a mother her son, a son his mother" (79). Tragic effect increases when some familial or emotional tie binds the characters. Of course, characters do not have to be related by blood for such a tie to exist, just a bond as strong as blood. Good screenwriters establish a strong connection before the tragic event. In *Reservoir Dogs,* for example, Tarantino builds a powerful brotherly relationship between Mr. White and Mr. Orange. By the time we reach the dramatic shootout at the end, Mr. White has put his life on the line in defense of Mr. Orange. Mr. White supports Mr. Orange's story about killing Mr. Blonde. Mr. White even draws down on his good friend Joe in defense of Mr. Orange. When the truth about Mr. Orange's identity finally comes out, Mr. White is forced to shoot the one man he least wants to shoot:

```
He [Mr. White] lifts Mr. Orange's head, cradling it in
his lap and stroking his brow.

                      MR. WHITE
                  (with much effort)
             Sorry, kid. Looks like we're gonna do a
             little time.

Mr. Orange looks up at him and, with even more of an
effort:

                      MR. ORANGE
             I'm a cop.

Mr. White doesn't say anything, he keeps stroking
Orange's brow.

                      MR. ORANGE
             I'm sorry, I'm so sorry.

Mr. White lifts his .45 and places the barrel between
Mr. Orange's eyes.

The CAMERA MOVES into an EXTREME C.U. of Mr. White.

The SOUNDS of outside STORM inside. We don't see any-
thing, but we HEAR a bunch of shotguns COCKING.
```

Aristotle, Aesthetics, and Critical Approaches

```
                    POLICE FORCE (OS)
         Freeze, motherfucker! Drop your fucking gun!

Mr. White looks up at them, smiles, PULLS the trigger.

BANG

We hear a BURST of SHOTGUN FIRE.

Mr. White is BLOWN out of frame, leaving it empty.
(100)
```

Tarantino even poses Mr. Orange and Mr. White in the pietà, visually stressing the familial bond that has developed between the two men and empowering the scene with mythic significance. Because it fuses Recognition with Reversal of the Situation, the scene is dramatically powerful. Like Spade and Brigid in *The Maltese Falcon,* Mr. White and Mr. Orange go from allies to enemies at the instant of Recognition.

The only weakness in the ending, according to Aristotelian principles, is that the Recognition relies on Mr. Orange's confession, rather than the events themselves. Of the five types of Recognition that Aristotle discusses, this is the second to least effective. Aristotle's five types of Recognition in order of artistic accomplishment are:

1. Recognition comes as a result of the events themselves.
2. Recognition comes as a result of reasoning (logic).
3. Recognition comes when an object awakens a feeling.
4. Recognition is invented by the will of the writer (e.g., a character simply tells who he is).
5. Recognition is a result of recognizing signs: scars, necklaces, and so on. (*Poetics* 84–86)

We seldom find Recognition in screenplays occurring as a result of the events themselves, but when the screenplay is structured this way, the result is often powerful and effective. For example, Jules's revelation in *Pulp Fiction* is not a result of reason, some object, forced recognition, or signs; Jules comes into understanding as a result of the Fourth Man's failed attempt to shoot him:

69

CHAPTER 3

INT. APARTMENT—DAY

The bathroom door BURSTS OPEN and the Fourth Man
CHARGES out, silver Magnum raised, FIRING SIX BOOMING
SHOTS from his hand cannon.

> FOURTH MAN
> Die . . . die . . . die . . . die. . . !

DOLLY INTO Fourth Man, same as before.

He SCREAMS until he's dry firing. Then, a look of confusion crossed his face.

TWO SHOT—JULES AND VINCENT
Standing next to each other, unharmed. Amazing as it
seems, none of the Fourth Man's shots appear to have
hit anybody. Jules and Vincent exchange looks like,
"Are we hit?" They're as confused as the shooter. After
looking at each other, they bring their looks up to the
Fourth Man.

> FOURTH MAN
> I don't understand—

The two men lower their guns. Jules, obviously shaken,
sits down in a chair. Vincent, after a moment of respect, shrugs it off. Then heads toward Marvin in the
corner.

> VINCENT
> Why the fuck didn't you tell us about that
> guy in the bathroom? Slip your mind? Forget
> he was in there with a goddamn hand cannon?

> JULES
> (to himself)
> We should be fuckin' dead right now.
> (pause)
> Did you see that gun he fired at us? It was
> bigger than him.

> VINCENT
> .357.

> JULES
> We should be fuckin' dead!

                    VINCENT
          Yeah, we were lucky.

Jules rises, moving toward Vincent.

                    JULES
          That shit wasn't luck. That shit was some-
          thin' else.

Vincent prepares to leave.

                    VINCENT
          Yeah, maybe.

                    JULES
          That was . . . divine intervention. You know
          what divine intervention is?

                    VINCENT
          Yeah, I think so. That means God came down
          from Heaven and stopped the bullets.

                    JULES
          Yeah man, that's what it means. That's ex-
          actly what it means! God came down from
          Heaven and stopped the bullets.

                    VINCENT
          I think we should be going now.

                    JULES
          Don't do that! Don't you fuckin' do that!
          Don't blow this shit off! What just happened
          was a fuckin' miracle!
          (Tarantino, *Pulp Fiction* 113–14)

This incident is the turning point for Jules's character, and it results in
his awareness near the end of the screenplay.

                    VINCENT
          When did you make this decision—while you
          were sitting there eatin' your muffin?

                    JULES
          Yeah. I was just sitting here drinking my
          coffee, eating my muffin, playin' the inci-
          dent in my head, when I had what alcoholics

71

```
refer to as a "moment of clarity."
(148)
```

Jules has moved from "ignorance to knowledge" (*Poetics* 72). Although what exactly he has become aware of is as mysterious as the contents of Marsellus's suitcase, it is nonetheless apparent that Jules has realized something life-altering. Aristotle would have, no doubt, preferred to know specifically what Jules has realized, but Tarantino is not an advocate of absolutes.

Screenplays in which Recognition is prompted by reason are much more common. Most detective dramas follow this rule. Sherlock Holmes, Miss Marple, Hercule Poirot, Sam Spade, Philip Marlowe, and the like, all reason to an understanding of events. But not *all* detective dramas operate this way. Robert Towne's *Chinatown,* for example, has Jake Gittes go through all the rational motions of a typical detective, but without reaching accurate conclusions. Gittes's realization comes as a result of Aristotle's fourth type of Recognition—Evelyn Mulwray simply tells him what has been going on.

Although movies such as *Pulp Fiction* and *Chinatown* meet structural criteria articulated in Aristotle's *Poetics,* they, like many movies in the past thirty years, stray from the philosophical belief in absolutes that underscores all of Aristotle's writing. The path to understanding—to the "truth"—is the same, but the nature of that truth and our understanding of it are radically different. This parallels a general philosophical trend at the end of the twentieth century that leans toward disruption, uncertainty, confusion, chaos, and indeterminacy, rather than balance, order, and certainty, as "many late twentieth-century thinkers, such as Lyotard, Derrida, Prigogine, and Delueze and Guattari," focused their thought on the realization that "the physical universe tends toward nonlinearity, dynamicism, indeterminacy, and unpredictability" (Boon 4).[9]

The two types of Recognition we have not yet discussed involve objects. The weakest form of Recognition comes when someone's identity is verified by an object: a scar, a necklace, a pendant, and so

---

9. I discuss this issue at length in *Chaos Theory and the Interpretation of Literary Texts: The Case of Kurt Vonnegut,* 3–34 and passim.

on. This technique is most common to fairy tales, comedies, and other more contrived literary forms: when Yogurt identifies Lone Starr as a prince based on Lone Starr's medallion in Mel Brooks's *Spaceballs,* for example, or when Robert Torn in *The Omen* identifies his son, Damien, as the antichrist based on the mark of the beast (i.e., 666) he finds on his scalp. The stronger of the two is when an object stirs a memory. Although Aristotle places this type of Recognition third in his hierarchy, it can be extremely effective if skillfully employed, as M. Night Shyamalan's tightly knit script for *The Sixth Sense* demonstrates:

ANNA
Why did you leave me?

MALCOLM
I didn't leave you.

Beat. She becomes silent. Anna falls back into deep sleep, her arm slides down. SOMETHING SHINY FALLS OUT AND ROLLS ON THE GROUND.

Malcolm's eyes watch as it comes to a stop . . . Beat. He gazes curiously at a GOLD WEDDING BAND laying [sic] on the wood floor.

Confusion washes over his face. He looks to Anna's hand. . . . An identical gold wedding ring sits on her finger.

Beat. Malcolm looks down at his own hand . . . HIS WEDDING RING IS GONE.

Malcolm is completely lost. He takes a couple steps back. Looks around in confusion . . . (112)

The wedding ring arouses emotions in Malcolm, emotions that accompany his dramatic realization. With this realization comes a reversal of his situation. Originally, the story was about Malcolm helping Cole come to terms with his unique situation, but when he sees the ring, this arrangement reverses and he and we learn that the opposite is also true: Cole has been helping Malcolm come to terms with his unique situation. Reversal of the Situation and Recognition in *The Sixth Sense* are bound together.

These five types of Recognition form a pattern. The events per se are privileged over all other possibilities, because "Plot . . . is the first and most important thing in Tragedy" (*Poetics* 65). Aristotle claims that plot is the "first principle, and . . . the soul of a tragedy" (63). As a structuralist, he is concerned with the form of the thing under examination. The closer we come to the thing in itself, the closer we come to the truth of the matter, and the closest we can come to the story is the specific sequence of events that make up the story. What Aristotle argues is that the story can, if well crafted, constitute a whole unto itself. The events can be complete. To be whole, a story must have "a beginning, a middle, and an end" (64), each of which carries unique characteristics: the beginning being that "which does not itself follow anything by causal necessity, but after which something naturally is or comes to be"; the end being "that which follows some other thing, either by necessity, or as a rule, but has nothing following it"; and the middle being that "which follows something as some other thing follows it" (65). These three parts may be judged as tightly structured or as haphazard based on their relationship to the issue of the story. One of Aristotle's three rules for judging a tragedy argues that a story should be "single in its issue" (76),[10] as are Shyamalan's *The Sixth Sense*, Orson Welles and Herman L. Mankiewicz's *Citizen Kane*, Ingmar Bergman's *The Seventh Seal*, Tarantino's *Reservoir Dogs*, Billy Wilder, Charles Brackett, and D. M. Marshman Jr.'s *Sunset Boulevard*, Huston's *The Maltese Falcon*, and a bevy of other great screenplays.

Most writers, especially mainstream screenwriters, understand the point Aristotle makes. Secondary and tertiary plotlines can often impose themselves on the primary thrust of a story, threatening to overrun it and dilute its focus. *Reservoir Dogs* is the story of how a failed heist leads to tragic consequences for Mr. Orange and Mr. White—a singular issue—just as *The Seventh Seal* is focused on Antonius Block's struggle to come to terms with death, *Citizen Kane* revolves around the

---

10. The other two rules are that the change in fortune must be good to bad (thus, qualifying it as a tragedy) and the change should come about out of some frailty, not vice. In the latter case, if the change is a result of some vice the hero possesses, the audience will not experience pity for his fall. The Lieutenant in Abel Ferrara and Zoë Lund's *Bad Lieutenant* is an example of a character who falls as a result of inherent vice.

struggle to sum Charles Foster Kane's life, and *The Maltese Falcon* outlines Sam Spade's ethical imperative.

The relationship between Mr. Orange and Mr. White is the heart of *Reservoir Dogs*. Although we must understand the motivation of the other characters because their actions must appear both plausible and necessary, *Reservoir Dogs* is not their story. What we learn about them is directly related to the actions they take that affect the experiences and actions of Mr. Orange in his relationship with Mr. White. The issue in *Reservoir Dogs* is single.

The issue in *Pulp Fiction*, however, is multiple. Although a primary storyline exists, other actions, which do not affect Jules and Vincent, dominate sections of the script. The core of the drama is framed by the change in Jules's outlook (and thus, on the events that facilitate that change), yet there are many actions in the screenplay that have no bearing on Jules or Jules's actions:[11] Mia's overdose, Butch's doublecross of Marsellus, the story of the watch, and so on. We can infer from the "Table of Contents" that Tarantino put at the beginning of the screenplay that he was aware that he was dealing with more than one story.[12]

It is important to note that the singularity Aristotle valorizes does not equate with simplicity. Although Aristotle argues that it is preferable to deal with "a single hero, a single period, or an action single," these should have "a multiplicity of parts" (*Poetics* 106). Complexity in an Aristotelian paradigm comes from a single source—the plot—but

----

11. Every source I've seen lists Vincent Vega as the main character and places Jules Winnfield in a supporting position. This is perhaps because the Academy nominated John Travolta for Actor in a Leading Role and Samuel L. Jackson for Actor in a Supporting Role. I have argued since the movie's release that Jackson in the character of Jules was actually the lead actor while Travolta played a supporting role. This distinction is perhaps incidental in every concern except screenwriting. As a screenplay, the drama turns on Jules, not on Travolta. Jules is the character that undergoes a change. He is the one whose character is affected by the actions of the film.

12. The table of contents (From *Pulp Fiction*, front matter, n.p.):
TABLE OF CONTENTS
PROLOGUE
VINCENT VEGA & MARSELLUS WALLACE'S WIFE
THE GOLD WATCH
JULES, VINCENT, JIMMIE & THE WOLF
EPILOGUE

"unity of plot does not, as some people think, consist in the unity of the hero" (67).

A unified screenplay is not obligated to present a main character in a complete manner. The main character may have unexplained characteristics or unresolved concerns as long as everything relevant to the central issue around which the plot is constructed is present. Aristotle argues that it is impossible to present any character completely, because "infinitely various are the incidents in one man's life which cannot be reduced to unity" (*Poetics* 67). Human beings are too complex, too varied, too overrun with psychological, emotional, and historical elements to be completely captured in a narrative. The best a writer can shoot for is to imply the richness of the character's life. In other words, in constructing characters to fit a story, a skillful writer avoids wholly representing characters, because the more complete the description (the less it implies unknown elements), the less realistic the character seems. This is significantly different from the way character is addressed in many creative writing circles. Often, writers, when learning their craft, are told to make their characters "fully realized" and are led to believe that E. M. Forster's "round character" is distinguished from a "flat character" by the fullness of his representation. Aristotle's position implies the inverse: a round character is one that implies much more than it presents, and a flat character is one that presents much more than it implies. How much we think we still don't know about a character tends to convince us of its authenticity, as is the case with Jules in *Pulp Fiction,* Charles Foster Kane in *Citizen Kane,* and Karl Childers in *Sling Blade:*

<pre>
                    VAUGHAN
        That's what I thought. I hope I haven't
        offended you in any way. You seem like a
        thinker. You seem to always be in deep
        thought. Tell me something. What are you
        thinking right now?

Karl looks up and stares for a moment.

                    KARL
        I was thinkin' I could use me another
        helpin' of these potaters.

                    VAUGHAN
        Oh. How about before that?
</pre>

76

```
                        KARL
        Before that I was thinkin' it'd be good if
        I could get another three or four cans
        of that potted meat if you got any extry.
        (Thornton n.p.)
```

Karl is an engaging character because we, like Vaughan, do not know what is going on inside his head. Billy Bob Thornton's dialogue implies much more than the character's scripted actions can possibly reveal. Vaughan asks the question for us: "What are you thinking?" And Karl's response is appropriately cryptic.

In addition to a long discussion of plot and character, the *Poetics* includes discussions of Aristotle's other four parts of a drama: thought, diction, song, and spectacle (in that order, from third in importance, behind plot and character, to least important). Of these four, song least concerns us here. Unlike ancient Greek tragedy, screenplays, unless they are specifically musicals, seldom use songs as an integral part of storytelling.[13] Exceptions exist, such as Woody Allen's original screenplay for *Mighty Aphrodite* (1995), which employs a Greek chorus, but they are rare.

Both thought and diction relate to dialogue. Thought, for Aristotle, "includes every effect which has to be produced by speech" (*Poetics* 93). Aristotle presumes a close relationship between thought and speech, and therefore makes little distinction between what a character thinks and what he says. Furthermore, what he says reflects his reasoning. Speech is the road to understanding his capacity for logic.

Although action for Aristotle is superior to speech, speech still functions in much the same way as action. Jules's speech at the end of *Pulp Fiction*, for example, exposes Jules's thought and influences the direction of the drama in a similar fashion to Jules's actions. But speech is not as powerful as action, despite the fact that "the only difference [between actions and speeches] is that the incidents should speak for themselves without verbal exposition" (*Poetics* 93). Words do not necessarily reflect a speaker's beliefs or reveal his intentions, because words

----

13. Although, an argument could be made that from *The Jazz Singer* in 1927 through the mid-1970s, many films contain an obligatory song, often placed midfilm, such as "Raindrops Keep Falling on My Head" in *Butch Cassidy and the Sundance Kid*.

can misrepresent their source. It is much more difficult to misrepresent oneself with actions (although it is possible), in the same way as one may say he likes monkey brains for dinner with a great deal more ease than he can actually consume them.

Aristotle broadly defines diction as "the expression of the meaning in words" (*Poetics* 64). His concern with diction is in how meaning is expressed, that is, what "mode of utterance" (94) the speaker employs (and in what context). For the most part, Aristotle excuses himself from any detailed discussion of modes of utterances (by which he means prayers, statements, threats, questions, answers, and such). Aristotle claims that, "The clearest style is that which uses only current or proper words" (101). By "current and proper," he means "one which is in general use among a people" (98). By conforming, at least partially, with common usage, dialogue gains "perspicuity" (102), it becomes lucid and easy to understand. This is not to say that dialogue should never rise above the level of the general audience. Aristotle points out that in "deviating in exceptional cases from the normal idiom, the language will gain distinction" (102), and that "diction should be elaborated in the pauses of the action, where there is no expression of character or thought" (110), but he is careful to note that character and thought are merely obscured by a diction that is overbrilliant" (110).

"Spectacle" would have meant essentially the same thing for Aristotle as it does for us, although the nature and quality of spectacle in ancient Greek drama differs drastically from the technology-driven special effects used as a matter of form today. Spectacle is, in Aristotle's view and in the opinion of many film critics, the least artful of the six parts of tragedy because "the production of spectacular effect depends more on the art of the stage machinist than on that of the poet" (*Poetics* 64). On these grounds, we could easily dismiss works such as David Koepp's screenplay for *The Lost World: Jurassic Park* (1997), which relies heavily on special effects to stimulate audience interest. As one person posted to the Internet Movie Database site, "once you've seen the T-Rex screech and eat people, it gets old really fast."[14] More recent films, such as Stephen Sommers's *Van Helsing* (2004), rely so heavily on com-

----

14. Message posted to www.imdb.com as user comment for *The Lost World: Jurassic Park* (3 Aug. 1998).

puter-generated imagery (CGI) that notable directors, such as George Romero, dismiss them as mere spectacle.

Special effects are the business of special effects artists, computer technicians, stunt coordinators, and so on. A writer of tragedy should, Aristotle stresses, "be the 'maker' of plots" (*Poetics* 69), and those plots should be well crafted. They should be complete unto themselves and they should incite emotional reactions (e.g., pity and fear) from their audience. Everything is subordinate to the sequence of incidents, and everything must serve the ends of the action. Furthermore, all incidents and dialogue must follow necessarily from preceding incidents and dialogue or to new incidents and dialogue until the denouement is reached. Aristotle's general outline relates to most mainstream screenplays. Aristotle even articulates five critical criteria that can be used to critique the worth of a work. Thus, if a screenplay contains things that are impossible, things that are irrational, contradictions, things contrary to "artistic correctness," or it is "morally hurtful" (115), we can, if we abide by Aristotle's *Poetics,* question its value.

It is true that, because most American films end happily, with a typical Hollywood ending, we rarely see a tragedy in the Aristotelian sense, but even with those, the happy ending is often tagged on to a traditional tragedy. Up to the point where Neo comes back from the dead, kills the bad guys, and finds instant love with Trinity, *The Matrix* follows a tragic plotline. And if we take back out the clichéd happy ending (not found in the screenplay) that the studio insisted on tacking onto the end of *Blade Runner,* it follows a tragic line. As do *Brazil, Barton Fink, The Godfather,* and scores of other films.

Boxing Aristotle

Primitive films were not Aristotelian, except to the extent films such as the Lumière brothers' *Les repas de Bébé* (1895), *La sortie des usines Lumière* (1895), and *Barque sortant du port* (1895) strive for realism. Even these, although they were the standard fare for the times, were not the only types of film being made. Georges Méliès's work, for example, did not attempt to imitate reality, and other than the most rudimentary attempt at a storyline in films such as *Le voyage dans la lune* (1902) many of his films, such as *L'impressionniste fin de siècle* (1899), ran contrary to Aristotelian principles.

But these films were made when film was still mostly a novelty, before Edwin S. Porter, D. W. Griffith, Charlie Chaplin, and others transformed film into a narrative medium. Once the primary function of film became storytelling, Aristotle's influence became more prevalent, so that we find traces of him in early features such as Erich von Stroheim's *Greed* (1924). Even *Das kabinett des Doktor Caligari* (1920) is strongly Aristotelian, despite its heavy use of German expressionism. When Francis identifies someone who is supposed to be dead to his listener, thus exposing himself as an occupant of the insane asylum rather than a visitor, we have Recognition and a Reversal of the Situation. Despite its surreal surface, *Caligari* is a conventional Aristotelian narrative.

Films like *Caligari* are still prevalent. David Webb Peoples and Janet Peoples's *Twelve Monkeys* (1995), for example, seems surreal, but the film's plot follows a conventional narrative, as do other similar films such as *The Matrix* and *Barton Fink*. Rather than challenging an Aristotelian narrative mold, they merely extend it. Instead of the death of a king, as in Oedipus, we get the death of a talented playwright's focus, à la *Barton Fink*, or the psychological conditions that lead a heroin-addicted writer to shoot his wife, à la *Naked Lunch*.

Bizarre or unusual qualities are not enough to exclude a film or a screenplay from Aristotelian paradigms. Aristotle might have argued that some films rely too heavily on spectacle, but the line of action is nonetheless conventional. We can find some variance from the form that the *Poetics* calls for, but that is because Aristotle was writing about a different medium and writing from a radically different perspective. In *Barton Fink*, for example, we are left dangling at the end.

```
CUT TO:
THE SURF

Crashing on the Pacific shore.

THE BEACH

Almost deserted at mid-day. A few bathers frolic at
the edge of the water. In the distance, Barton's lone
overcoated figure can be seen making his way across the
sand. The paper wrapped parcel swings from the twine in
his left hand.
```

Aristotle, Aesthetics, and Critical Approaches

BARTON

He walks a few more paces and sits down on the sand, looking out to sea. His gaze shifts to the side.

HIS POV

Down the beach, closer to the water. A bathing beauty, sitting on the sand, gazing out at the water. She looks much like the picture on the wall in his hotel room.

The surf crashes in the background, the sound washing over the track obliterating everything except the occaisional [sic] cry of a gull.

BARTON

Staring at her. Transfixed.

THE GIRL

She is exceptionally beautiful, backlit by the sun, her hair piled up on top her head, her hand cupped over her eyes. The sea glitters beyond her, stretching to a distant horizon.

BARTON

Still staring.

CLOSE ON THE GIRL

Rising to her feet. The wind blows her hair down as she walks along the shore.
EXTREME CLOSE ON THE GIRL

Bending to pick a shell off the sand. She looks up and sees Barton.

Their eyes meet.

She says something but her voice is lost in the crash of the surf.

Barton cups his hand to his ear.

> Beauty
> (above the crash of the surf)
> I said it's a beautiful day . . .

                         Barton
          Yes . . . It is . . .

                         Beauty
          What's in the box?

Barton shrugs and shakes his head.

                         Barton
          I don't know.

                         Beauty
          Isn't it yours?

                         Barton
          I . . . I don't know . . .

She nods, sitting down on the sand several paces away
from him facing the water but looking back over her
shoulder at Barton.

                         Barton
          . . . You're very beautiful. Are you in
          pictures?

She laughs.

                         Beauty
          Don't be silly.

She turns away to look out at the sea.

WIDER

Facing the ocean. Barton sits in the middle foreground,
back to us, the box in the sand next to him.

The bathing beauty sits, back to us, in the middle
background.

The surf pounds.

The sun sparkles off the water.

FADE OUT (Coen and Coen, 123-25)

This ending is open-ended, and avoids any sense of absolute resolution,
thus dodging Aristotelian notions of a tightly knit plot. Yet, the ending

does complete a circuit of imagery, returning the reader to the image on the wall of Barton's room at the Hotel Earle.

```
We pan up to a picture in a cheap wooden frame on the
wall above the desk. A bathing beauty sits on the beach
under a cobalt blue sky. One hand shields her eyes from
the sun as she looks out at a crashing surf.

The sound of the surf mixes up.

BARTON

Looking at the picture

TRACKING IN ON THE PICTURE

The surf mixes up louder. We hear a gull cry.

The sound snaps off with the ring of a telephone.

THE HOUSE PHONE (13-14)
```

Throughout their screenplay, the Coen brothers skillfully set up this final scene so that, when it arrives, it resonates an "uncanny" sense, as Tzvetan Todorov (and Freud before him) used the term to describe a disintegration of the boundary between real and unreal.[15] The imagery in the picture introduced at the beginning of the screenplay becomes the imagery of the scene described at the end of the screenplay—the unreal image becomes the real image. We are left to wonder what the imagery signifies in both cases. We feel we should understand it, even though it cannot be understood.

Despite the open ending, *Barton Fink* functions as a tragedy in the Aristotelian sense because the penultimate scene concludes with Lipnik lambasting Barton, dismissing his "talent," and effectively roadblocking his career. This scene has Recognition and Reversal of the Situation and operates very much in an Aristotelian dramatic sense. Like the upbeat conclusions that Hollywood insists on tacking on to the end of most

----

15. See Tzvetan Todorov's *The Fantastic* (passim) and Sigmund Freud's entry on the uncanny in *The Standard Edition of the Complete Psychological Works of Sigmund Freud* (219–52).

mainstream releases, the last scene in *Barton Fink* exists beyond the end of the tragedy, and therefore cannot be said to significantly discount all the dramatic elements found in the previous 123 pages.

Some screenplays challenge Aristotle's *Poetics* at a more fundamental level. Aristotle argues that, "In Tragedy we cannot imitate several lines of action carried on at the same time" (9, 108). However, as Kristen Thompson points out, the "double plotline" is a "distinctive feature of the Hollywood cinema" (14). The double plotline represents a core difference between Aristotle's poetics and the conventional Hollywood narrative. But works such as Robert Altman and Frank Barhydt's *Short Cuts* (1993) and Altman and Barbara Shulgasser's *Prêt-à-Porter* (*Ready to Wear*) (1994) extend the number of plotlines far beyond Aristotle's one and Thompson's two. *Short Cuts,* in particular, is structured in a nontraditional, and distinctly non-Aristotelian paradigm. In order to bring Raymond Carver's short stories to the screen, Altman creates a pastiche of plots, characters, incidents, and settings—some scenes being linked by no more than a shared character. Instead of presenting one story, *Short Cuts* presents many. The result is a sense that the whole (Los Angeles during a spraying for Medfly infestation) is too large to capture, implying that there are myriad interesting and important stories going on in the city that we do not find on the page. Robert T. Self discusses this type of narrative in Altman at length in *Robert Altman's Subliminal Reality,* in which he points out that Altman "describes the 'perfect movie' as a nonlinear, atmospheric, rationally baffling evocation of 'subliminal reality'"(3). Altman's description applies equally well to other films, such as Paul Haggis and Robert Moresco's *Crash* (2004) and Richard Linklater's *Slacker* (1991).

Aristotle considers this manner of storytelling inferior to the singular narrative of tragedy, and devalues epic poetry for the very reason that it introduces more than it is able to thoroughly cover. Fragmented narratives, such as the one we find in *Short Cuts,* produce in narrative a similar structure to montage, as we find it in Sergei Eisenstein. In place of the individual shots of montage, we find entire scenes, so that the scenes collide like individual images rendering narrative effect. Yet, even with *Short Cuts,* we have to grant Aristotle that it was not overly popular with audiences.

Altman is not alone. Jim Jarmusch's *Night on Earth* follows a similar form, and much of his writing resists Aristotelian principles. The same can be said of much of Wim Wenders's work, and the screenplays of Peter Greenaway. Greenaway, in particular, has spent his career exploring new methods of narrative. His *Prospero's Books* is as inventive as it is intellectually inviting. But perhaps we may still orient these radically different narratives to the *Poetics,* insomuch as screenplays always seek to imitate something, and thus satisfy the "instinct for imitation" (53) that Aristotle claims we all have. Even if we resist Aristotle's absolutism, Aristotle's *Poetics* offers us insight into the mystery of how many powerful and effective stories are made.

2 Critiques

4

Dialogue as Action

Discourse, Dialectics, and the Rhetoric of Capitalism in David Mamet's *Glengarry Glen Ross*

David Mamet is among a surprisingly small number of contemporary American screenwriters with the rare ability to generate and maintain dramatic tension primarily through the use of dialogue. Nearly everyone writing about film, particularly popular film, is quick to note that film is a medium of motion—*moving* pictures. Syd Field, for example, points out that "good character is the heart and soul and nervous system" of a screenplay (*Workbook* 54), and that "action is character; [that] what a person does is who he is, not what he says" (*Workbook* 55). Field is generally correct. What a character does (the actions he or she takes) reveals more about the nature of that character than what he says. But screenwriters often exaggerate this principle, resulting in characters who eschew dialogue in favor of action, and screenplays that are little more than a string of action sequences. The dialogue in most blockbuster screenplays is so sparse that a number of the film industry's biggest action stars are willing to forgo millions of dollars in order to perform in films by writers with a strong command of dialogue. Consider Bruce Willis's fervent desire to work with Tarantino in *Pulp Fiction,* or Sylvester Stallone, who agreed to work for scale in James Mangold's *Cop Land.* Actors, such as these, realize that well-written dialogue can become the action by which character is defined.

Audiences appreciate good dialogue and respond positively when scripts such as Christopher McQuarrie's *The Usual Suspects,* Quentin Tarantino's *Pulp Fiction,* and David Mamet's *Glengarry Glen Ross* make it to the screen. While most screenwriters are struggling to pen another *Twister* or *Jurassic Park,* trimming dialogue to the bone to keep the visuals active, a few gifted writers are writing scripts that offer active dialogue. The impulse to cut as much dialogue as possible is based on a misunderstanding of the function of dialogue. Action tells more about character than dialogue only when the dialogue to which we are referring is didactic. When a character says he is nurturing, for example, all an audience knows is that the character is the type of person who says he is nurturing. If audiences trust the character, then they believe the character thinks he is nurturing. They do not, however, necessarily believe he is nurturing. The character must engage in nurturing behavior before audiences will judge him to be nurturing.

Didactic dialogue is inferior to action. It lectures audiences about what they are supposed to think, drawing their conclusions for them. Its primary weakness is that it keeps conclusions external. Audiences do not decide if characters are evil or good; they are told. But all dialogue is not didactic. Dialogue can take on the characteristics of action. Active dialogue is as much about where it is occurring and between whom it is occurring as it is about what is being said. Like action, it is context-driven. Audiences recognize the context of the dialogue and draw conclusions based on what type of person would say such things to those particular people at that particular time and place. Unlike the externally determined conclusions drawn from didactic dialogue, conclusions drawn from active dialogue are internally determined, thus increasing an audience's personal involvement with the overall production of meaning.

In Tarantino's *True Romance,* when Vincenzo Coccotti (Christopher Walken) confronts Clifford Worley (Dennis Hopper) in order to locate Worley's son Clarence (Christian Slater), Worley engages in a long monologue about the history of Sicilians, tracing their mixed bloodline with peoples of African descent. Worley does not raise a hand to Coccotti; yet, the monologue operates as a slap across Coccotti's face. The dialogue functions like a condemned man spitting into the face of his executioner. By indirectly narrating Coccotti's heritage, Worley takes *verbal* action, which is inseparable from context, and which generates a greater dramatic tension than if he had taken physical action.

Active dialogue usually results in a more complex dynamic between a film and its audience than films relying on physical action. Many of the films that make best use of active dialogue come from playwrights. This is not surprising when we consider that playwrights do not begin their work with the infinite canvas that film offers. When writers such as Neil Simon, Sam Shepard, David Mamet, and Harold Pinter (who helped arrange for the London production of *Glengarry Glen Ross*) write plays, they are spatially limited. Visual tricks and special effects must play a substantially smaller role because everything takes place on stage. Characters do not have vast areas in which to wander around. The dramatic tension must be generated by characters engaged in limited action; therefore, the bulk of the dramatic weight rests on what the characters say and how they say it, the conversations they engage in, and the dynamic relationships among speeches within the context of the play. Just as with a screenplay, every word counts; however, in a stage play, characters do not have the option of remaining mute. A film, we might argue, is a thing made of images, while a play is a thing made of language. When the level of attention paid to dialogue in a stage play finds its way into a screenplay, the result is often quite remarkable, and this is precisely the complex dialogue we find in David Mamet's screenplay for *Glengarry Glen Ross.*

Dialogue, Discourse, and Dialectics

In order to examine the dramatic context of Mamet's dialogue in *Glengarry Glen Ross,* we need to clarify our terminology. Up to this point, I have been using the term "dialogue" primarily to refer to a conversation between or among two or more people. However, this definition alone is too simplistic to offer us much insight into the complex dynamic at play in Mamet's writing. Discourse is a more functional term for referring to Mamet's dialogue.

The term "discourse" has become a buzzword in recent scholarship, resulting in a dilution of its specificity, but it carried particular significance for the early writers on rhetoric. The etymology of the term associates it with movement across time and speech. The Latin *cursus* literally means race or racecourse. The Spanish *discurso* combines speech with time, indicating that discourse is speech across time. But there is a third connotation of the term that is often overlooked in popular usage. For example, in Aristotelian views of discourse, discourse has a dialectic quality. People enter into discourse in order to convince others of the truth of their suppositions. And "truth" for Aristotle is not relativistic. Therefore, for Aristotle, discourse is a means by which *truth* (in an absolute sense) is approached. The object of discourse is to facilitate a movement toward *skopos*, the "one goal . . . at which . . . [private individuals and all people generally] aim in what they choose to do and in what they avoid" (*Rhetoric* 57). The presumption is that the more we move toward this universal human goal, the more we achieve happiness.

In *On Rhetoric*, Aristotle divides happiness[1] into its parts. He equates happiness with success[2]—obtaining a life that is pleasant and secure, while accumulating an "abundance of possessions" (57). This "success" is coupled with "virtue," and cannot be achieved without practical wisdom, courage, temperance, and justice (57n97). A happy man cannot be amoral or unethical. A lack of ethics would disqualify a man from gaining success and happiness.

Aristotle claims that happiness consists of the following parts:

- good birth (legitimate and descended from a line of honorable ancestors)
- numerous and worthy friendships
- good and numerous children
- good old age
- health
- beauty
- strength
- physical stature
- athletic prowess
- reputation
- honor
- good luck
- virtue

Rhetorical discourse is the means by which "truth" is obtained, and in obtaining "truth," a person gains happiness. Therefore, Aris-

----

1. The transliterated term from the Greek is *eudaimonia*.
2. *Eupraxia*.

totle's characteristics of happiness are the ultimate aim of rhetorical discourse. Furthermore, although it is possible to make a rhetorical argument on both sides of an issue, Aristotle argues for a "natural" tendency toward the true and just. Note the ethical tone Aristotle employs when addressing this issue: "One should be able to argue persuasively on either side of a question, just as in the use of syllogisms, not that we may actually do both (for one would not persuade what is debased) but in order that it may not escape our notice what the real state of the case is and that we ourselves may be able to refute if another person uses speech unjustly" (*Rhetoric* 34). Aristotelian theory goes so far as to claim that if a speaker manages to persuade someone of something that is not true, then both the speaker *and* the listener are nonvirtuous (as with the dialogue between Aaronow and Moss discussed at length later in this chapter). A virtuous speaker would not attempt to persuade someone of something that is not "just" and "true," and a virtuous listener could not be persuaded of something that is not "just" and "true" because the "true and the just are by nature stronger than their opposites, so that if judgments are not made in the right way [the true and the just] are necessarily defeated [by their opposites]. And this is worthy of censure" (*Rhetoric* 34).[3]

Discourse without ethics cannot direct a speaker or his audience toward happiness, thus, unethical speech cannot be successful and successful discourse is necessarily ethical. But what are we to make of Mamet's *Glengarry Glen Ross* where much of the dialogue between and among the characters is clearly unethical? Yet, the screenplay itself is not without ethics, inviting us to examine how a screenplay in which all the characters are unethical manages to construct an ethical viewpoint. In an Aristotelian universe, characters engaged in unethical discourse cannot achieve truth, cannot improve their perception of the "real." The characters in *Glengarry Glen Ross* could not, then, be articulating the ethics of the discourse.

To understand the power of Mamet's dialogue we must look at discourse as it relates to the production of meaning; we must question where the production of meaning is located. The site of meaning in *Glengarry Glen Ross* is not exclusively, or even significantly, positioned

---

3. Bracketed comments belong to George A. Kennedy (cf. Aristotle, *On Rhetoric*).

between or among the characters engaging in dialogue. What much of the dialogue *means* for the characters is found outside syntactic and semantic categories. The characters themselves are not the recipients of the "meaning" of the dialogue because they are too unethical to make those distinctions, too absorbed in their corrupt lives to distinguish the true and just from the untrue and unjust. None is any more ethical or moral by the end of the screenplay than he was in the beginning. Although lives change, especially Levene's life, the changes are not ideological.

The primary site where meaning is engendered in the screenplay is between the audience and the characters in dialogue. The audience does more than observe conversations between characters; it enters into moral interpretation. The audience, not the characters, is in the position to judge what, in an Aristotelian sense, is true and just, thus the audience provides the moral critique of the discourse. This is what I will examine, specifically as it relates to dialogue between Moss and Aaronow; but first we need to look at what adulterated the characters' discourse, what led the characters to their present state, for that is at the heart of Mamet's screenplay and represents the chief focus of his critique.

Capitalism and the Death of Community

In *Glengarry Glen Ross,* Mamet raises issues about the effect of capitalism on the communal American spirit. For him, "the purpose of theater [in general] is not primarily to deal with social issues . . . it is to deal with spiritual issues" (qtd. in Bigsby 111), and *Glengarry Glen Ross,* in specific, is about "a society based on business" (qtd. in Bigsby 111). This begs the question of what spiritual issues *Glengarry Glen Ross* deals with, and what effect capitalist enterprise has on those issues.

In an interview with C. W. E. Bigsby, Mamet speaks of a "frontier ethic" encoded into American consciousness. This ethic promised "something for nothing" to those venturing west under the misguided assumptions that they would find easy fortunes there. This myth was, Mamet points out, a "way of enslaving the common man and woman . . . playing on their greed" (qtd. in Bigsby 111). Capitalism enslaves because it entraps its devotees in a lie, that wealth equals happiness, that capital alone will purchase the other characteristics of happiness in Aristotle's definition: good birth (legitimate and descended from a line of honorable ancestors), numerous and worthy friendships, good and numerous children, good old age, health, beauty, strength, physical stature, athletic prowess, reputation, honor, good luck, and virtue. Under capitalist doctrine, the solitary aim of the individual is to increase his "abundance of possessions." Wealth becomes narrowly defined by material goods, and all other qualities are consumed by that one overarching objective. Consider Blake's response when Moss asks him his name at the sales meeting in an attempt to humanize the rapacious representative of Mitch and Murray:

<pre>
                        MOSS
          What's your name?

                        BLAKE
          Fuck <u>you,</u> <u>that's</u> my name. You know why,
          Mister? 'Cause you drove a Honda to get
          here tonight, I drove a sixty-thousand
          dollar B.M.W. <u>That's</u> my name, and your name
          is you're <u>wanting,</u> and you can't play in the
          man's game, you can't <u>close</u> them, then go
          home and tell your wife your troubles.
          Because One Thing Counts In This Life: Get
          Them To Sign On The Line Which Is Dotted.
          You hear me, you faggots . . . ? I <u>know</u> your
          war stories. I <u>know</u> the bullshit excuses
          that are your lives. What do <u>you</u> know
          . . . ? What do <u>you</u> know . . .
          (12)
</pre>

Blake is a new character added for the screenplay. He is not found in the original stage play, most of which remains intact in the adaptation. Blake symbolizes the force that drives all the characters. Blake's presence angers them, not because of who he is, but because they are not him. He reinforces the lie underlying their lives. They see him as a man who, like Mitch and Murray, appears to get something for nothing, someone for whom selling is a simple matter. The way Blake describes it, the buyers are *"sitting* out there, waiting to give you their money" (13), and Blake parades his wealth to prove how easy it is.

Blake has what they all aspire to have—an abundance of possessions, and, seemingly, the life those possessions promise, a promise that

Mamet's screenplay shows us is never realized because it is based on the fallacy of capitalist greed.

When Moss questions whether or not Blake is a "hero," Blake once again responds by flaunting the value of his possessions:

```
ANGLE—MOSS

looking disgruntled

                                    MOSS
            You're such a hero, you're so rich, how come
            you're coming down here, waste your time
            with such a bunch of bums?

ANGLE—CU BLAKE

impassive.

ANGLE—BLAKE HOLDS UP HIS WRIST

shoots the cuff. Monogrammed cuff, gold cufflinks, a
gold Rolex watch.

                                BLAKE (O.S.)
            You see this watch . . . ?

ANGLE—BLAKE TALKING TO THE MEN

                                BLAKE (CONT'D)
            You see this watch? This watch cost more
            than your car. I made Nine Hundred Seventy
            Thousand Dollars last year. What did you
            make? . . .
                        (pause)
            You see, Pal . . . ? That's who I am, and
            you're nothing. Nice Guy? I don't give a
            shit. Good Father? Fuck you. Go home to your
            kids. You want to work here? Close. You
            think this is abuse . . . ? You think this
            is abuse, you cocksucker . . . ? You can't
            take this, how can you take the abuse that
            you get on a sit? You don't like it, you
            leave. I can go in there, tonight, the
            materials you got, make myself fifteen
            thousand dollars. Can you? Can you?
            (14)
```

Blake is his expensive Rolex watch. He is his expensive BMW. He is what he owns, and everyone in the room believes him because they are slaves to the same capitalist propaganda. Being a "nice guy" doesn't matter, because friendships don't matter. Being a "good father" doesn't matter, because children don't matter. All sense of community and all human relationships are lost to avarice, ironically in the hope that wealth comes with meaningful relationships. Michael Hinden points this out when he writes, "To pervert intimacy by using friendship as a lure for business is to traduce communal values and represents for Mamet the key to Roma's self-disgust, his excremental vision of the world. The alternative might be defined as the communal vision, whose power is felt in Mamet's play by the absence more often than its presence" (37). Capitalism appropriates all desire under its banner and disempowers communal values. This is at the heart of Mamet's script, a point Dennis Carroll makes when he argues that in Mamet's fiction there are "tensions between the spirit of 'business' and communion" (175). Friendships and familial relationships are all sacrificed to the one object of desire presumed to assure happiness. As Hinden goes on to say,

> the dramatic context [of Mamet's drama] leads us toward the . . . conclusion that compared to this [modern avarice], the old communal circle around the campfire was anything but vicious, and that the substitution of the cash nexus for the tribal unit which functions as an extended family might have been a retrograde development in human affairs.
>
> Nowhere is Mamet's view on this subject expressed more forcefully than in Richard Roma's monologue on individualism and moral relativism in the opening of scene 3 of *Glengarry Glen Ross*. As rhetoric, the function of this speech is to ensnare a prospective client. (36)

The speech Hinden refers to appears in the script as follows:

```
INT. THE RESTAURANT—NIGHT

Roma at a booth with James Lingk.

                    ROMA
        You know something, you know something? All
        train compartments smell vaguely of shit.
```

```
You take a train, you're paying for a com-
partment, luxury, all this, all of the time,
the thing smells like, it vaguely smells,
and you ignore it.
         (beat)
That's the worst thing that I can confess.
You know how long it took me to get there,
a long time. When you die, you're going to
regret the things that you don't do. You
think you're queer? I'm going to tell you
something: We're all queer. You think that
you're a thief? You get befuddled by a mid-
dle-class morality? Get shut of it. Shut
it out. You fuck little girls? So be it.
There's an absolute morality? May be. And
then what? If you think there is, then be
that thing. Bad people go to hell? I don't
think so. If you think that, act that way. A
hell exists on earth? Yes. I won't live in
it. That's me . . . (50)
```

In this speech, Roma articulates the amorality underlying Blake's reductive capitalism. The luxury in Roma's world smells of shit. Something is foul. But he chooses to ignore it. He lives the life Blake preaches:

```
ANGLE—THE BLACKBOARD

writes huge in chalk: "A.B.C."

                    BLAKE (O.S.)
A.B.C.
A. Always
B. Be
C. Closing, Always Be Closing.
(12)
```

Roma understands the world of Blake, so it is not surprising that, even though he missed the meeting, he rearticulates Blake's main missive while listening to Levene recount his sale:

```
                  LEVENE
What we have to do is admit to ourself that
we see that opportunity . . . and take it.
         (pause)
And that's it. And we sit there.
```

```
                  (pause)
           I got the pen out . . .

                              ROMA
           Always be closing . . .
           (86)
```

Roma isn't in Blake's meeting because he already has the message. Ironically, while the other salesmen are being told to always be closing, Roma is the one man who is at that moment closing a sale. What we see in his life and the lives of all the other characters is a world without virtue, a world that smells vaguely of shit, a world driven by greed, or, as Mamet states it, a world "set deeply in the milieu of capitalism, obviously an idea whose time has come and gone" (qtd. in Bigsby 111).

Capitalism proffers material possession as a panacea for all life's ills, a ticket away from existential angst—instant happiness. Yet we see that no one in the screenplay, from the best closer, Blake, to the worst, Levene, is happy. Although the thesis of the discourse is not expressly stated by any of the characters, the audience can infer it from their dialogue. The dialogue, as active object in the discourse between audience and film, manages to produce meaning by skillfully manipulating the moral and ethical leanings of the audience. What we hear in the dialogue is the patter of salesmen struggling to excel in their profession; what we learn is that capital does not equal contentment, and that the agendas of capitalism are incongruous with the goals of community.

Speaking of Talking . . .

One of the most interesting, ingenious, and insightful dialogues in the script occurs between Aaronow and Moss. The conversation exposes the mutual culpability of characters enslaved to the lie of capitalism, characters who are deceived by the very same delusion they use to sell their clients. Ann Dean addresses this when she says that, "In the same way as the salesmen's endless quest for spurious success is essentially a chimera, so the goods they sell are probably quite worthless. The salesmen are, therefore, exploiting those who, like them, need to dream and to believe in a brighter future. It is a vicious circle" (189).

Moss *sells* Aaronow on the idea of stealing the premium leads from the real estate office and selling them to Graff. Aaronow *buys* into

Moss's proposition in the abstract because of an assumption that resides outside the syntactic and semantic boundaries of the discourse. Moss presents his plan explicitly, though Aaronow perceives that Moss is only "talking" and not seriously intending to rob the sales office. Moss leads Aaronow into a discussion of the robbery (in effect, plans the robbery with him) without explicitly revealing his intention. He gripes about work conditions, leading Aaronow to agree that "they" are responsible for the problems Moss and Aaronow are having closing enough sales to get "on the board":

```
INT. THE EMPTY DOUGHNUT SHOP—ANGLE—MOSS AND AARONOW

go up and sit down at the counter.

                        MOSS
                (sighs)
        My mistake, I shouldna' took the lead in the
        first place.

                        AARONOW
        You had to.

                        MOSS
        Yeah? Why?

                        AARONOW
        . . . to get on the . . .

                        MOSS
        To get on the Board. Yeah. How'm I gonna get
        on the Board trine' a sell a doctor?
. . . . . . . . . . . . . . . . . . . . . . . . . . . .

The WAITRESS brings the coffee and doughnuts.

                        MOSS (CONT'D)
        We all . . . remember when we were, when we
        were selling Glen Ross Farms . . .

                        AARONOW
        Huh . . .

                        MOSS
        Didn't we sell a bunch of that?
```

David Mamet's *Glengarry Glen Ross*

```
                  AARONOW
. . . they came in and they, you know . . .

                   MOSS
Well, they fucked it up.

                  AARONOW
They did.

                   MOSS
. . . they killed the goose.

                  AARONOW
They did. (38-39)
```

After obtaining Aaronow's agreement that "they" are to blame, Moss becomes more specific and directly implicates their managers.

```
                   MOSS
And I'll tell you what the hard part is, is
to stop thinking like a Goddamn slave: you
say "The Nazis in Europe . . ." "They came
in my door, I'd . . ." well, bullshit . . .
you know what I mean? The time is now: what
do you do now, some guy pissing in your
face, cocksucker—wants to break your rice-
bowl. Mitch. And Murray . . . fuck you, what
I say, fuck you, and sittin' on the good
leads. These are men here . . .⁴
(46)
```

Moss's move from the general "they" to the specific (Mitch and Murray) represents a sales ploy wherein a salesman leads a prospect from vague general assertions to specific actions that are in line with the salesman's agenda. From the prospect, a salesman manipulates a series of progressively more specific agreements (called "commitments" in the sales trade) that lead to his original objective. A salesman uses language to obtain a series of commitments from a prospect until the prospect finally commits to a salesman's original objective and the salesman is said to have "closed" the sale. During this process, the prospect moves

----

4. Moss's speech as filmed ends with the line, "George, we're men here . . . ," which has Moss establishing an even more personal bond with Aaronow.

CHAPTER 4

from casual observer (or "listener") to active participant. The prospect, in effect, becomes complicit in the sale once he is verbally maneuvered into a position where one of two actions must be taken: either he must "buy" whatever the salesman has been selling, or he must contradict himself by recanting the series of commitments he has already made and walk away from the sale. If the salesman is a skilled communicator, the prospect will find the second option substantially more stressful than the first.

Once Moss has gotten Aaronow to accept Mitch and Murray as the source of their mutual dissatisfaction, Moss begins to lead Aaronow in the direction of a solution by first introducing Jerry Graff—the man Moss has already arranged to sell the premium leads to once they steal them—as a positive figure.

```
                         MOSS
        Starting up. Standing up, breaking free
        of this bullshit, this, this enslavement
        to some guy, because he's got the Upper
        Hand. This is the difference. Listen to me,
        George, now: Jerry Graff: he went in busi-
        ness for himself. He said "I'm going on my
        own," and he was free, you understand me
        . . . ? (47)
```

Key in this speech is the association of freedom with Graff. Moss, here, is planting the idea in Aaronow's mind that Graff is a savvy businessman who knows how to take care of himself, the same attitude Aaronow will need in order to go through with the robbery for which Moss is clandestinely priming him.

Moss's lengthy interchange with Aaronow leads Aaronow to the subject Moss has wanted to discuss all along. The discourse turns when Moss says, "I want to tell you what somebody should do." Here again, as with "they," Moss begins with general terms to tell Aaronow that "someone should stand up and strike *back*," that "somebody . . . should do something to *them*" (47). Moss negotiates the conversation from general assumptions to specifics:

```
                         MOSS
        And I want to tell you what somebody should
        do.
```

                          AARONOW
What?

                           MOSS
Somebody should stand up and strike back.
          (pause)
Somebody . . .

                          AARONOW
Yes . . .?

                           MOSS
Should do something to <u>them</u> . . .

                          AARONOW
What?

                           MOSS
Something. To pay them back. Someone should
hurt them. Mitch and Murray.

They start to walk down the street.

                          AARONOW
. . . someone should hurt them . . .

                           MOSS
Yes.

                          AARONOW
. . . how?

                           MOSS
. . . someone . . . should <u>do</u> something
. . . to hurt them. Where they live.

                          AARONOW
. . . what . . . ?

CAMERA DOLLIES BACK in front of Moss and Aaronow, who
are crossing the street, the office behind them.

                           MOSS
          (pause)
Someone should rob the office.

                          AARONOW
Huh.

                           103

```
                    MOSS
    . . . that's what I'm saying. If we were, if
    we were that kind of guy: to knock it off,
    and trash the joint, it looks like robbery,
    and take the fucking leads out of the file,
    and go to Jeff [sic] Graff.


                    AARONOW
    Huh!


                    MOSS
    And take the fuckin' Glengarry Leads . . .
    (47-48)
```

Moss introduces his sales objective. But, he is careful not to reveal his intention.[5] Moss begins to reap the seeds he sowed earlier by stressing "saying," thus implying to Aaronow that these are just words he is saying, words without any *real* intent behind them, words *not* actions. Moss rhetorically presents his plan with the language of speculation. He has already gotten a commitment from Aaronow that Mitch and Murray are to blame for their current difficulties with sales quotas, now he points out that "if" he and Aaronow were the "kind of guys" to commit the crime, then justice would be served, thus probing Aaronow to determine his disposition regarding robbing the office. Moss does not want to undermine his objectives, give himself away, until he has reason to believe that Aaronow might go along with the plan. When the script later returns to the conversation, Aaronow reveals his interest, and in doing so makes himself vulnerable to Moss's plan.

```
                    AARONOW
    What could we get for them?


    Beat.


                    MOSS
        For . . . ?


                    AARONOW
        For the leads.
```

----

5. Importantly, the audience, as well as Aaronow, is unaware of Moss's actual intention. Like Aaronow, the audience is also maneuvered into a sales situation; the audience is also being "sold."

```
                           MOSS
What could we get for the leads . . . ?
          (pause)
I don't know. Buck a throw, buck-a-half a
throw, I don't know.
          (pause)
For the leads, you're saying, say somebody
took 'em, went to Jeff [sic] Graff.

                           AARONOW
Yes. (51)
```

As the conversation moves to a discussion of how much is to be gained by the robbery, Aaronow begins to seemingly direct the conversation, but it was Moss that led him there by appealing to Aaronow's encoded capitalist desire for easy money. Moss lies to Aaronow about not knowing how much the leads are worth, because it is not advantageous to his "sales objective" to reveal his political agenda without more commitment from Aaronow. Significantly, the more Aaronow is drawn into the "sale," the longer Aaronow's dialogue becomes and the shorter Moss's becomes. Aaronow is beginning to take verbal action, and Moss is moving toward a "close." The less he says the less likely it is he will say something to upset the "sale." Aaronow, from this point on, traps himself by pursuing specifics. Each assertion he makes operates as an acceptance in principle of the robbery being discussed.

```
                           AARONOW
. . . How many leads do we have?

                           MOSS
The Glengarry? The Premium Leads . . . ?
I've got to think they've got five thousand,
say, five thousand leads.

                           AARONOW
And a fellow, you're saying, a fellow could
take and sell those leads to Graff . . .

                           MOSS
The leads to Graff, yes. I was saying, yeah.
A guy could take, like anything else, it
seems to me, that is negotiable . . .
          (pause)
A guy could sell 'em . . .
```

Pause.

> AARONOW
>
> How do you know he'd buy 'em?

> MOSS
>
> Graff . . . ? Because I worked for him.
> (51–52)

Aaronow is now moving in the direction that Moss intended him to move. The two men are in effect planning the robbery although Aaronow is still not yet aware that he is being manipulated into participating in the crime. However, Aaronow is becoming suspicious that there is more to this exchange than can be divined directly from the things being said.

> AARONOW
>
> You haven't <u>talked</u> to him . . .

> MOSS
>
> No. What do you mean? Have I talked to him about this . . . ?

> AARONOW
>
> Yes. I mean, are you actually <u>talking</u> about this, or are we just . . .

> MOSS
>
> . . . no, we're just . . .

> AARONOW
>
> We're just "talking" about it.

> MOSS
>
> . . . we're just "speaking" about it.

> AARONOW
>
> As an idea.

> MOSS
>
> Yes.

> AARONOW
>
> We're not actually <u>talking</u> about it.

MOSS

No.

AARONOW

. . . talking about it, as a . . .

MOSS

No . . .

AARONOW

. . . as a Robbery.

MOSS

. . . as a "Robbery" . . . no . . .

The two of them laugh.

AARONOW

Weeellll . . .

MOSS

Hey!

Pause.

AARONOW

So all this, uh, you didn't, actually, you didn't
actually call, call Graff, you didn't talk to . . .

MOSS

Not actually, no.

Pause.

AARONOW

You didn't?

MOSS

No, not actually.

AARONOW

Did you?

MOSS

What did I say?

AARONOW

What did you say?

                    MOSS
I said "not actually." The fuck <u>you</u> care, George?
We're just "talking."

                   AARONOW
    We are?

                    MOSS
    Yes.

Pause.

                   AARONOW
    Because, because, you know, it's a <u>crime.</u>

                    MOSS
    Robbery. That's right. It <u>is</u> a crime.

Aaronow reaches for a cigarette, finds he is out. Gets
up off the stool and starts for the cigarette machine.
Moss follows him. CAMERA MOVES with them.

                    MOSS
           (sotto)
    It's also very safe.
    (52-54)

Aaronow points out that the language he and Moss are using can have vastly different significance depending on whether they are "talking" about the robbery as an "idea" or whether they are "talking" about the robbery as a physical act. The confusion here is not in the language being used, is not at the syntactic or semantic level of the discourse; the confusion is in the gap between rhetoric and ideation. Aaronow is confused because he is not sure to what these speech acts are referring; he cannot reconcile the felicity of the idea they are discussing, and he does not yet realize that speaking is action even though, ironically, his profession as a salesman is based on active speech.

Aaronow appears to be slipping away from Moss's control when he stresses the criminality of the act under discussion. By pointing out that "it's also very safe," Moss reasserts his manipulative position in an attempt to redirect Aaronow back toward his objective. This time Moss reveals himself to Aaronow and Aaronow begins to decode Moss's actual objective.

Aaronow moves closer to Moss, in the alcove of the cigarette machine. They whisper.

> AARONOW
>
> You're actually <u>talking</u> about this.

> MOSS
>
> . . . that's right.

> AARONOW
>
> You're going to steal the leads . . .

> MOSS
>
> . . . have I said that?

Pause.

> AARONOW
>
> Are you?

> MOSS
>
> Did I say that? . . .

> AARONOW
>
> . . . did you talk to Graff?

> MOSS
>
> . . . is that what I said?

> AARONOW
>
> . . . what did he say?

> MOSS
>
> . . . what did he say? He'd <u>buy</u> them.

> AARONOW
>
> . . . you're going to steal the Glengarry Leads and sell the leads to him.

> MOSS
>
> Yes. (54)

Because Aaronow has caught on to his scheme, Moss finally exposes his intention to steal the leads and sell them to Graff. Although the sale (Moss getting Aaronow to agree to participate in the robbery) does not close smoothly, it does close. Even though Aaronow objects to *actually* robbing the office as opposed to just "talking" about it, Moss points out to Aaronow that Aaronow is already an "accessory" (60) merely for engaging in conversation about it. Aaronow, in talking with Moss about the robbery, tacitly accepts the ethical principles underlying the robbery. He aligns himself with Moss, identifies with a capitalistic desire for easy money. Talking is action. By the time Moss reveals his true intention, Aaronow is already trapped by his own avarice.

```
ANGLE-POV-THE OFFICE

                        MOSS (O.S.)
          Tonight is the thing, talk about a chance, is
          when a chance presents itself . . .

ANGLE-MOSS AND AARONOW

                        AARONOW
          So, you're saying, that you have to go in there
          tonight, and . . .

                        MOSS
          You.

Beat.

                        AARONOW
          . . . I'm sorry?

                        MOSS
          You.

Pause.

                        AARONOW
          Me . . . ?

                        MOSS
          You have to go in. You have to get the
          leads.

Pause.

                        AARONOW
          I do . . . ?

                        MOSS
          It's not something for nothing, George. I took
```

you in on this, you have to go. That's your thing.
I've made a deal with Graff. I <u>can't</u> go in. I've
spoken out on this too much.

. . . .

                         AARONOW
    <u>Dave</u> . . .

                          MOSS
    Yes.

                         AARONOW
    . . . you want me to break into the office to
    night and steal the leads?

                          MOSS
    Yes.

Beat.

                         ARRONOW
    No. (57-59)

Aaronow tries to refuse Moss, but Moss points out to him that he is
already an accomplice.

                         AARONOW
    Me . . . ?

                          MOSS
    Absolutely.

                         AARONOW
    . . . that's ridiculous.

                          MOSS
    Well, to the law, you're an accessory, before
    the fact.

                         AARONOW
    I didn't ask to be.

                          MOSS
    Then Tough Luck, George, because you are.

CHAPTER 4

```
                  AARONOW
Why? Why? Because you only told me about it.

                   MOSS
That's right.
                  AARONOW
Why are you doing this to me, Dave? Why are you
talking this way to me? I don't understand. Why
are you doing this at all?


                   MOSS
That's none of your fucking business, pal. Just
In or Out. You tell me.
        (beat)
You're out, you take the consequences.


                  AARONOW
I do . . .


                   MOSS
Yes.


                  AARONOW
And why is that . . . ?


                   MOSS
Because you listened.
(60-61)
```

Aaronow is culpable because he engaged in the discourse, because he entertained the idea. As in Aristotle's paradigm, Aaronow is guilty because he listened to unethical discourse without distinguishing it as untrue or unjust. Listening without moral judgment is a crime just as much as robbery is a crime. Aaronow's crime is rhetorical. This directly parallels the salesmen themselves, who are all guilty of rhetorical crimes. They "talk" their prospects into buying presumably worthless real estate. Their weapon is speech. They operate as if they are guiltless—just men doing business. Yet, they work without ethical or moral principles. Moss feels no moral obligation to be fair to Aaronow any more than Roma feels an obligation to be fair to Lingk, or Williamson to Levene, or any character to another. Thus, *Glengarry Glen Ross* is about language more than anything. It exposes us to a world where capitalism has reduced discourse down to a single amoral objective— the accumulation of more capital. And capital, Karl Marx tells us, "is

112

dead labor, which, vampire-like, lives only by sucking living labor, and lives the more, the more labor it sucks" (342). The characters in *Glengarry Glen Ross* are its victims and its emissaries, prisoners and proponents of capitalist rhetoric.

Mamet's screenplay employs active dialogue to expose language as action, placing the audience in a position similar to Aaronow's. Like Aaronow, we must determine if the rhetoric of capitalism is unethical, or dismiss it as just "talking." Mamet skillfully puts us in a position in which we must either judge the rhetorical acts of these characters as unjust or become accomplices in the pervasive spread of blind avarice and the resulting decay of communal values.

Implied in Mamet's screenplay are issues of race and gender. Although the point is never expressly indicated in the screenplay, none of the main characters are women and the breadth of ethnicity among those characters is narrow. *Glengarry Glen Ross* only presents the rhetorical actions of white men. Race and gender, as inescapable components of all screenplay narrative, are integral to any critical examination of the screenplay, and it is to those that we now turn.

5

Scripting Gender, Representing Race

No precise accounting of women screenwriters in the early days of film is possible, but it is clear that "women dominated the industry's screenwriting departments" well into the 1920s (Abrams 77). Some estimates place the number of women screenwriters during the period as high as 90 percent. More conservative estimates place the number around 50 percent;[1] however, there is little debate that the majority of early screenwriters were women and that women played a key role in the early development of screenwriting.

Some of these early women writers (directors and producers), such as Lois Weber, gained "enormous respect and substantial creative control" during these early days of film (Stamp 141). Even MGM, which had a "reputation for devaluing the role of the screenwriter" and whose "executives insisted upon collaborations, multiple versions, a wide and baffling array of critical perspectives, and constant rewrites" (Smyth 162), gave a relatively free hand to Anita Loos and Frances Marion, two of Irving Thalberg's most valued screenwriters. One of the reasons for this trust from studios was that women screenwriters were reliable and prolific. Lois Weber wrote more than one hundred scenarios from 1911 to 1919. Frances Marion, who won an Academy Award for *The Big House* (Best Adapted Screenplay, 1930) and was the highest paid screen-

----

1. See Denise D. Bielby and William T. Bielby's "Women and Men in Film: Gender Inequality among Writers in a Culture Industry," 252.

writer during the 1920s, wrote over 130 scenarios between 1915 and 1929. Gene Gauntier, who was brought into the film writing business by Marion, wrote more than three hundred scenarios while working for Kalem and Biograph.

The overall number of scripts by women declined in the decade after sound, as the industry shifted away from women writers. Weber wrote approximately nine scenarios in the 1920s and only one produced scenario in the 1930s (*White Heat,* 1934). Marion's prodigious output dropped off to twenty-seven in the 1930s, and only five more of her scripts were produced after the 1930s. By the 1930s, the percentage of women screenwriters working in Hollywood dropped to around 15 percent. Bielby and Bielby note that Hollywood screenwriting in the mid-1930s experienced a "'male' invasion of the profession" (253), partly as a result of the rise of the studio system and partly as a result of the improving reputation of film industry professionals. The more acceptable the profession became, the more men supplanted women. By the end of the 1930s, screenwriters working for the big five (RKO, Warner Brothers, 20th Century Fox, MGM, and Paramount) and the little three (Columbia, Universal, and United Artists) were predominately white men. Despite a rise in the percentage of women screenwriters beginning in the 1970s, the number of women screenwriters lagged behind men screenwriters and the divide between the two continued to increase well into the 1990s (cf. Bielby and Bielby analysis of WGA West membership roles from 1935 to 1992, 253).

Early women screenwriters were highly instrumental in the evolution of the screenplay, as evident in Jeanie Macpherson's comments to the *New York Telegraph* (October 21, 1917) about the emerging literary form. "I have watched the scenario work from the beginning, from the days when the main purpose of the script was to keep some prominent object moving before the eyes of the delighted audience. Naturally at that time any subtlety of motion would be wasted on a plot whose main situation took the form of a ball rolling down the hill with a frenzied mob chasing it. I now feel that scenario work is coming into its own" (qtd. in Francke 18).

Despite their significance to the early days of screenwriting and their immeasurable contributions to the form, women were subject to cultural and professional influences that aimed the scripting of gender toward mainstream stereotypes. Lizzie Francke argues that for Marion,

Scripting Gender, Representing Race

these influences may have eventually won the battle for her creative inclinations. Francke quotes an article on adaptation that Marion wrote for *Photoplay* in the 1920s.

> A producer buys a story because it is a "big seller." Sometimes it is a splendid story for a man. The woman plays an important role in it, but a passive role. He hands it over to us poor picked-on scribes and says: "Make this a great vehicle for Norma Talmadge, or Gloria Swanson, or Mae Murray!" . . . What happens to the author's story? . . . We tear it down, we reconstruct it, we make the woman dominate, and the male character as passive as every woman would like to have her husband. We end up with a splendid vehicle for a woman star. (41)

Francke notes that a mere decade later, Marion's seeming advocacy for powerful women characters appears to have succumbed to other influences, and she "seemed happy to endorse conservative story-lines" (40), as evident in her 1937 book *How to Write and Sell Film Stories*, in which "Marion suggests two successful storylines: 'The wife who earns more than her husband loses her love,' and 'A woman's need for romance makes her an undependable factor in business'" (38).

Unlike women screenwriters, who at least enjoyed some measure of dominance during the early days of film, writers of color were marginalized from the beginning of the industry. The earliest African American screenwriters were associated with The Lincoln Motion Picture Company, a black production company, which formed in 1915. But black productions were not able to attract the white audiences they needed to survive; thus, writers such as George Johnson (story) and Dora Mitchell (scenario) who wrote *The Right of Birth* (1921) for Lincoln had limited careers. Despite the presence of African American controlled films such as Oscar Micheaux's full-length *Birthright* (1918) and Emmett J. Scott's full-length *The Birth of a Race* (1918–19),[2] the economically sensitive Hollywood film industry embraced the less realistic depictions of black life that white audiences preferred, making financial

---

2. Both *Birthright* and *The Birth of a Race* were reactions to D. W. Griffith's blatantly racist *The Birth of a Nation*.

successes of films such as D. W. Griffith's *The Birth of a Nation* (1915).

African Americans have been depicted in film throughout the industry's history, beginning with early actualities, such as Edison's "The Morning Bath" (1896), a short twenty-two-second film depicting a black woman bathing a black infant in a tub of white suds. Sometimes, black faces dominated the screen, as in productions such as the 1929 "all-Negro" musical, *Hearts in Dixie,* and King Vidor's *Hallelujah,* also released in 1929. But the creative forces behind the screen remained white, and though characters were sometimes black, they were "directed by whites in scripts authored by whites and then photographed, dressed, and made up by whites" (Bogle 27). Donald Bogle argues that this "blackface fixation" continued long after blackface came off (27). By 1921, after only six years, the first African American production company (the aforementioned Lincoln Motion Picture Company) came to an end.

Oscar Micheaux was the first African American screenwriter to manage a lasting career. In 1919, Micheaux wrote and directed *The Homesteader,* becoming the first African American to write and direct a feature-length motion picture. He went on to write and direct between thirty and forty feature-length screenplays between 1919 and 1948, but Micheaux's films remained largely peripheral to Hollywood's more dominant offerings. The first mainstream film with a script written by black authors did not appear until 1939 when Langston Hughes and Clarence Muse wrote *Way Down South.* But the appearance of *Way Down South* does not mark a significant trend among mainstream audiences. In the same year that *Way Down South* was released, Mickey Rooney appeared in blackface in the more popular *Babes in Arms.* According to box-office receipts, blackface was still more popular than black faces. Other than some additional dialogue for the 1940 film *Broken Strings,* Clarence Muse did not write another produced screenplay and Langston Hughes did not receive another screen credit until he wrote the book for the 1959 musical *Simply Heaven.*

In the 1960s, African American screenwriters began to make tentative inroads into the film industry. Gordon Parks received writing credits for the documentary *Flavio* in 1964 and the screenplay adaptation of his 1963 novel *The Learning Tree* in 1969. Advances made by the civil rights movement opened more movie industry doors for African

American writers. Maya Angelou wrote *Georgia, Georgia* in 1972 and co-wrote the screen adaptation of her book *I Know Why the Caged Bird Sings* with Leonora Thuna in 1979. Charles Burnett wrote *Killer of Sheep* in 1977. Unlike the African American screenwriters who preceded them, African American screenwriters in the 1970s saw opportunities increase rather than dwindle. But the 1970s were not a period of positive representation for African Americans. The popularity (and profitability) of Blaxploitation films did much to waylay positive African American images. Although Blaxploitation films often presented blacks in strong roles—detectives, superheroes, cowboys, and so on—these depictions were largely two dimensional, but they did provide African American writers with some—albeit limited—access to Hollywood. A *Newsweek* cover story about the black movie boom points out that "talented black actors, directors and writers were suddenly plucked out of studio back rooms, modeling agencies and ghetto theaters, and turned loose on new black projects" (qtd. in Bogle 241). Despite this advertised interest in "black movies," ultimately, whites wrote many of the black movies shot during the 1970s.

The first major breakthrough for African American screenwriters did not come until the 1980s when Spike Lee wrote, produced, and directed *She's Gotta Have It* (1986), *School Daze* (1988), and *Do the Right Thing* (1989) and Robert Townsend wrote, produced, and directed *Hollywood Shuffle* (1987), which revealed an audience for stories depicting African American life from an African American perspective. Despite the increased access to the Hollywood system that the success of these works facilitated, African American screenwriters still faced (and continue to face) a more reluctant audience in white producers and studio heads. As Charles Burnett points out in a 1995 interview, "For us, being people of color, everything has to be exact. Everything counts. I don't think you [African American screenwriters] have the luxury of being too experimental at the studio level" (29). Carol Munday Lawrence points out that "there are almost 8,000 writers in the [Writers] Guild, but there are only 264 who are people of color, of whom only 112 are black" (69). Not until the end of the twentieth century did screenplays, such as John Singleton's *Boyz N the Hood* (1991), begin to be regularly produced—screenplays written by African American screenwriters, which exhibited fidelity to the lived lives of African American culture.

The Politics of Racial and Gender Inscription

Filmmakers have long held the notion that distinctions can be drawn between film representations that are "true" to some external "reality" and film representations that are pure artifice. Around the time the Lumière brothers were "documenting" the world with their early short films, in a style said to "present an unmediated view of reality" (Fell 300), Georges Méliès was creating film fantasy with his cinematic sleight of hand. One category of film work was said to reflect, while the other was said to construct. In the first part of the twentieth century, the distinctions between the two were presumed to be self-evident. However, there are many examples of how, even then, categories of "true" representation and "pure" artifice broke down under scrutiny. The public response to D. W. Griffith's *Birth of a Nation* (1914), for example, exposed the difficulties inherent in any attempt to distinguish "true" representation from storytelling. While some, such as President Woodrow Wilson, claimed the film was "like history written with lightning" (qtd. in Mast and Kawin 62), others recognized the work as virulent racist propaganda. Griffith's sought to use film to "represent" life as it actually was and was surprised when the veracity of his work was vehemently questioned. What *Birth of a Nation,* and all film, demonstrates is that what film mediates is a *presumed* "reality" (or realities)—a "real" written to the reel, rather than objective truth. "True" representation is merely a subjective political judgment. Representations that align with existing belief systems are perceived as "true," while representations that challenge belief systems are perceived as artificial; the closer a representation aligns with our politics, the truer it seems. Laura Mulvey addresses this issue when she points out that, "As an advanced representation system, the cinema poses questions about the ways the unconscious (formed by the dominant order) structures ways of seeing and pleasure in looking" (15). Mulvey's work expanded film theory with its recognition (and sometimes attribution) of gender to cinematic experience, leading to our "understanding that film viewing always involves gendered identities" (Humm 17). In her illumination of female subjectification, Mulvey must also contend with male gaze. The man/woman binary is the yin/yang of cultural perceptions of gender. Just as gender cannot be omitted from issues of human reproduction, it cannot be excised from film production and its apparatuses. Neither can gender be separated from screenwriting. It is the screenplay, after all, that filmmakers translate into film. Thus, it is the screenwriter who first shapes representation, who first frames the gaze. The screenwriter is always the first audience for a story, the first to judge a story's verisimilitude; it is the screenwriter who first determines to what extent his/ her story does or does not "represent" the cultural milieu from which it emerges. And it is the screenwriter who determines which representations s/he will inject into the conversations of culture.

Since the latter half of the twentieth century, the ability of a representation to reflect any transcendent "reality" has increasingly been criticized. To what extent can a fictional character, for example, remain true to some external referent? Most late twentieth-century thinkers would dismiss the idea that some pure ideal of "male" or "female" exists outside the cultural factory. Without a "pure" ideal, how then can a representation be judged "true" or "accurate?" As with Griffith's *Birth of a Nation,* the question always arises: true or accurate to what (or *whose*) standard?

Writers are employed in the enterprise of shaping representations of race and gender. The form their characterizations take both reflects culture and constructs it. Questions of whether or not film constructs or perpetuates stereotypes are moot—writing cannot *not* construct stereotypes. When a writer sits before a computer creating a female or male character s/he shapes that character based on perceptions of what constitutes female or male. The same may be said of race, and the writer's perceptions of race and gender are always partial. All characteristics exhibited by a particular group cannot be completely enumerated, much less captured in one character. It is impossible for one Southern female to represent *all* Southern females, or one black male to represent *all* black males. Therefore, the act of creating a character is always reductive. Characters are often condemned for not being "fair" to a particular group, but that is not a function of the character's verisimilitude;[3] rather, it is a function of how closely that character meets the expectation of a select audience. A writer cannot write "whole"

----

3. Alice Walker, for example, frequently comes under fire for her seemingly negative portrayals of black men. But is Walker obligated to be fair to all black men? If one black man resembles her characterizations, is she then justified in a narrow presentation? A former colleague of mine, in a discussion of William Faulkner's *Sanctuary,* once

characters, no matter how hard s/he may try; therefore, writers cannot be "fair" to particular groups. A tremendous amount of diversity exists within racial, political, and cultural groups. People categorized on the basis of one or more shared characteristics may differ greatly in other ways. If we define stereotypes as unfair generalizations attributed to entire categories of people, then the construction of any fictional character is inherently an act of stereotyping. Redaction is reductive.

Yet, some characters are more believable than others; some are more complex, and more interesting. James Cameron and Gale Anne Hurd's terminator (*The Terminator,* 1984) is a flat character without much depth. Conversely, Robert Towne's Jake Gittes (*Chinatown,* 1974) is complex and intriguing. What makes one character seem more real than another is the character's complexity. A strong, interesting character is not strong and interesting because s/he is realistic or more realistic than other characters; what makes a character interesting is the extent to which that character implies that a rich and complex psychological network is operating below the surface of the character's words and actions.

Ultimately, we must admit that film and the screenplay do not, in any reliable way, present the world; they map cultural perceptions (and unconscious predilections), which are largely controlled by hegemonic constructions; they are inescapably political. The economics of capitalist production that fuel mainstream filmmaking pressure screenwriters to reproduce past success, thus the repetition of gender and race representations that we find in mainstream cinema tend to perpetuate the cultural perceptions of the dominant gaze, and these perceptions can be mapped.

Paradigms at Play—Making Males: Heroes and Rogues

Mainstream American cinema has been primarily about the lives of white men: swashbucklers, lawyers, gunfighters, politicians—men of decisive action, men of intelligent restraint. The range of male characterizations has been broad and rich, yet most male characterizations

---

asked the same question of Faulkner's obligation to white Southern women. If one woman somewhere exists who is similar to the character of Temple Drake, does that justify Faulkner's fictional representation?

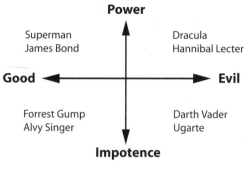

Fig. 4.

can be summarized by their relationships to two axes on a Cartesian plane: one axis for power, one axis for morality (fig. 4).

Mainstream American screenwriters tend to present male characters based on these two parameters: Is he a *good* man or a *bad* man? Is he powerful or weak? Note how Tod Browning and Garrett Fort quickly locate the character of Dracula with respect to these axes.

```
A-34          INT. HALL-LONG SHOT
```

. . . He [Dracula] is a tall, thick-set man of distinguished appearance. His lips are pale, but his large, luminous eyes burn with an unholy light, and upon closer inspection can be identified with those of the mysterious driver of the coach. He is wearing formal attire, and wears a decoration. His manner is invariably suave—his bearing one of distinction. As he comes slowly down the stairs, CAMERA SWOOPS UP TO LARGE CU (Crane Shot) and he pauses, looking down at Renfield:

```
A-35          INT. MAIN HALL
              MED. SHOT RENFIELD
```

As seen from Dracula's point of view. He [Renfield] is staring up at Dracula, open-mouthed and startled.

```
A-36          INT. LARGER CLOSEUP
              DRACULA
```

He bows and smiles as he says,

DRACULA

I am Dracula—

```
A-37        INT. MED. CLOSE
            RENFIELD
```

He is too frightened for the moment to say anything—
he looks around nervously and then looks back at
Dracula. (n.p.)

In this early scene in which Dracula and Renfield meet for the first time, Dracula is quickly established as a man of great power. He is described as "distinguished," and "suave," implying social power; his "bearing" is said to be "one of distinction," implying a powerful physical presence. Dracula's power is so overwhelming that he instantly strikes fear into Renfield, causing Renfield to grow nervous and avert his gaze in a primal domination ritual. Dracula is the more powerful man, as the remainder of the screenplay illuminates. But Dracula's power is not the only characteristic described; his power is coupled with "luminous eyes that burn with an unholy light." Dracula is powerful *and* evil. Both qualities are necessary to establish his character. Gerald Mast refers to this *type* as the mythic villain. Mast offers as an example the Michael Douglas character, Gordon Gekko, in *Wall Street,* whom he calls a "tremendously powerful antagonist, a takeover artist who incarnates every evil known to capitalism" (516). Gekko is an economic vampire who bleeds the poor working class of its livelihood. This character type finds its apex in the central figures of slasher films: Michael Myers from John Carpenter's *Halloween,* Freddy from Wes Craven's *Elm Street,* and Jason from an army of *Friday the 13th* films—all powerful characters without moral conscience capable of indiscriminate carnage, all capable of reaching beyond the grave and feeding off innocent life without compunction, and all male.

Joan Mellen traces this prototypical male character back to the close-up of actor George Barnes firing his gun at the audience, which ends *The Great Train Robbery* (1903). Mellen claims that "whatever his moral posture, his prowess suggests that only comparable brutality will be sufficient to best him. Above all, there can be no doubt about his maleness. Overpowering, intensely physical, and unrelenting" (31). Mellen's description of the George Barnes character pinpoints the two primary axes of male construction in screenwriting: power and moral-

Fig. 5. Screenwriters Tod Browning and Garrett Fort establish
Dracula's power by introducing him descending a flight of stairs.

ity. Power for the male hero is linked to his capacity for direct action.
His morality relates to his motives for those actions.

Compare these powerful and evil characters to Ugarte (*Casablanca*,
1942), a character who is impotent and evil. In Ugarte's first conversation with Rick in the script, Julius Epstein and co-writers clearly mark
his character.

                    UGARTE (fawning)
        Watching you just now with the Deutches Bank,[4]
        one would think you had been doing this all
        your life.

                    RICK (stiffening)
        What makes you think I haven't?

----

4. A German banker to whom Rick has just refused entrance to the back-room
casino of Rick's Café Americain.

CHAPTER 5

          UGARTE (vaguely)
Oh, nothing. When you first came to
Casablanca, I thought—

          RICK (coldly)
Yes?

     UGARTE (fearing to offend RICK, laughs)
What right have I to think? (hastily changing
the subject) Too bad about those German
couriers, wasn't it?

          RICK (indifferently)
They got a break. Yesterday they were just
two German clerks; today they're the Honored
Dead.

          UGARTE (shaking his head)
You will forgive me for saying this, M'sieur
Rick, but you are a very cynical person.

          RICK (shortly)
I forgive you.

[Bartender comes into the scene and sets two drinks
down in front of Rick and Ugarte]

          UGARTE (his eyes lighting up)
Oh, Rick—you are going to drink with me?

               RICK
No.

               UGARTE
You despise me, don't you?

          RICK (indifferently)
If I gave you any thought, I probably would.

               UGARTE
You object to the work I do. But think of the
poor refugees who must rot in this place if I
did not help them. Is it so bad that through
ways of my own I provide them with exit
visas?

          RICK (staring at his drink)
For a price, Ugarte, for a price.

Fig. 6. An evil, impotent Ugarte (Peter Lorre) fails to impress the good, powerful Rick Blaine (Humphrey Bogart) in *Casablanca* (1942).

```
                        UGARTE
        Yes—but those poor devils who cannot meet
        Renault's price, I get it for them for half.
        Is that so parasitic?

RICK turns to look at UGARTE
                        RICK
        I don't mind a parasite. I object to a cut-
        rate one. (131-32)
```

In this scene, a dominant/submissive binary relationship is outlined between Rick and Ugarte. Ugarte is without power, a man with no right to think. Even Ugarte's private, psychic machinations submit to the forceful presence of Rick. Ugarte hopes to impress Rick with his slaughter of the German couriers and theft of the exit visas, to raise his status in the herd, but Rick only finds Ugarte loathsome—a cut-rate parasite who, like Dracula and Gordon Gekko, feeds off the misfortune of others. Ugarte is an object of disdain, a man without a moral conscience to counterbalance his lack of power. In killing the couriers,

Ugarte has attempted to increase his power, but his action was unctuous and avoided the standards of fair combat among honorable men, and his motives for action were selfish.

In Woody Allen's Alvy Singer (*Annie Hall*, 1977), we find that a moral conscience offsets a lack of power and engenders identification from an audience. The character is powerless to affect his environment, yet he maintains hope that somehow things will improve, that people will wake up one day and the world will be a better place in which to live. Characters like Alvy Singer don't ask, as moral characters *with* power ask (e.g., the Lone Ranger, Superman), "What can I do?" They ask, "Why doesn't someone do something?" Because he lacks the power to act alone, he becomes the voice of the common man.

Allen establishes Alvy Singer's powerlessness in the second scene of the screenplay:

```
CUT TO:
INTERIOR. DOCTOR'S OFFICE—DAY.

Alvy as young boy sits on a sofa with his mother in an
old-fashioned, cluttered doctor's office. The doctor
stands near the sofa, holding a cigarette and listen-
ing.

                    MOTHER
          He's been depressed. All of a sudden, he
          can't do anything.

                    DOCTOR
          Why are you depressed, Alvy?

                    MOTHER
          Tell Dr. Flicker. (Young Alvy sits, his
          head down. His mother answers for him)
          It's something he read.

                    DOCTOR
          Something he read, huh?

                    ALVY
          The universe is expanding.

                    DOCTOR
          The universe is expanding?
```

                    ALVY
Well, the universe is everything, and
if it's expanding, someday it will break
apart and that would be the end of
everything!

Disgusted, his mother looks at him.

          MOTHER (*Shouting*)
What is that your business? (*She turns
back to the doctor*) He stopped doing his
homework.

                    ALVY
What's the point?[5]
(*Four Films* 4-5)

Alvy's concerns are immense (the inevitable destruction of the universe), which elevates his impotence to universal levels. If the universe cannot be steered from its terminal course, "what's the point" of doing anything? All actions are empty; all efforts are futile. But, behind Alvy's fatalistic facade, beneath a rampage of one-liners and clever witticisms, is a deep moral conscience. After Annie and Alvy watch *The Sorrow and the Pity*, a film about the Nazi occupation of a French town in World War II, a movie they had seen before, a movie Alvy insisted on seeing again, they have the following conversation:

CUT TO:
INTERIOR. BEDROOM—NIGHT

Annie is sitting up in bed reading.

                  ALVY (OS)
Boy, those guys in the French Resistance
were really brave, you know? Got to listen to Maurice Chevalier sing so much.

                    ANNIE
M'm, I don't know, sometimes I ask myself
how I'd stand up under torture.

----
5. I have taken the liberty of cutting many of the dialogue markers from this scene, as they tend to be unnecessary and cumbersome in these transcriptions, and are almost always added by the publisher.

```
                    ALVY (OS)
          You? You kiddin'? (He moves into the
          frame, lying across the bed to touch
          Annie, who makes a face) If the Gestapo
          would take away your Bloomingdale's
          charge card, you'd tell 'em everything.

                    ANNIE
          That movie makes me feel guilty.

                    ALVY
          Yeah, 'cause it's supposed to.
          (17)
```

Beneath the humor of the scene, moral distinctions between Alvy and Annie are outlined. Annie does not want to confront the Holocaust over and over again. She feels guilty and, although she goes to see the movie, it is clear that she would prefer not to, that she would prefer to put the ugliness of the past behind her, to move on. Alvy, on the other hand, cannot forget, cannot put aside the hideous immoral treatment of the Jews at the hands of the Nazis, partly because he is Jewish, but also because a strong moral sense will not let him avert his eyes away from injustice and brutal inhumanity. For Alvy, the Holocaust is a metaphor for a universe expanding toward its eventual destruction, a destruction he has no power to avert. He knows something must be done, but he lacks the power to do it.

Male characters with the power to act on their moral imperatives receive the highest heroic status in screenplays. They are often superheroes: men with nearly unlimited abilities, virtually indestructible characters committed to the protection of moral and ethical values. The archetypal powerful and moral character is arguably Superman—an essentially flat character who does not offer easy dramatic opportunities because conflict is difficult to establish for characters who have few external physical threats and fewer internal psychological tensions. But not all moral and powerful characters are like Superman, Batman, Captain America, and other superheroes. Some, such as John McClane (*Die Hard*, 1988), are physically vulnerable when pitted against seemingly insurmountable odds. John McClane operates on the side of the law; he is a representative of justice and, though he is mortal, his testosterone-driven determination to do something about the evil terrorists allows him to overcome overwhelming obstacles.

Scripting Gender, Representing Race

A surprising number of male characters can be defined by their position on the two axes of power and morality. Importantly, this paradigm, like all paradigms, is *artificial;* it is a construct, a creation. It does not encapsulate maleness; it manufactures points of view about what men are. Joan Mellen notes in *Big Bad Wolves: Masculinity in the American Film* that "male stars are people manufactured from the raw material of humanity to appear as supermen overcoming women and lesser men by sheer determination and will, involving, in varying permutations, competence, experience, rationality—and charm" (3). Mellen points out that this masculine heroic construction has existed since the early days of film. She cites rare exceptions, such as King Vidor's 1928 version of *The Crowd* (28), but notes that, even in instances where the male protagonist appears to be weak, he often succeeds by adopting the aggressive behaviors of the contrived masculine hero. Benjamin, in *The Graduate,* for example, appears aimless and weak, but "his 'triumph' consists finally in a conventional pursuit and conquest of Mrs. Robinson's daughter, Elaine" (Mellen 276). Benjamin assaults Elaine's wedding, and Elaine translates his aggression into signs of devotion.

Often male types are set in contrast, as in Waldo Salt's screenplay for *Midnight Cowboy* (1969), where the powerful and (somewhat) moral cowboy, Joe Buck, is set in contrast against the weak and immoral Ratso. In Eugene Solow's screenplay for *Of Mice and Men* (1939), the powerful and moral George is set against the weak and moral Lennie. In *Casablanca* (1942), the powerful and moral Rick is set against the weak and immoral Ugarte. The morality of characters such as Joe Buck and Rick Blaine rests not in their adherence to external, preexisting notions of morality. Buck is, after all, a prostitute, by choice, and Rick runs an illegal casino and deals with the black market. But both do follow a code of their own. They are like Hemingway's heroes, men who live correctly according to their own standards of honor. The play among these four types—high power/high moral, high power/low moral, low power/high moral, and low power/low moral—constitutes much of the male interaction found in the mainstream American screenplay.

Paradigms at Play—Forming Females: Vestals and Vamps

Women characters generally operate across a narrower range than male characters for several reasons. First, and perhaps foremost, mainstream cinema is patriarchal, like the cultural milieu in which cinema is formed. For one hundred years, the film industry has been controlled by men, concerned primarily with "male" issues of power and morality, and has tended to define "female" by its relationships to patriarchal hegemonic standards of sexuality and the male view of a woman's relationship to male desire. It is the woman who is subjected to the male gaze, not the other way around. As Christina Lane points out, the male gaze "positions men as active subjects and women as passive objects" (15).

Although women have been involved in film from early on, their roles have tended to be subordinate (assistants to men) or marginal (independent of the Hollywood studio system). The attempt of women filmmakers to gain a foothold in the film industry has thrown into question traditional views of women and the role film plays in the construction of gender. This, Laurie Ouellette argues, is necessary. Ouellette points out that in order to "subvert the hidden mechanisms of patriarchal ideologies. . . . films by women would require a revolutionary counter-aesthetic, one that revealed how film itself operates as a signifying practice" (29). Ouellette's call is for reflexive awareness on the part of women filmmakers. She implies that, in order to be effective, feminist cinema must expose the relationship between film and ideology. At the level of the screenwriter, the relationship between language and ideology must also be questioned. All screenwriters, male and female, are influenced by gender dynamics in their construction of characters.

While female characters, like male characters, are definable by variant levels of power and morality, they seldom, in mainstream cinema, escape sexual definition. The power of a female character and the morality of a female character are often linked to the character's sexuality, and that sexuality is usually oriented to male desire. The pattern creates a chiasma that sets female power in direct opposition to morality. In this patriarchal view, the more powerful a female character becomes, the less moral she is. Conversely, the weaker she becomes, the greater her morality. All of this is in direct proportion to her sexuality (fig. 7). This pattern is at the heart of the Madonna/whore myth that equates female sexuality with issues of morality.

Carl Foreman prefaces his script for *High Noon* with a section titled "Some Notes about This Story." His descriptions of the two primary

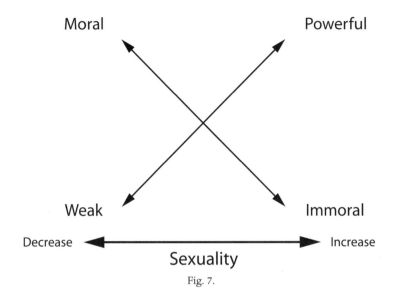

Fig. 7.

female roles in the film (Helen Ramirez and Amy Doane) strongly link morality to sexual activity and exemplify this paradigm in practice.

> HELEN RAMIREZ. She is two or three years older than [Will] Doane, a victim of an era and environment with rigid social standards. To begin with, Helen is half Mexican, and thus neither acceptable to the "pure" American women of the region, nor eligible for a "good" marriage. Consequently, in addition to being intelligent, shrewd and strong-willed, she is also hard and resentful. Physically, she is handsome, full-breasted, passionate. More, she has style, personality.
> (41)

Helen, whom Foreman tells us "still cannot forgive Will Doane" for ending their "lengthy affair" (41), is morally "unacceptable" to Will Doane. She is described as impure and unfit to be a wife. Yet she is "a good business woman" (41). Helen is a boundary creature with economic power who is nonetheless morally deficit. Thus, her sexuality is pronounced: she is described as "full-breasted" and "passionate." Helen is the "whore" to Amy Doane's "Madonna"—a sexually active woman who operates outside culturally mandated standards for women (standards that Will, as a man, is not subject to). Helen's first appearance in the script frames her as an object of male desire, a sexual creature.

```
MED. CLOSE SHOT—HELEN RAMIREZ—through the window into
her sitting-room. She is in negligee, still languorous
from sleep, her long black hair cascading down over her
shoulders. She stretches luxuriously. There is the o.s.
SOUND of the approaching horses. HARVEY PELL enters
the scene from behind her, and draws her back into the
room. (45)
```

Like the opening of *Psycho*, Helen Ramirez is introduced in *High Noon* in a way that suggests a flawed moral character. She is dressed in a negligee as if she has just risen from bed, and she is in the company of a man to whom she is not married.

Foreman's description of Amy Doane, conversely, lacks references to her physical sexuality.

```
    AMY DOANE is, without knowing it, one of the
new women of the period, women who are beginning to
rebel against the limitations and restrictions of
the Victorian epoch. Young, attractive, intelligent,
strong-willed, Amy is determined not to be a sheltered
toy-wife but a full partner in her marriage, and it is
she who has planned their [Will and her] future. More,
Amy has strong emotional and intellectual convictions
against any form of violence, because her father and
brothers were killed while taking part in Vigilante
[sic] action, and she has since embraced the Quaker
faith. Marriage to Doane would have been unthinkable
had he remained a peace officer. (41)
```

Although described as a "rebel against . . . the Victorian epoch," Amy is virginal. Foreman foregrounds the fact that Amy does not kiss Will until they are married, and when Will gets her alone immediately after the wedding ceremony, Amy is described as "embarrassed but amused" (51). Foreman implies that Amy will be a "full partner in her marriage," but Will ends up with the power. In his long discussion with her over his need to stand up to the Jordan bunch, Will is matter-of-fact about what he is going to do. Amy pleads with him, but Foreman leaves little doubt that Will is in control and that ultimately Amy will have to live with whatever Will decides.

<pre>
                    AMY
Will, I'm begging you—please! . . . Let's
go . . . !

                    DOANE
I can't . . .

                    AMY
          (angry)
Don't try to be a hero! You don't have to
be a hero—not for me!

                    DOANE
          (losing his temper)
I'm not trying to be a hero! If you think
I like this, you're crazy!
          (he masters himself)
Amy, look. This is my town. I've got
friends here. Toby and Harvey'll be here.
I'll swear in a bunch of special depu-
ties. With a posse behind me, maybe there
won't even be any trouble . . .

                    AMY
          (defeated)
You know there'll be trouble.

                    DOANE
Then it's better to have it here. . . .
I'm sorry, honey. I know how you feel
about it—

                    AMY
          (harshly)
Do you?

                    DOANE
          (awkwardly)
Of course I do. I know it's against your
religion and all—Sure I know how you feel
about it.

                    AMY
          (bitterly)
But you're doing it just the same.
</pre>

```
                        DOANE
              (helplessly)
    Amy . . .
```

Amy comes to him, her heart in her eyes, deliber-
ately throwing all she has of magnetism and sex at
him.

```
                        AMY
              Will, we were married just a few minutes
              ago—doesn't that mean anything to you?
              We've got our whole lives ahead of us.
              . . . * * * Doesn't that mean anything
              to you.
```

With an effort, Doane gently pushes her aside. Amy
is shattered. (63-64)

Amy's lack of power is juxtaposed with her inability to seduce her husband. The relationship between sex and power is presented as "natural"; no self-reflexive interrogation of the relationship exists. Amy does
not have the power to influence her husband because she does not have
the power to seduce him. The very "purity" that makes Amy a suitable
bride for Will renders her powerless. The implication is clear: a suitable
wife is one without power, one who must accept the man's decisions,
regardless of how drastically those decisions contradict her desires.

In *Casablanca*, when Ilsa makes her first major attempt to get Rick
to understand why she left him at the train station in Paris, Rick responds by implying that she was on a moral par with a prostitute.

```
                        ILSA
              Can I tell you a story, Rick?


                        RICK
              Has it got a finish, honey, has it got a
              twist?


                        ILSA
              I don't know the finish yet.


                        RICK
              Maybe one will come to you as you go
              along.
```

Scripting Gender, Representing Race

                    ILSA
It's about a girl who was very young. She
had just come to Paris from her home in
Oslo. At the house of some friends she
met a man—a very good man. They became
friends—he became her teacher. She had
been brought up very provincially, and he
opened up for her a whole beautiful world
of knowledge and thoughts and ideals.
Everything she ever knew or ever
became was because of his goodness. And
she looked up at him and worshipped him
with a feeling she supposed was love—

          RICK (definitely interrupting)
I heard a story once. In fact, I've heard
a lot of stories in my time. They went
along with the sound of a tinny piano in
the parlor downstairs. "Mister, I met a
man when I was only a kid," they'd always
begin.

ILSA, *shuddering, gets up.*

Fig. 8. Ilsa (Ingrid Bergman) and Rick (Humphrey Bogart)
face off in *Casablanca* (1942).

137

CHAPTER 5

```
                          ILSA
            I'll go now. (Epstein et al. 146)
```

Rick characterizes Ilsa's narrative as if Ilsa is making excuses for immoral behavior. Her romance with Laszlo is reduced to an immoral
sexual encounter. Rick's anger with Ilsa is tied directly to her leaving
him in Paris, an assertion of independence. When Ilsa makes decisions
regarding her life, and what is best for herself, Rick, and Laszlo, Rick
attacks her moral character. Later, in her strongest assertion of power,
she points a gun at Rick and demands he hand over the letters of transit.
Her inability to shoot Rick is immediately followed by the resurrection
of her moral character and a reduction in her power. Ilsa pits her will
against Rick's and fails, after which she explains that she was married to
Laszlo and had thought he was dead when she became involved with
Rick. Thus, her story reenters the boundaries of an acceptable male
narrative of female desire. It is appropriate for a woman to take on a
new lover after her husband dies, and it is morally appropriate for her
to immediately return when she discovers he is alive. In a conventional
sense, Ilsa is "faithful" to both Rick and Laszlo to the best of her knowledge. Once her moral character is vindicated, her power dissipates.

```
                          RICK
            It's still a story without an ending.⁶
            (looks at her directly) What about now?


                          ILSA
            (simply) I'll never have the strength to
            go away from you again.
```

Shortly later she adds:

```
                          ILSA
            I can't fight it any more. I ran away
            from you once. Some morning I may wake up
            to find that you've gone, and if it lasts
            fifty years or ten days I know there'll
            be more heartache in it than happiness.
            I don't know what's right any longer.
```

----

6. Rick's reference to the end of the story recalls the previous scene.

```
You'll have to think for both of us,
Richard—for all of us. (161)
```

Phallic power is passed back to Rick at the expense of Ilsa's autonomy. By the end of the film she is weak but moral.

Major Hollywood scripts that attempt to disrupt this gender paradigm tend to begin by factoring morality out of the equation. In Callie Khouri's *Thelma and Louise* (1991), for example, Thelma's escape from her restrictive relationship with Darryl parallels her sexual awakening with J. D. Syd Field summarizes Thelma's transformation in *Four Screenplays: Studies in the American Screenplay:* "Louise is still sitting in the booth as Thelma joins her for coffee. 'Her energy and volume is several notches higher than the rest of the people in the coffee shop,' the script reads, and we know it must have been fantastic for her. She can't wait to share it with Louise. . . . Thelma is totally into it: 'I can't believe it! I just can't believe it! I mean I finally understand what all the fuss is about. This is a whole 'nother ball game!'" (46). While Thelma's power is still linked to her sexuality, the moral stigma is absent. Her adulterous liaison with J. D. is liberating and fulfilling. The same is true for the heroine of Jane Campion's *The Piano;* she is a woman who is empowered by the discovery of her own sexuality, not marginalized by it.

Just as characters are subject to screenwriters, screenwriters are subject to the pervasive paradigms that influence their writing. What appears real or natural is often only what parallels their personal biases. Writers who are conscious of the paradigms that influence the way they construct characters are free to challenge those paradigms, to create male characters that do not operate within conventional systems of power and morality, and to construct female characters that are not defined by their sexuality. While pure representation is not possible and screenwriters can never present men and women as they "actually" are, screenwriters do open up the range of possibilities for their characters when they challenge conventional points of view, which can only result in a richer, more diverse cinema.

Race and Ethnicity

The representation of African Americans in mainstream screenplays is no less subject to cultural mandates from the dominant hegemony than issues of gender. The precursors to black representation in early screenplays were the blackface performers who worked in traveling road shows and circuses in the first half of the nineteenth century. Beginning with the Virginia Minstrels in New York (1843), scripted minstrel groups purported to present a view of plantation life, but they were, as Rudi Blesh has noted, a "travesty," despite their appearance as "a sort of tribute to the charm and power of the real thing" (84). The characters of the minstrel show—Brudder or Mister Bones, Tambo, Mr. Interlocutor, and M.C.—were grotesque exaggerations of the life African Americans led at the time, and their dialogue (often scripted) parodied rather than mimicked black dialects. These characters were often depicted "singing, loafing, attending massa or missus, making love, [and] hunting coon or possum" (10), and engendered their white, working-class audiences with a comic sense of superiority.

The appearance of motion pictures at the end of the century did little to alter the misrepresentation of African Americans. There was, of course, no spoken dialogue during the first three decades of film, so the "black" dialects found in minstrel shows were reduced to altered spellings on title cards, such as "Yo' northern low down black trash, don't try no airs on me," from *The Birth of a Nation*. Mainstream cinema clung to white, working-class notions of African Americans. Behind the black face was white perception. This was the case for white actors in blackface, such as Al Jolson in *The Jazz Singer,* and for characters portrayed by African American actors, such as Bert Williams in *Darktown Jubilee* (1914), who also performed his role in blackface. Mike Chopra-Gant acknowledges that Jolson engaged "in a distinctly *white* American performance of black identity," and that blackface performance was more a "ritualized performance of a conception of blackness constructed by and for whites" than a depiction of black ethnicity (59). Bernard Wolfe claims that this ritualized performance was the same for black and white performers, noting that "the truth about the Negro performer is that he is required to be a *Negro impersonator . . .* [by a] Southern caste etiquette, which requires each individual Negro to personify the white man's image of the composite Negro" (62).

When sound was introduced, blackface slowly disappeared and black actors were increasingly hired to play black characters; nevertheless, blackface remained more popular than realistic black portrayals. Even when black performers were finally able to appear without blackface, their popularity was precipitated on the adoption of white, working-class stereotypes. Actors such as Stepin Fetchit, Bill "Bojangles" Robinson, and Hattie McDaniel were forced to play fools, butlers, black mammys, and servants if they wanted to find regular work. Serious black actors, such as Paul Robeson, often had to go overseas for more realistic roles. It is telling that, by 1932, the top-grossing film of the silent era was *Birth of a Nation,* which brought in over $10 million in domestic and foreign revenue, and the top-grossing sound film was Al Jolson's *Singing Fool,* which had earned over $5 million by 1932.

White screenwriters often crafted black characters in bestial terms, as in the following description from Curt Siodmak and Ardel Wray's script for *I Walked with a Zombie* (1943), which claims to be "based on scientific information from articles by Inez Wallace" (title page):

```
                    HOLLAND
        It's easy enough to read the thoughts of
        a newcomer. Everything seems beautiful
        because you don't understand. Those fly-
        ing fish—they are not leaping for joy.
        They're jumping in terror. Bigger fish
        want to eat them. That luminous water—it
        takes its gleam from millions of tiny
        dead bodies. It's the glitter of putres-
        cence. There's no beauty here—it's death
        and decay.

                    BETSY
        You can't really believe that.


        A star falls. They both follow its flight
        with their eyes.

                    HOLLAND
                (pointing to it)
        Everything good dies here—even the stars.


        He leaves his position by the mast and walks
        aft.


        The group of negroes at the mainmast. They have
        stopped singing and they sit about the charcoal
        brazier. They are eating, tearing at the meat
        with cruel, greedy, animal gestures. Holland
        walks past them on his way aft.
        (n.p.)
```

The black West Indies is presented as a dangerous place full of decay, its inhabitants as bestial, uncivilized people full of dark knowledge. This bestial imagery is frequent in screenplay depictions of African American characters prior to the 1980s. Ernest Tidyman's 1970 screenplay for *Shaft*, for example, uses the same type of bestial imagery to depict Shaft. Shaft is a man who "doesn't have a mother" (35), "a man in tune with his body" (2), a big eater who stuns Anderozzi by easily putting away "five dogs [hot dogs] and two root beer[s]" for lunch (34). His physicality is distinctly animalistic. Note how Anderozzi describes Shaft to the commissioner:

```
               ANDEROZZI (cont'd)
     But his value is that he doesn't stop to think a
     lot. He moves—and every ounce of that man is mus-
     cle and hate when he's up against it. (79)
```

Shaft is dominated by the bestial impulses of his own body, summoning the characterization of black slaves by white slavers. When Shaft strips off his clothes, he reverts to a physical nature that cannot be suppressed by the trappings of civilization.

```
     INT. McBURNEY YMCA—LOCKER ROOM—NIGHT

     WAIST-LEVEL SHOT of Shaft stripping, the three bullet
     scars in his lef side visible. He seems almost frantic
     to get out of his clothes.
                                        SLOW DISSOLVE TO:


     INT. McBURNEY YMCA—LOCKER ROOM—NIGHT

     INTO MONTAGE OF DOUBLE AND TRIPLE EXPOSURES of Shaft
     working out—running the track, hand over hand on an
     overhead ladder, dribbling a basketball across an empty
     court, driving his fists into a heavy bag—gasping for
     breath as he strains and sweats it out. (26)
```

Immediately following this montage of physical power, Shaft makes love to Ellie, his white "girlfriend." In the heat of passion, she screams out:

```
               ELLIE (fiercely)
          You're an animal! You're a god-damned
          animal. (27)
```

142

This presentation of Shaft as muscle and bestial impulses is hardly an improvement over centuries of degrading racial characterizations, which argue that the black form "approaches that of the beast" (Cuvier 105). As Donald Bogle points out in *Toms, Coons, Mulattoes, Mammies, and Bucks,* the racial stereotyping of black men is not limited to buffoons ("Coons"), such as Stepin Fetchit, and submissive servants ("Toms"). The "Buck" character is also prevalent and no less repressive than the others. A Buck is brutal and savage, with an overactive libido and an insatiable sex drive.

Shaft does not embody black culture; rather, he personifies the anxiety of dominant white culture and differs from what Bogle labels the "pure black bucks" in *The Birth of a Nation* only in the unmarginalized status of his role (13). Bogle describes Griffith's archetypal pure black bucks as "always big, baadddd [*sic*] niggers, oversexed and savage, violent and frenzied as they lust for white flesh" (13). He categorizes them with "black brutes," claiming that the "differences between the two are minimal" (13). He defines the black brute as "a barbaric black out to raise havoc . . . subhuman and feral . . . [and] full of black rage" (13). The same characteristics inform Tidyman's construction of John Shaft. The screenplay *Shaft* is the story of a story, a metanarrative that reaffirms seductive and dangerous misperceptions about the qualities of difference that mediate black/white discourse. Nevertheless, films such as *Shaft* showed African Americans as key players in the narrative and demonstrated to economically minded studio heads that movies about African Americans could be financially lucrative. Commercial potential may very well be critical to the nature of African American representation in screenplays, both as a cultural construct and a contributing factor to cultural construction.

A number of "race movies" were made between 1927 and 1948 with black casts. Many of these were white productions designed to cash in on urban, black audiences, primarily in the North. In those rare instances, during the early days of film, when a a black screenwriter wrote a screenplay, the African American protagonists often exhibited glimmers of nobility rare among characters written by white screenwriters. In Oscar Micheaux's *Lying Lips* (1939), the character of Benjamin Hadnot quits his job managing a club rather than contribute to the corruption of singer Elsie Bellwood.

GAROTTI

Now, this Elsie girl. She's very attractive. Some
of our customers want her to sit in on a little
party now and then. You understand. After the place
closes. Now, we like to oblige our customers. So we
think that you should—

HADNOT

Listen, Mr. Garotti. [. . .] It's up to her. But I
hire her to sing and dance here in the place, not
to go out on private parties. Now if you want to
try and persuade her to, that's your business. But
I won't.

GAROTTI

Oh, you won't, heh? Well what do you think we got
you hired for besides managing the place? We can do
the managing. We . . . (softer) You know the girls
better than we do. You talk the same language.
We've been after this girl to help us out a long
time. Now we say, you'll get her to or—

HADNOT

QUIT! That's okay by me.

FARINA

Now, now, Hadnot. You don't have to do that. Let's
talk it over. You see I try to get—

Hadnot and Garotti stand.

HADNOT

You've both made your positions very clear. And
there's no alternative but to do what you want me
to or resign. I'm resigning. You can get plenty of
men in my race to do what you want to do, so why
waste your time on me? As far as Miss Bellwood's
concerned, she's a lady. I've too much respect for
her and myself to try and persuade her to do what
you know and I know is wrong. As to you two, if you
had any respect for the unfortunate members of my
race, especially the girls that are forced to work
here, you wouldn't try to make them do ugly things.
But since you haven't, I don't like your attitude.
I'm quitting. Good day!
(n.p., transcribed from the film)

The human sensitivity Hadnot exhibits is undercut somewhat by Farina's and Garotti's ethnicity. In the 1930s, Italian Americans were the recipients of suspicion as a result of Mussolini's fascist ambitions and the "increased interference of Fascist officials in Italian-American communities after 1933" (Cannistraro 30). In 1939, when *Lying Lips* was made, an African American standing up to an Italian American would have been seen as less threatening than an African American standing up to an Anglo-American. Nevertheless, Hadnot is less of a caricature than black depictions scripted by white writers.

Actor Mantan Moreland, who found steady work in films from his 1933 appearance in *That's the Spirit* to his performance in *The Young Nurses* in 1973, the year he died, was frequently cast in white-scripted roles that Bogle describes as calling for "a round-faced, wide-eyed, cherubic coon" (72). Moreland appeared as the character of Birmingham Brown in eight Charlie Chan movies, always exhibiting the same characteristics: a fondness for drink, unreasonable fear and superstition, and a childlike naïveté. His character functioned solely as comedic relief, with bits that poked fun at qualities attributed to his ethnicity by white writers and audiences, such as the following exchange from *The Shanghai Cobra* (1948), written by George Callahan and George Wallace Sayre.

> CHAN
> You get illegal U-turn ticket?

> BIRMINGHAM
> Mr. Chan, I'll tell you just how . . .
> Tommy, you tell him.

> TOMMY
> I warned you, Birmingham. I said no U-turn
> here.

> BIRMINGHAM
> Yeah, that's what you said: "No, you turn
> here."

> TOMMY
> I said, "No U-turn here."

> BIRMINGHAM
> That's what I did. You said, "No, you turn
> here."

CHAPTER 5

```
                    TOMMY
Pop, I told him.  I said, "No U-turn here."

                  BIRMINGHAM
Yeah, that's what you said: "No, you turn
here." And I did.

                    TOMMY
See what I mean, Pop? I said, "No U-turn
here."

                  BIRMINGHAM
Mr. Chan, did you hear? He said, "No you—"

                    CHAN
              (INTERRUPTING)
Please, PLEASE! You turn so many U-turns you
have my head spinning like merry-go-round.
You remain here until I find doghouse big
enough to hold both of you. Please. Please.
```
(n.p., transcribed from the film)

The tendency may be to read individual scenes such as this one as merely reflective of the same type of humor we find in nonminority comedy routines—in an Abbott and Costello or Laurel and Hardy skit, for example—but the presentation of minorities by white writers during the first half-century of film tended to *only* present them as caricatures authorized by white hegemonic perceptions. Stepin Fetchit's characters, for example, were always dim-witted, superstitious, unreliable, lethargic servants prone to drink. Even in the hands of African American screenwriters, characters did not escape stereotyping. Elsie, in *Lying Lips*, is so moved by Hadnot's sacrifice on behalf of her honor that she offers the following soliloquy while taking a bath.

```
                    ELSIE
Well, Benny my man, I saw you give up your
job tonight to defend a girl's honor. A girl
almost a stranger to you. But she's a good
girl, Benny. And you stood up for her and
believed in her at the price of your job.
That's what I call a man. You're all right,
Mr. Hadnot. I'd like to see some other col-
ored man give up his job on account of any
```

146

girl. Why, he'd throw her at anybody that'd
show him fifty cents, I'm sorry to say. And
then take her back for himself. Pretty rot-
ten setup. But you're out of a job, Benny.
You've got to live and get along until you
find another one. Now you may have this job
that you mention, and you may have just said
it to console me, but I'll find out. I've
seen plenty of women taking care of men.
Worthless, trifling, good-for-nothin' men.
And I've hated 'em for it. Isn't it funny.
I want to take care of one now, too. You,
Benny. But you're such a good man, Benny.
But this is different. You've just got to be
all right. I've just got to do this. I want
to give you everything that I make and let
you give me what you want me to have. Will
you promise me you'll do this, dear? It'll
make me so happy.
(Micheaux n.p., transcribed from the film)

Despite the more human depiction of blacks, in general, in films by African American screenwriters during the first decades of film, black women characters were often subjected to the same stringent gender roles as white women characters. Early in her soliloquy, Elsie seems to be critiquing the inequity of gender stereotypes when she praises Had-not's noble act and condemns men who live off of women. Yet, by the end of her dialogue, Elsie has subsumed her economic value beneath Hadnot and articulated her willingness to assume a subservient role.

Integrated screenplays that deal with racial bigotry and the friction between white and black did not begin appearing until the end of the 1940s. By the 1950s, mainstream audiences were exposed to black MDs (e.g., Sidney Poitier in *No Way Out*, 1950) and black educators (e.g., Dorothy Dandridge as a teacher and Harry Belafonte as a school prin-ciple in *Bright Road*, 1953). In the 1960s, African American depictions and African American and integrated storylines produced a number of excellent screenplays: *A Raisin in the Sun* (1961), *Lilies of the Field* (1963, for which Sidney Poitier won a Best Actor Oscar), *Black Like Me* (1964), and *Guess Who's Coming to Dinner* (1967) among them.

"The study of race and ethnicity in film," Robyn Wiegman points out, "has taken shape according to the formation of race and ethnicity in US culture more widely, reflecting not a cross-ethnic political agenda geared to white supremacy's massive deployment, but the discrete histories and political projects of specific identity sites" (158). Wiegman's observation may reflect a shift in the function of African American characters in the American screenplay, away from a purely oppositional critique that pits white hegemony against black identity toward a more complex, less homogenous view of racial representation, a view that acknowledges that the misreading of the black form is part and parcel of the white mythology that underscores racism, while recognizing that white mythology, as Don Belton notes, was authored by whites and blacks (3), and that both whites and blacks, having constructed it, are seduced by its seeming veracity.

The American screenplay's representation of gender and race is part of the complex of American culture. Audiences cannot shield themselves from the political and social bias that shapes a screenplay's content any more than screenwriters can avoid the political and social influences of culture. Just as screenplays are inseparable components of the culture they comment upon, culture can no longer be apprehended without considering the pervasive presence of ideologies that have been prescribed by screenplays. If, as Jean-Louis Comolli and Jean Narboni assert, "every film is political" (45), and that "cinema is one of the languages through which the world communicates itself to itself" (46), then the same must be said of the American screenplay.

6

The Screenplay Adaptation

Huston, Hammett, and the Thing(s) from Another World

No other literary form relies as heavily on adaptation as the screenplay. Linda Seger calls "adaptation [. . .] the lifeblood of the film . . . business" (xi), accounting for most of the stories that eventually make it into production. Seger further notes in *The Art of Adaptation* that "85 percent of all Academy-Award winning Best Pictures are adaptations" (xi). The first Academy Award for writing, which went to *The Jazz Singer,* was for Alfred A. Cohn's adaptation of Samson Raphaelson's short story "The Day of Atonement."

Screenplay adaptations vary broadly, ranging from screenplays that closely echo their sources (e.g., John Huston's *The Maltese Falcon,* Larry McMurtry and Diana Ossana's *Brokeback Mountain*) and works that bear almost no resemblance to their sources (e.g., Woody Allen's *Everything You Always Wanted to Know about Sex but Were Afraid to Ask,* Charlie Kaufman's *Adaptation*), but even the most direct adaptations require artistic judgment. Robert McKee acknowledges that, because of "story complexity" (365–70), adaptation is almost never simple. Syd Field argues that "adapting a novel, book, play, or article into a screenplay is the same as writing an original screenplay" (*Screenplay* 204).

Screenwriter Charlie Kaufman's self-reflexive *Adaptation* playfully sheds light on the nature and potential artistic difficulties of screenplay adaptation. Consider the following passage:

```
Orlean looks at him. After a long silence, Laroche
muses:

                    LAROCHE (cont'd)
          You know why I love plants? Because
          they're so mutable. Adaptation is a
          profound process. It means you figure
          out how to thrive in the world.
          People can't sometimes.

                    ORLEAN
          Well, it's easier for plants; they
          have no memory. They just move on to
          what's next. For a person, it's al-
          most shameful to adapt. It's like
          running away.

89  INT. AGENT'S OFFICE-DAY  89

Kaufman sits with his agent Marty in a glass-walled
office.

                    KAUFMAN
          I don't know how to adapt this. I
          should've just stuck with my own
          stuff. I don't know why I thought I
          could— (48)
```

Here Laroche's comments on the "natural" process of biological adaptation are juxtaposed with the act of literary adaptation, implying that screenplay adaptation is an unnatural act. Frequent references to Darwin highlight distinctions between the lengthy process of natural evolution and the process of screenplay adaptation. Susan Orlean's *The Orchid Thief,* the book Kaufman—both writer and character—has been hired to adapt, does not evolve into a screenplay. It becomes a screenplay only when it is transformed into Kaufman's own creative work. Just as the ghost orchid inspires Orlean's book, Orlean's book ultimately inspires Kaufman's screenplay. The parallel illustrates the inherent relationship between a work and its adaptation. The second work, as Kaufman's screenplay cleverly shows, is not a natural evolution of the first. The second work is an autonomous literary creation limited only by the talent of the screenwriter. "Adapting someone else's work is certainly an opportunity to think differently" (Kaufman 10), the character of Valerie tells Kaufman in the screenplay.

Fig. 9. Charlie Kaufman (Nicolas Cage) struggles
with writer's block in *Adaptation* (2003).

All adaptations are not as intelligent and well educated as Kaufman's *Adaptation*. Some are weak and grossly inferior to the works on which they are based. But poor adaptations are not a valid justification for devaluing all adaptations, as Andrew Horton and Joan Magretta note in the introduction to their edited collection of essays on the art of adaptation in post–World War II European filmmaking: "Most adaptation studies have shown, rather disdainfully, how great books become inferior movies. In fact, Hollywood has been notoriously crass and shameless in its commercial exploitation of serious writers and their work. But if we want to learn about the rich possibilities of film *art*, very little will be gained by studying the worst that has been accomplished" (1). It could be argued that some screenplays, such as David Koepp's *Stir of Echoes,* based on Richard Matheson's novel, or Stanley Kubrick and Diane Johnson's *The Shining,* based on Stephen King's novel, surpass their source material in aesthetic merit.

Nearly every type of source material can and has been adapted into a screenplay. The most common source materials are the novel and the stage play. Novels, such as *The Maltese Falcon, Catch 22,* and Frank Norris's *McTeague* (which inspired Eric von Stroheim's *Greed*) and stage plays such as *Who's Afraid of Virginia Woolf? Chicago,* and *A Streetcar Named Desire,* have been fertile ground for the film industry since story

151

first became part of filmmaking. Equally significant as source material are novellas and short stories. John Milius and Frances Ford Coppola's screenplay for *Apocalypse Now* is an adaptation of Joseph Conrad's novella *Heart of Darkness* and Raynold Gideon and Bruce A. Evans's screenplay for *Stand by Me* is an adaptation of Stephen King's novella *The Body.* John Michael Hayes's screenplay for *Rear Window* (1954) is an adaptation of Cornell Woolrich's short story "It Had to Be Murder"; Dudley Nichols and Ben Hecht's screenplay for *Stagecoach* (1939) is an adaptation of Ernest Haycox's short story "Stage to Lordsburg"; and Ronald Shusett, Dan O'Bannon, and Gary Goldman's screenplay for *Total Recall* is based on Philip K. Dick's short story "We Can Remember It for You Wholesale." A full list of the number of novels, novellas, short stories, and stage plays that have been adapted into screenplays would easily fill its own book.

Nonfiction book-length works are also frequently adapted. Akiva Goldman's screenplay for *A Beautiful Mind,* which won the 2002 Best Picture Academy Award, is an adaptation of Sylvia Nasar's scholarly biography of Nobel Prize–winning mathematician John Nash. Woody Allen's screenplay for *Everything You Always Wanted to Know about Sex but Were Afraid to Ask* is an adaptation of David Reuben's popular nonfiction book by the same title. Martin Scorsese and Nicholas Pileggi's screenplay for *Goodfellas* is based on Pileggi's true-life account of the life of mobster Henry Hill.

Novels, novellas, nonfiction books, short stories, and stage plays are the most common sources, but there are quite a few other sources for adaptation that have received less attention. Some screenplays are adaptations of a person's life, rather than a single published biography, such as Stephen J. Rivele, Christopher Wilkinson, and Oliver Stone's screenplay for *Nixon.* Some are adaptations of television shows, such as Laurice Elehwany, Rick Copp, Bonnie Turner, and Terry Turner's screenplay *The Brady Bunch Movie* and Marianne Wibberley, Cormac Wibberley, Jay Scherick, and David Ronn's screenplay for *I Spy.* Some are adaptations of current events, such as Victor Colicchio, Michael Imperioli, and Spike Lee's *Summer of Sam* and Reggie Rock Bythewood's *Get on the Bus.* Comic books, such as Batman, Spiderman, and Superman have been adapted, as have video games, such as *Resident Evil, Mortal Kombat,* and *Final Fantasy.* Popular songs have also been adapted, such as Herman Raucher's *Ode to Billy Joe,* a screenplay adaptation of a

1967 song by Bobbie Gentry. Even poems have been adapted, as is the case with Richard Matheson's screenplay *The Raven,* which is an adaptation of Edgar Allan Poe's poem.

Close examination of the diverse and various screenplay adaptations that exist throws into question the term itself. To adapt is to make fit; that is, "the process of modifying a thing so as to suit new conditions" (OED). The term implies the work is a "reproduction of anything modified to suit new uses" (OED). The term "adaptation" is a bit of a misnomer. A film based on a screenplay is more consistently an adaptation than a screenplay based on or inspired by another work, although we encounter the same difficulties in claiming that a film is an adaptation of a screenplay as we run into when we attempt to justify a screenplay as an adaptation of another work. The etymology of the term "adaptation" does not well suit how it has been traditionally used. A screenplay adaptation is more accurately labeled as the Academy of Motion Pictures titles its corresponding Oscar category: "screenplay based on material previously produced or published." Nevertheless, the term "adaptation" has currency in film and screenplay literature and is too ingrained into the discourse of the screenplay to expect it to change in the foreseeable future, but the term should be used as one of convenience, not as an accurate term for the actual result of screenplay adaptation. The worst "adaptations" might fit the term, but the best certainly do not, and Horton and Magretta are right—"very little will be gained by studying the worst that has been accomplished" (1).

A screenplay adaptation should be critiqued on its own artistic merit. Source material is relevant, and can offer insight into the work under examination, but source material should not automatically receive preferred status. Kaufman's *Adaptation* is clear evidence of Field's claim that "an adaptation must be viewed as an original screenplay. It only *starts* from the novel, book, play, article, or song. That is the *source* material, the starting point. Nothing more" (*Screenplay* 205).

The primary complication in the examination of an adaptation involves the attribution of authorship. Screenplays that closely reproduce their source materials can complicate authorial attribution. However, this should not necessarily negate the literary contributions of the screenwriter. We might question, for example, how closely Mary Joseph Farnham, June Mathis, and Erich von Stroheim's screenplay for *Greed* parallels Frank Norris's *McTeague,* upon which it is based, especially when we consider von Stroheim's commitment to realism. How closely do von Stroheim and collaborators adhere to Norris's novel? Where do they stray? How do they redact the material? Examinations of this type can be illuminating, as is the case with John Huston's adaptation of Dashiell Hammett's *The Maltese Falcon,* for which Huston received an Academy Award nomination for best screenplay.

Huston's mixed and varied career as a screenwriter is not without its laurels. Hired to write for Universal in the early 1930s, Huston wrote scripts for films such as *Jezebel, The Killers, Moby Dick, The African Queen, Key Largo,* and *Wuthering Heights.* He received Oscar nominations for co-writing *Dr. Ehrlich's Magic Bullet* (1940) and *Sergeant York* (1941). However, his screenplay for *The Maltese Falcon* raises questions about how much of the brilliance of the screenplay we should attribute to him and how much rightfully belongs to Dashiell Hammett for his cinematically compatible novel.

Howard Hawks is reportedly the person who first gave Huston the idea of adapting Dashiell Hammett's novel for Huston's first stint as director. Hawks advised Huston to "go and make *The Maltese Falcon* exactly the way Hammett wrote it, use the dialogue, don't change a goddamn thing and you'll have a hell of a picture" (qtd. in Finler 109). Huston took Hawks's advice to heart, producing a screenplay that faithfully follows the course set by the novel. Huston makes few changes to the original story, and, although he does make several significant cuts, he adds no additional material, no new characters, and no original dialogue. Even Hammett's linear organization is reproduced almost exactly as it is laid out in the novel.

Huston's distinction as a director, I acknowledge without reservation, and his competence as a screenwriter is not in debate. My goal here is to look exclusively at Huston's adaptation of Hammett's novel, an important work that set the standard for film noir and the hardboiled detective film, launched Huston's career as a director, and helped to establish Humphrey Bogart as a major screen talent.

Novel form is substantially different from screenplay form, making the adaptation of a novel to the screen a tricky and often foreboding task. Regardless of how well executed a screenplay adaptation may be, it frequently pales in comparison to the novel, for the novel offers writers a much broader palette, allowing them to write about psychological states and to make extensive use of metaphor and figurative language. Both are difficult, if not impossible, in film. James Joyce or Thomas Pynchon can spend pages describing a character's single thought, but film, as a visual medium, cannot provide access into a character's mind except through action and dialogue; that is, except through implication. Even fantasy sequences and flashbacks are relayed through action and dialogue.

When Stanley Kubrick and Diane Johnson adapted Stephen King's *The Shining* for the screen, they had to come up with a way to visually present Jack Torrence's descent into madness. Unlike King, Kubrick and Johnson could not tell us that Torrence was going insane, could not narrate what was going on inside Torrence's head; they had to write visuals that show us Torrence's state of mind. One of the ways they managed this feat was to add a scene in which Wendy Torrence discovers that the manuscript her husband has been laboring over for months consists of hundreds of pages that repeat the same phrase, "All work and no play makes Jack a dull boy." This scene visually confirms what the audience has suspected, that Torrence has drifted into madness.

Because of the difficulties inherent in turning a novel into a screenplay, we would expect a screenplay based on a novel to display scars left by the screenwriter's scalpel as he reworks the body of the novel for a visual medium, and we would expect to find evidence of substantial revision. Perhaps the most interesting idiosyncrasy of Huston's *The Maltese Falcon* is there are virtually no signs that the screenplay is an adaptation. Scene by scene, line by line, the script is, as nearly as we could expect any script to be, a precise recounting of Hammett's novel. The tight narrative, the incisive visual pacing, the terse dialogue, and the skillful characterizations of the script can all be found in Hammett's novel. Huston's screenplay unquestionably benefits from the enormous labor Hammett put into crafting *The Maltese Falcon,* which William Marling notes is "the distillation of two years' worth of writing" and over a quarter of a million words (127).

With few exceptions, Huston duplicates Hammett's dialogue verbatim and co-opts much of his narrative. Note the following passage from Hammett's novel describing part of Sam Spade's first meeting with Joel Cairo:

CHAPTER 6

Cairo turned his hat over, dropping his glove into it, and placed it bottom-up on the corner of the desk nearest him. Diamonds twinkled on the second and fourth fingers of his left hand, a ruby that matched the one in his tie even to the surrounding diamonds on the third finger of his right hand. His hands were soft and well cared for. Though they were not large their flaccid bluntness made them seem clumsy. He rubbed his palms together and said over the whispering sound they made: "May a stranger offer condolences for your partner's unfortunate death?"

"Thanks."

"May I ask, Mr. Spade, if there was, as the newspapers inferred, a certain—ah—relationship between that unfortunate happening and the death a little later of the man Thursby?"

Spade nodded with eyebrows lifted to indicate attentiveness.

"The ornament is a statuette," Cairo went on, selecting and mouthing his words carefully, "the black figure of a bird."

Spade nodded again, with courteous interest.

"I am prepared to pay, on behalf of the figure's rightful owner, the sum of five thousand dollars for its recovery." Cairo raised one hand from the desk-corner and touched a spot in the air with a broad-nailed tip of an ugly forefinger. "I am prepared to promise that—what is the phrase?—no questions will be asked." He put his hand on the desk again bedside the other and smiled blandly over them at the private detective.

"Five thousand is a lot of money," Spade commented, looking thoughtfully at Cairo. "It—"

Fingers drummed lightly on the door.

When Spade had called, "Come in," the door opened far enough to admit Effie Perine's head and shoulders. She had put on a small dark felt hat and a dark coat with a grey fur collar.

"Is there anything else?" she asked.

"No. Good night. Lock the door when you go, will you?"

Spade turned in his chair to face Cairo again, saying: "It's an interesting figure."

The sound of the corridor-door's closing behind Effie Perine came to them.

Cairo smiled and took a short compact flat black pistol out of an

156

inner pocket. "You will please," he said, "clasp your hands together at the back of your neck." (43–44)

Now compare Hammett's prose to Huston's screenplay, and mark how closely Huston followed Hammett's text.

Cairo turns his hat over, drops his gloves into it and places it, bottom up, on the corner of the desk. Diamonds twinkle on the second and third fingers of his left hand. A ruby, surrounded by diamonds, like the one in his cravat, is on the third finger of his right hand. Cairo rubs his palms together, then, in a high-pitched thin voice:

                    CAIRO:
          May a stranger offer condolences for
          your partner's unfortunate death?

                    SPADE:
          Thanks.

                    CAIRO:
          May I ask, Mr. Spade, if there is, as
          the newspapers infer, a certain—ah—rela-
          tionship between that unfortunate hap-
          pening and the death a little later of
          the man Thursby?

Spade does not reply. When it is obvious to Cairo that Spade does not mean to answer, he rises and bows.

                    CAIRO:
               (punctiliously)
          I beg your pardon.

He sits down and puts his hands side-by-side flat on the corner of the desk.

                    CAIRO:
          More than idle curiosity prompted my
          question, Mr. Spade. I am trying to re-
          cover an—ornament that has been, shall
          we say, mislaid. I thought, and hoped,
          you could assist me.

Spade nods once, briefly.

CHAPTER 6

> CAIRO:
> The ornament is a statuette—the black
> figure of a bird.

Spade nods as before.

> CAIRO:
> I am prepared to pay on behalf of the
> figure's rightful owner, the sum of five
> thousand dollars for its recovery.

He raises one hand from the desk corner and touches a
spot in the air ever so lightly with his fore-finger.

> CAIRO:
> I am prepared to promise that—what
> is the phrase?—"No questions will be
> asked."
> > (he puts his hand back on the desk
> > beside the other and smiles blandly)

> SPADE:
> (Thoughtfully)
> Five thousand dollars is a lot of money.

OVER scene there is a light rapping on the door.

> SPADE:
> (calls)

Come in.

The door opens enough to admit Effie Perine's head and
shoulders. She is wearing a small dark felt hat and a
dark coat with a gray fur collar.

> EFFIE:
> Is there anything else?

> SPADE:
> No. Goodnight. Lock the door when you
> go, will you?

> EFFIE:

Goodnight.

She disappears behind the closing door. Spade turns in
his chair to face Cairo again.

The Screenplay Adaptation

```
                    SPADE:
      It's an interesting figure . . .

The SOUND of the corridor door closing comes OVER
scene. Smiling, Cairo takes a short, compact, flat
black pistol out of an inner pocket.

                    CAIRO:
      You will please clasp your hands to-
      gether at the back of your neck.
      (35-37)
```

Huston's script is so close to Hammett's text that one might suspect a scriptwriting software program automatically reformatted the prose. Furthermore, this particular excerpt is not unique. With very few exceptions, you can match any section of the novel to its sister section in Huston's screenplay and discover twins. These similarities, however, do not depreciate Huston's standing as a screenwriter. Instead, they indicate that he had the good sense not to fiddle with a work that was already masterfully written and skillfully organized into a chain of highly visual dramatic events.

Huston's wisdom in his writing of *The Maltese Falcon* script is that he took Hawks's advice and, for the most part, left Hammett's story alone.

Huston's screenplay consists of 125 scenes. Hammett's novel is made up of twenty chapters. The following breakdown outlines the relationship between Huston's scenes and Hammett's novel, indicating the chapters in which each scene can be found.

NOVEL	SCREENPLAY
Chapter	Scenes
One	1–3
Two	4–13
Three	14–16
Four	17–1/2 20
Five	1/2 20–23
Six	24–40
Seven	41–48
Eight	1/2 49

Nine	1/2 49 (50–51 omitted)
Ten	52–62
Eleven	63–67
Twelve	69–70, **74–75**
Thirteen	71
Fourteen	72–73, 76–77
Fifteen	**68**
Sixteen	78–96
Seventeen	97–1/2 114
Eighteen	1/2 114–1/2 115
Nineteen	1/2 115–121
Twenty	122–125

In this chart, "1/2" indicates that the scene crosses chapter breaks and boldface denotes scenes that fall out of sequence with the novel. Although several of Hammett's scenes are absent from Huston's script, every scene in Huston's screenplay can be found in the novel. None is original to Huston. Furthermore, of the scenes that are included, nearly all of them correspond to the same linear pattern as Hammett's novel; the material is ordered according to Hammett's original organizational structure. Only three scenes out of 125 fall out of sequence. Scene 68, which recounts Spade's meeting with Bryan, the district attorney, appears earlier in Huston's script than in Hammett's novel, and scenes 74–75, in which Effie informs Spade that Brigid never arrived at her house, are moved later.

Scene 68 serves two functions: it gives Spade's character another opportunity to demonstrate the umbrage he experiences whenever he is questioned by figures of authority, and it implies that perhaps Spade is really in danger of having a crime or two pinned on him. The first function is a repetition of what we have already learned from Spade's interaction with Polhaus and Dundy, although, presumably, the district attorney is more serious business than two police detectives. The second function intensifies Spade's predicament, adding strength to Spade's final argument with Brigid in which he finally coerces the truth from her about Archer's death:

```
He [Spade] turns, takes three swift steps toward Brigid
O'Shaughnessy. The girl, startled by the suddenness of
his approach, lets her breath out in a little gasp.
Spade, face to face with Brigid, looks at her hard of
jaw and eye.

                        SPADE:
        They'll [Gutman et al.] talk when
        they're nailed—about us. We're sitting
        on dynamite. We've only got minutes to
        get set for the police. Give me all of
        it fast. (Huston 137)
```

If we believe that Spade is in real danger from the authorities, that his luck may have run out, then we see that when Spade resists Brigid's temptations later in this scene, he is not only upholding his personal code of honor by fulfilling his obligation to "do something about" his partner's murder regardless of what he thought of the man, but he is also protecting his own skin (142). In moving scenes 74–75 later into the script, Huston sets up Brigid's desperate call to Spade's office. Thus, Brigid's disappearance and the seeming risk to her safety propel us into the third act and the screenplay's ultimate conclusion. It improves the pacing of the story.

In Hammett's novel, Brigid makes the call to Spade's office before Gutman's long exposition tracing the history of the Maltese Falcon. Therefore, shortly after Brigid, the love interest, falls into apparent danger, Spade, the hero, sits through Gutman's lengthy lecture on the falcon. The story loses momentum. Huston wisely places the scenes after all the key points of exposition have been relayed. Thus, the final act is a rush toward resolution, unhindered by the need to fill in missing narrative gaps.

Several key scenes from the novel are noticeably absent from the screenplay. We might question whether or not Huston willingly cut these scenes or whether he was responding to pressure from the Hays office (The Motion Pictures Production Code of 1930) to clean up the more salacious sections of Hammett's novel. The Maltese Falcon was produced during the age of the big Hollywood studios, before the Motion Picture Producers and Distributors of America (MPPDA) had become the Motion Picture Association of America (MPAA). At the

Fig. 10. Sam Spade (Humphrey Bogart) puts honor before love in John Huston's
faithful adaptation of Dashiell Hammett's *The Maltese Falcon* (1941).

time, all major studios let Production Code Administration (PCA) rulings alter content, and according to the Code, movies were to "avoid depicting any kind of sexual promiscuity (unwedded, extramarital, or 'unnatural')" (Mast 225). These are precisely the types of scenes that Huston cut.

The largest and perhaps most significant cut involves the relationship between Spade and Brigid. By the end of the film, we are to believe that Brigid and Spade may be in love. Yet, throughout the movie, they have little romantic contact. This is not the case with Hammett's novel. Spade and Brigid's relationship in the novel is substantially more intimate. For example, chapter nine, where Spade attempts to coax the real story of what is going on from Brigid, ends suggestively.

> Her eyelids drooped. "Oh, I'm so tired," she said tremulously, "so tired of it all, of myself, of lying and thinking up lies, and of not knowing what is a lie and what is the truth. I wish I—"

The Screenplay Adaptation

She put her hands up to Spade's cheeks, put her open mouth hard against his mouth, her body flat against his body.

Spade's arms went around her, holding her to him, muscles bulging his blue sleeves, a hand cradling her head, its fingers half lost among red hair, a hand moving groping fingers over her slim back. His eyes burned yellowly. (Hammett 89)

The corresponding section in Huston's script (scene 49), as written, is similar.

```
                         BRIGID:
                    (her eyelids droop)
          Oh—I'm so tired.
                    (then tremulously)
          So tired . . . of lying and thinking up
          lies and not knowing what is a lie and
          what is the truth. I wish I. . . .

     She puts her hands up to Spade's cheeks, her mouth
     hard against his mouth—her body flat against his body.
     Spade's arms go around her, holding her to him. Muscles
     [. . .]  (67)
```

The following page of the script marks the omission of the next two scenes, 50 and 51. Hammett's novel gives us an idea of what may have been in those scenes, enabling us to infer why they were omitted.

In the novel, chapter ten begins with the next day.

Beginning day had reduced night to a thin smokiness when Spade sat up. At his side Brigid O'Shaughnessy's soft breathing had the regularity of utter sleep. Spade was quiet leaving bed and bedroom and shutting the bedroom-door. He dressed in the bathroom. Then he examined the sleeping girl's clothes, took a flat brass key from the pocket of her coat, and went out. (Hammett 90)

The Production Code would never have allowed two unmarried people to share the same bed. It is reasonable to infer from the omission of scenes 50–51 and the fact that Huston wrote scene 49 as it appears in the book that he would have preferred to stay with Hammett's novel and include these scenes. Because Huston is so faithful to Hammett elsewhere, these changes stand out.

The argument that outside influences may have motivated Huston's major changes to Hammett's story is strengthened by the fact that scene 49 was not shot as scripted. Almost every scene in the screenplay is shot exactly as Huston scripted it except for scene 49. As it was shot, Brigid does not move to Spade; he bends toward her and then, just as he is *about* to kiss her, he glances through the window and notices Wilmer outside on the street. Here the scene ends. The morning-after sequence is completely excised.

Although cut from the script, the bedroom scene with Spade and Brigid is important to the story. It helps define their relationship and establishes a more intimate bond between them than the film manages to establish. Furthermore, this scene alludes back to an earlier scene in the novel when Brigid offers her body as a negotiating chip.

> "I've given you all the money I have." Tears glistened in her white-ringed eyes. Her voice was hoarse, vibrant. "I've thrown myself on your mercy, told you that without your help I'm utterly lost. What else is there?" She suddenly moved close to him on the settee and cried angrily: "Can I buy you with my body?"
>
> Their faces were a few inches apart. Spade took her face between his hands and he kissed her mouth roughly and contemptuously. Then he sat back and said: "I'll think it over." (Hammett 57)

A reader of the novel is left to wonder if, when Spade and Brigid do have sex, Spade has thought it over and decided to accept her offer. This increases the dramatic pressure of the all-important final conversation between Brigid and Spade. Our suspicion that Spade may have fallen prey to Brigid and might actually let her go is increased by these earlier sexual negotiations. Thus, Spade's determination to give her over to the police at the end of the novel represents a larger sacrifice and is therefore more intense in the screenplay than in the film.

Scene 49 (and 50–51 by implication) is not the only sexually charged scene to be trimmed. Note the following scene in which Gutman retrieves the envelope containing ten $1,000 bills.

```
Brigid's eyes question Spade. Spade nods. She puts her
hand inside her coat, takes out the envelope, gives it
to Spade. He tosses it into Gutman's lap.
```

                    SPADE:
Sit on it if you are afraid of losing
it.

                    GUTMAN:
                    (suavely)
You misunderstand me. It is not that at
all but business should be transacted in
a business-like manner.
                    (he opens the envelope,
                    takes out and counts the
                    bills, then chuckles)
For instance, there are only nine bills
here now.
                    (he spreads them on his
                    knee)
There were ten when I handed it to you,
as you very well know.
                    (his smile is broad,
                    jovial and triumphant)

                    SPADE:
                    (looks at Brigid)
Well?

She shakes her head. Her lips move slightly. Her face
is frightened. Spade holds out his hand to Gutman and
the money is put into it. Spade counts the money—nine
bills—and returns it to Gutman. Spade picks up the
three pistols from the table, rises.

                    SPADE:
                    (matter-of-factly)
I want to know about this.

Cairo looks at Spade with questioning eyes. The boy
beside him does not look up. He is leaning forward,
head between hands, elbow between knees, staring at the
floor.

                    SPADE:
                    (to Gutman)
You palmed it.

                    GUTMAN:
                    (chuckles)
I palmed it?

                                165

CHAPTER 6

```
                    SPADE:
Yes.
                (he jingles the pistols
                in his hand)
Do you want to say so or do you want to
stand for a frisk?


                    GUTMAN:
Stand for . . . ?


                    SPADE:
You're going to admit it or I'm going to
search you. There's no third way.


Gutman rocks back in his chair, laughs delightedly.


                    GUTMAN:
By Gad, sir, I believe you would. I re-
ally do. You are a character, sir—if you
don't mind my saying so.


                    SPADE:
You palmed it.


                    GUTMAN:
Yes, sir, that I did.
(Huston 127-28)
```

The scene, as it appears in the script, is relatively tame. In this confrontational scene between Spade and Gutman, Spade has little doubt that Gutman palmed the bill. His trust tips in favor of Brigid. However, in Hammett's novel, Spade distrusts both Gutman and Brigid equally and believes both of them capable of taking the $1,000. Thus, the section in the novel skillfully places Spade between the two other characters, forcing him to question where his loyalties lie. In the screenplay, his loyalties clearly lie with Brigid. In the novel, he is forced to take action to determine who is playing him. The action he takes in the novel is sexually suggestive, making it impossible for Huston to script the scene as Hammett wrote it without violating the Production Code. In the novel, Spade does not automatically believe Brigid, and insists on strip-searching her in the bathroom. Hammett describes the interaction between Brigid and Spade in the bathroom as follows.

In the bathroom Brigid O'Shaughnessy found words. She put her hands up flat on Spade's chest and her face up close to his and whispered: "I did not take that bill, Sam."

"I don't think you did," he said, "but I've got to know. Take your clothes off."

"You won't take my word for it?"

"No. Take your clothes off."

"I won't."

"All right. We'll go back to the other room and I'll have them taken off."

She stepped back with a hand to her mouth. Her eyes were round and horrified. "You would?" she asked through her fingers.

"I will," he said. "I've got to know what happened to that bill and I'm not going to be held up by anybody's maidenly modesty."

"Oh, it isn't that." She came close to him and put her hands on his chest again. "I'm not ashamed to be naked before you, but—can't you see?—not like this. Can't you see that if you make me you'll—you'll be killing something?"

He did not raise his voice. "I don't know anything about that. I've got to know what happened to that bill. Take them off." (195–96)

Only after Spade strip-searches Brigid does he go back into the room and accuse Gutman of palming the bill. Gutman confesses and the story continues. Although the scene provides us with insight into Spade's character, Huston had little choice but to cut it. What the strip search indicates is that even toward the end of the story, Spade still does not trust Brigid. This adds force to his later claim that if he were to let her go, he could never be sure his actions would not come back to haunt him; he could never be sure he had not provided Brigid with a powerful weapon she could use to manipulate him.

Also falling victim to the Production Code is the character of Joel Cairo. Hammett's novel unmistakably presents Cairo as a homosexual. Spade, when talking to Wilmer, even refers to Cairo as a "fairy" (94). Although the screenplay strongly implies that Cairo is homosexual—based on stereotypes of gay men as perfumed, meticulously groomed, prone to tears, and wimpy—most of Hammett's references and many of his allusions to Cairo's homosexuality are cut. Even the few that

167

made it into the script failed to make in onto the screen. Cairo's character in the film comes off more as a fop than a homosexual.

The most substantive changes in Cairo's actions occur toward the end of the screenplay when Gutman, Brigid, Wilmer, Spade, and Cairo are all together and Spade is suggesting they let Wilmer take the fall for the murders. Huston writes the scene as Hammett crafted it, with Cairo rushing first to Wilmer's defense and then remaining by his side to comfort him.

> Spade drive's his left fist against the boy's chin.
> The boy's head snaps back. When it comes forward Spade
> drives his right fist against the boy's chin. Cairo
> drops the boy's arm letting him collapse against Gut-
> man's round belly. Cairo springs at Spade, clawing at
> his face. Tears are in the Greek's eyes and his lips
> work angrily but no sound comes from between them.
>
>   SPADE:
>   (laughing)
>   Cairo, you're a pip!
>
> He cuffs the side of Cairo's face with an open hand,
> knocking him over against the table. Cairo regains his
> balance, springs again. Spade stops him with a long
> rigid arm, the palm flat against Cairo's face. Cairo,
> failing to reach Spade, flails his shorter arms at
> empty air.
>
>   SPADE:
>   (growls)
>   Stop it! I'll hurt you!
>
> Cairo backs away. [. . .] Gutman, who has put the boy
> in the rocking chair, stands looking down at him with
> troubled eyes. Cairo goes down on his knees beside the
> chair, begins to chafe the boy's limp hands. [. . .] He
> [Spade] lifts the boy without apparent effort, carries
> him to the sofa. Brigid O'Shaughnessy gets up quickly.
> Spade places the boy on the sofa. [. . .] Cairo comes
> over and sits down beside the boy's hand. [. . .]
> Cairo, sitting on the sofa, rubs the boy's temple and
> wrists, smooths his hair back from his forehead, peers
> anxiously at the white, still face.
> (123-24)

In the scene as it was shot, Spade slugs Wilmer once, then Cairo and

Spade carry Wilmer to the couch. Cairo stays away from Wilmer through the rest of the scene. All actions implying that Cairo has an "unnatural" sexual interest in Wilmer are completely whitewashed.

Another significant change from the novel is the elimination of Gutman's daughter, Rhea. Although Gutman's daughter is mentioned elsewhere, she only makes one appearance in Hammett's novel. When Brigid calls Spade's office pretending to be in peril, she tells Effie that she is at the Alexandria. Spade, after checking the falcon at the Pickwick Stage terminal, rushes to the hotel where he finds the seventeen-year-old daughter of Gutman apparently drugged.

Hammett describes Rhea as a "small fair-haired girl in a shimmering yellow dressing-gown, a small girl whose face was white and dim and who clung desperately to the inner doorknob with both hands" (161). In the novel Rhea directs Spade to 26 Ancho by claiming that that is where her father and his accomplices have taken Brigid. Rhea makes a graphic case for her sincerity when she shows Spade how she managed to stay awake until he arrived. Hammett writes:

> She twisted convulsively around in his arms and caught at one of his hands with both of hers. He pulled his hand away quickly and looked at it. Across its back was a thin red scratch an inch and a half or more in length.
>
> "What the hell?" he growled and examined her hands. Her left hand was empty. In her right hand, when he forced it open, lay a three inch jade-headed steel bouquet-pin. "What the hell?" he growled again and held the pin up in front of her eyes.
>
> When she saw the pin she whimpered and opened her dressing gown. She pushed aside the cream-colored pajama-coat under it and showed him her body below her left breast—white flesh criss-crossed with thin red lines, dotted with tiny red dots, where the pin had scratched and punctured it. (163)

The self-mutilation of a young, seemingly innocent, fair-haired girl would not have made it past the PCA, nor would it likely have been well received by audiences in 1941. Huston understandably cut the scene and cut the character. Nevertheless, Rhea serves a significant function in the novel. Her self-mutilation forces us to redefine Casper Gutman's character. Without Rhea, Gutman comes off as an otherwise congenial man who happens to be obsessed with the Maltese Falcon. However, Rhea adds a dark new dimension to Gutman. Rhea is seventeen years old, exactly the length of time that Gutman has been chasing the falcon. This raises questions about how attentive of a father Gutman could have been, chasing the black bird the entire time his daughter was growing up. Gutman's attitude regarding Rhea's mutilation cements our suspicions.

Shortly after Spade and Brigid enter Spade's apartment and find Gutman, Cairo, and Wilmer waiting, Spade says to Gutman, "That daughter of yours has a nice belly, . . . too nice to be scratched up with pins," to which Gutman smiles, a smile Hammett describes as "affable if a bit oily." Then Gutman says, "Yes, sir, that was a shame, but you must admit that it served its purpose" (173).

Gutman's comments are shocking. They expose the evil that lurks at the heart of his character. Gutman is the kind of man who would let his own daughter be mutilated in order to get his hands on a valuable statue. He is a man selfishly driven by his fetish attachment to a lifeless artifact to the abandonment of his paternal instinct and, by extension, his humanity.

When Gutman agrees to let Wilmer, whom he claims to care for as if he were his own son, take the fall for the murders, we understand why. Gutman, who has no remorse for his own daughter, would not be expected to show concern for a young man with whom he shares no bloodline. The explanation Gutman offers Wilmer also applies to Gutman's daughter. In the screenplay, Huston scripts Gutman's explanation just as Hammett wrote it:

> GUTMAN:
> Well, Wilmer, I am sorry indeed to
> lose you and I want you to know that I
> couldn't be any fonder of you if you were
> my own son. But, well, by Gad, if you
> lose a son, it's possible to get another
> and there's only one Maltese Falcon!
> (126)

Without the Rhea character, Gutman's claim that he cares about Wilmer as if he were his own son loses certainty. He could be lying to Wilmer. However, once we have learned that he let his own daughter be mutilated because of his avaricious desire for the falcon, we have no trouble believing that Gutman's claims to Wilmer are sincere (albeit ironic).

Dashiell Hammett's novel is a scriptwriter's dream. Like other hard-boiled writers such as James M. Cain and Raymond Chandler, Hammett keeps each moment in the novel charged with expectation and cloaked in mystery. Like other "plain-writing" writers of the modern era who worked to capture an objective view of the world, writers such as Ernest Hemingway and F. Scott Fitzgerald, Hammett maintains narrative distance throughout the novel, enabling him to present events and characters in a visual, cinematic style that translates easily into screenplay format. Adapting a novel such as *The Maltese Falcon* into a screenplay is primarily a matter of remaining loyal to the novel's text. Howard Hawks was wise to recommend Hammett's novel to Huston, and Huston was wise to follow Hawks's advice. The result of Huston's effort is a film that, like the elusive black bird, is of incalculable value; however, when we scratch beneath the surface of this Maltese Falcon, unlike Gutman, we find pure gold.

Scripting *The Thing*

In situations where we have more than one adaptation of a work, as is the case with John W. Campbell's short story, "Who Goes There?" examinations of both adaptations can be fruitful. It might be tempting to approach Bill Lancaster's screenplay for John Carpenter's *The Thing* (1982) as an adaptation of Charles Lederer's screenplay for Howard Hawks's *The Thing from Another World* (1951), and we do find some overlap of the first work in the second work, but Lancaster's and Lederer's screenplays are more accurately freestanding adaptations of John W. Campbell's short story (*Astounding Science Fiction*, 1938), on which both screenplays are based.

Neither screenplay has received much attention, but the two films are often set in opposition: Hawks's[1] version is praised and Carpenter's

---

1. Directorial credits for *The Thing from Another World* are shared with Christian Nyby. Precisely how much Nyby contributed to the final version of the film and how much credit belongs to Hawks is a subject of much debate. Michael Goodwin states, "Although Christian Nyby is officially credited as director, there can be little question in anyone's mind but that 'producer' Howard Hawks is primarily responsible" (n.p.).

version is reviled.[2] Many reviewers claim that Carpenter's film is a "failure" (Jenkins 158) and "a bore" (Keneas 4). Even more disconcerting
are reviews that assert that "Carpenter blows it" (Ansen 73). Contrast-
ing these scathing critiques of Carpenter's *Thing* is a blizzard of effusive
praise for Hawks's earlier version. Few reviewers have anything dis-
paraging to say about Hawks, and even fewer have anything laudatory
to say about Carpenter (Archer Winsten of the *New York Post* is one
notable exception [42]), and neither position is well argued.[3]

Objections to *The Thing* fall loosely into three categories. The first,
and the most untenable of the three, is criticism of what Linda Gross
at the *Los Angeles Times* refers to as the "visceral and vicious special
makeup effects" (15). Apparently, Rob Bottin's graphic effects disturb
many critics. They claim, as Carrie Rickey does, that the film is "pro-
grammed to gross out its audience with its technical savvy, but forgets
to develop a story" (50). There are two problems with this argument.
Firstly, condemning a sci-fi/horror film for its graphic effects is a bit like
condemning a pizza for its cheese. Graphic special effects have been
the lifeblood of sci-fi/horror films for over twenty-five years, ever since
The Exorcist (1973) redefined gore for mainstream audiences.[4] The only
valid criterion for judging the visceral qualities of a film is to question
their relationship to the narrative. If graphic effects are integral to the
subject matter, if they help advance the story, then they are warranted.
Someone's susceptibility to them is a matter of personal preference,
not an authoritative basis for an objective appraisal of the overall quality of a film.

----

2. I frequently refer to Carpenter and Hawks when discussing criticisms of the film
because the critics are positing these two as the authors of the films. Some of the criticism, however, applies equally to Lederer's and Lancaster's screenplays. Steve Jenkins's
criticism of the presentation of scientists, for example, is more relevant to a discussion
of the screenplay than the film, yet he refers to Carpenter and not Lancaster in his
critique.

3. Anne Billson argues that "the poor reception of *The Thing* can in part be chalked
up to the critical generation gap, which was even more pronounced back in 1982 than
it is now" (9).

4. George Romero's *Night of the Living Dead* technically redefined gore five years
earlier, but *The Exorcist* enjoyed a much broader release and reached a wider audience
in 1973 than *Night of the Living Dead* managed to reach in 1968. *Night of the Living Dead*
redefined gore for the horror film and its fans, but *The Exorcist,* I contend, redefined
gore for the general film-going public.

The Screenplay Adaptation

Second, Bill Lancaster's script does deliver a story. True, it is not a boilerplate sci-fi story about some young buck hot-rodding across the universe with a phallic light saber, and it does not duplicate the hero-antics audiences have come to expect from films, but these, I would argue, are strengths, not weaknesses. They speak to the film's originality, and they help to protect the genre from vapid replication.

The Thing recounts a man's struggle to maintain his individualism in the presence of malicious and chaotic forces. Not unlike Terry Gilliam, Charles McKeown, and Tom Stoppard's *Brazil*, or W. D. Richter's *Invasion of the Body Snatchers*, at the center of *The Thing* are questions as old as the Athenian scholars: *Who am I?* And *What makes me* me? It is a story rooted in existentialism, which may explain why some people feel it doesn't have a story. Lederer's version of *The Thing*, like most contemporary American screenplays, foregrounds Platonic ideals: familiar notions of community, teamwork, and patriotism. All ideas that existentialism denounces, as Nietzsche notes: *"Basic error:* to place the goal in the herd and not in single individuals! The herd is a means, no more! But now one is attempting to understand the herd as an individual and to ascribe to it a higher rank than to the individual—profound misunderstanding!" (*Will* 403). For Nietzsche, the individual is the source of everything new, the wellspring of creativity, and the individual "derives the values of his acts from himself" not from communal initiatives or social outcomes (*Will* 403). Captain Henry in Lederer's *Thing* is an American soldier whose loyalty to his country, his military, his gender, and his species, come before his loyalty to self, and Lederer sentimentalizes Henry's self-sacrificial attachment to the herd. MacReady in Lancaster's *Thing* is an existential hero, whose loyalty to self supersedes all other concerns. Thus, the two films are ideologically opposed. Lederer values community, while Lancaster venerates the individual. Lederer pits the human race against an alien race in a battle for species superiority, while Lancaster pits MacReady against the Thing in a clash of individual wills.

Nietzsche argues that "every living thing reaches out as far from itself with its force as it can, and overwhelms what is weaker: thus it takes pleasure in itself" (*Will* 403–4). This impulse is central to what he considers the primary driving force in a person—the will to power. The Thing in Lancaster's script personifies this will to power. Its sole objective is the assumption of weaker life forms. It has no goal other than

173

the expansion of self. Its drive to reach out and overwhelm all other life forms is unadulterated, and it functions in the script as a foil against which we measure the force of MacReady's will.

MacReady qualifies as a heroic character, because, through the strength of his will, he manages to maintain his individuality. He resists appropriation into the communality of the Thing.

Nietzsche says of the self: "Active, successful natures act, not according to the dictum 'know thyself,' but as if there hovered before them the commandment: *will* a self and thou shalt *become* a self" ("Assorted" 366). This is precisely what MacReady does. The strength of his individualism is the manifestation of the strength of his will. He asserts his individuality without hesitation. For example, during the blood test he has no doubt that the test will come out in his favor.

```
He cuts himself with the scalpel and begins collecting
his own blood.

                    MAC READY
                   (continuing)
        Now I'll show you what I already know.

He heats the wire and puts it to his plate. The same
harmless hissing. All eyes continue to watch as he
tries again. The same result. (Lancaster, The Thing 102)
```

MacReady's certainty in his self is his most heroic characteristic. When the other characters are tested, they all betray a lack of confidence in who they are.

```
MAC READY

perspiring profusely, his hand trembling slightly, pre-
pares to continue the test. He heats the wire.

The men are pouring sweat, white-knuckled.

One of the smaller torches is pointed at Nauls. He
closes his eyes. MacReady places the heated wire into
his plate. Hiss. MacReady exhales. Nauls opens his
eyes.

MAC READY

unties Nauls with one hand, while the torch stays glued
to the others.
```

```
MAC READY
heats the wire once again. Both he and Nauls have
torches aimed at Sanchez. Sanchez is near tears.

The wire is dipped into the plate . . . Hisssss.

Sanchez breaks down and sobs.

CHILDS


sits stoicly [sic], while he watches the preparations
for his turn.
                        CHILDS
            Let's do it, Bwana.

Nauls and Sanchez take aim five yards away. Fierce, de-
termined. The wire comes off the flame into the plate
. . . the harmless hissing.
The muscles in Childs's face melt into a sigh.


                     ̄ CHILDS
                      (continuing)
            Muthafu.  . . . (104)
```

Nauls, Sanchez (Windows in the film), and Childs are all uncertain about their own essential selves. Nauls closes his eyes, unable to face the possible truth. Sanchez sobs with relief when he discovers he has not been taken over. Even Childs, for all his macho bravado, is relieved when the test shows him to be human. These three men need the test to reassure them that they are still themselves. Their need for external validation distinguishes them from MacReady. Only MacReady faces the test without flinching. Only he is certain of the fidelity of his self. The test he performs on himself is not for him, it is for the others. He is already sure of who he is, and the strength of his conviction frames the story and propels the action. Any claim that *The Thing* lacks a story overlooks this point.

The second type of objections to Carpenter's *Thing* involves attacks against Carpenter and gratuitous comparisons of the film to Hawks's version. John Preston goes so far as to claim that Carpenter is "patently no Hawks" (24). Strangely, when critics criticize Carpenter, the very elements they argue are weak in Carpenter's film are all doubly present in Hawks's version. For example, when Linda Gross complains about a "notable . . . lack of female characters" (15), she forgets that the only female in Hawks's *Thing* is Nikki, whose primary function is as a foil to accent Henry's virility. In Charles Lederer's script, when Nikki tries to keep Henry from Carrington's notes, Henry "puts an end to it by sending a short right into her stomach." Even more horrifying, Nikki does not resent the physical assault. She says to Henry, "I'm glad you—did what you did. I'm very glad" (104). Lederer's script not only presents women as objects of desire for men, it subjugates them to male dominance, and presents them as physical targets for male aggression.

On another front, Steve Jenkins takes offense at Carpenter's treatment of scientists. He compares Carpenter's scientist, Blair, to Hawks's Carrington (cf. footnote 2 above). Jenkins cites Robin Wood's claim that "Professor Carrington is . . . never made absurd; [that] he is . . . consistently presented as intelligent, dedicated and courageous," and he blindly accepts Wood's argument that Carrington's portrayal allows us to "sense Hawks' respect for professionalism in whatever cause" (158). Jenkins's objective is to, by comparison, criticize the portrayal of Blair, and by extension, Carpenter; however, he overlooks the fact that Carrington's character is a stereotype, a sci-fi cliché—the scientist so blinded by his own lust for knowledge that he foolishly jeopardizes lives. The film sets Carrington up as an object of ridicule. It does not praise his actions; it condemns them. Carrington's assessment of the Thing is presented as naïve and dangerous. This is most apparent near the end of the film when Carrington tries to communicate with the Thing and it strikes him dead. This scene demonstrates the fallibility of Carrington's methodology and the foolishness of his scientific rationale. Lederer's screenplay doesn't present scientists as pantheons of professionalism. It presents them as children, "six-year-old Einsteins" (61), mucking around in matters better left to men. Notice how the soldiers' dialogue derides the scientists.

```
                    EDDIE
        I'm just wondering if the professors will
        try to rush us, Pat.

                    HENRY
                  (grimly)
        Might relieve the monotony if they did.

                    EDDIE
        I'd hate to have to shoot down seventeen of
```

```
                 the world's greatest geniuses. You know
                 somethin?

                         HENRY
                 What?

                         EDDIE
                 They're kids, all of them. Nine year olds
                 drooling over a new fire engine. Scientists!
                 Did you ever notice those two double domes
                 who started crying—when we left the table?
                 (47)
```

Nowhere in the script is this position subverted. From fade-in to fade-out, the message is that scientists are boys and soldiers are men. The film does not glorify scientific professionalism; it glorifies brutish, militaristic masculinity.

The third type of objections to *The Thing* addresses the film's dark quality, and is, ironically, the most enlightening. Not for what it illuminates in Lancaster's screenplay, but for what it shows us about audience expectation. *The Thing* disheartens a number of reviewers, because it "traffics in paranoia" (Gross 15) and "misses many positive qualities of the 1951 version" (Sterritt 18). Gross sums these objections well when she says, "Instead of providing us with love, wonder, and delight, 'The Thing' is bereft, despairing and nihilistic" (15). Apparently for Gross, and critics who share her views, screenplays are obliged to uplift and instill optimism in audiences. The problem with this notion should be obvious. If the function of quality storytelling is to provide us with "love, wonder, and delight," what do we do with Kafka's *Metamorphosis*? Nabokov's *Lolita*? Fitzgerald's *Gatsby*? Steinbeck's *Of Mice and Men*? For that matter, what do we do with screenplays such as Gérard Brach, Roman Polanski, and David Stone's *Repulsion* and Robert Towne's *Chinatown*? Pupi Avati, Roland Barthes, Maurice Blanchot, and Sergio Citti's *Salò*? Herman J. Mankiewicz and Orson Welles's *Citizen Kane*?

Mainstream American audiences, in general, want their expectations fulfilled, and Hollywood goes to great lengths to make movies that fulfill those expectations, because it wants to attract those audiences. The problem with this paradigm is that those movies then go on to shape audience expectation. It's a cycle. If we judge the quality of films based on their adherence to formulaic optimism, we end up stifling narrative innovation. This is one of the points Michael Tolkin makes in *The Player*: that cliché is the backbone of the Hollywood blockbuster, and that cliché is not conducive to creativity.

Large studios frequently eschew the poignantly tragic conclusion of films such as *El Mariachi*. When they financially back films like *Desperado* (*El Mariachi's* big budget sequel), they pressure screenwriters for the happy endings to which Western audiences have been conditioned. The result in the case of *Desperado* is a film lacking in the mythic qualities of its predecessor. Hampton Fancher and David Webb Peoples's *Blade Runner* faced a similar fate. The initial release in 1982 contained a voice-over written by Roland Kibbee. The voice-over was added because the studio felt audiences were too limited to follow the story without it. The studio also added a happy ending wherein Deckard and Rachael literally ride off together toward a blue horizon. When Ridley Scott released his director's cut ten years later, he pulled out the voice-over and cut the cheery ending, allowing us to finally glimpse his original vision, one that is much darker and more powerful than the altered first release allowed us to see.[5]

Some critics pan Carpenter's version of *The Thing* because Lancaster's script is not a rehash of stale ideological predispositions. It does not reaffirm sacred notions of human superiority or valorize communal values, and MacReady does not rise up in defense of all that is holy about traditional Western thought. The screenplay is dark. It is tragic. And it raises uncomfortable philosophical questions about the nature of human existence.

Critics vehemently dislike Carpenter's film because it lacks Spielbergesque sentimentality (as David Sterritt notes, it is "a far cry from *E.T.*" [18]), and it is a tragic appraisal of the human condition. As Ian Conrich puts it, "the monstrous force and the apocalyptic all-consuming threat posed by Carpenter's indiscernible Thing, could not compete

---

5. Scott intentionally shot *Blade Runner* so that the only moment of brightness in the entire film would be when Roy Batty (Rutger Hauer) releases the dove on top of the roof at the moment of his death. This plan was completely destroyed by the addition of a bright, sunny conclusion. A good example of why Harlan Ellison calls the TV/Film arena "an art-form by committee, a cobbled-up Frankenstein's Monster of arbitrary rules, imbecile decisions, cowardly rationalizations, and tasteless pandering to the lowest possible common denominators of public mass taste" (23).

with a mass market that had been seduced by the appealing wide-eyed features of a compassionate alien drawn to friendship with a young boy" (97).

The major change Lancaster made to Campbell's novella is the failure of the Antarctica team to defeat the Thing. In Campbell's story, the research team locates the fourteen duplicates via a blood test and disposes of them. As Norris explains, they win "by the grace of God, who evidently does hear very well, even down here, and the margin of half an hour, we keep our world, and the planets of the system, too" (Lancaster 353). There is no such divine providence in Lancaster's script. No reestablishment of order. No clear victory for the hero. It is not even certain that the world has been protected from the Thing or that the efforts of the team in Lancaster's screenplay have done anything more than delay the creature's assimilation of the human race. At the end, two members of the team are left alive: MacReady and Childs. But we do not know if Childs has been taken over. Thus we, like MacReady, cannot get closure.

The final dialogue between MacReady and Childs is marvelously open-ended.

CHILDS
Are you the only one who made it?

MAC READY
I'm not the only one.

CHILDS
Did you kill it?

MAC READY
Where were you, Childs?

CHILDS
I thought I saw Blair. I went out after him. Got lost in the storm. (beat) Fire's got the temperature up all over the camp. Won't last long, though.

MAC READY
Neither will we.

CHILDS
How will we make it?

179

CHAPTER 6

```
                        MAC READY
        Maybe we shouldn't.

                         CHILDS
        If you're worried about me—

                        MAC READY
        If we've got any surprises for each other, I
        don't think we're in much shape to do any-
        thing about it.

                         CHILDS
        Well, what'll we do?

                        MAC READY
        Why don't we just . . . wait here for a
        little while. See what happens.
```
(Lancaster, transcribed from the film)

After all the destruction and death, we are still left wondering if anything was accomplished. MacReady is still uncertain about whom,
other than himself, he can trust, and the outlook for humanity is still
bleak. Thus Lancaster's script narrates a descent into chaos from which
there is no return.

Early in the script, MacReady records a message in his quarters,
foreshadowing the end of the screenplay. In the message, he notes the
loss of trust among his companions.

```
                        MAC READY
        I'm gonna hide this tape when I'm finished.
        If none of us make it, at least they'll be
        some kind of record. The storm's been hit-
        ting us hard now for 48 hours. We still have
        nothing to go on. One other thing, I think
        it rips through your clothes when it takes
        you over. Windows found some shredded long
        johns, but the name was missing. They could
        be anybody's. Nobody . . . nobody trusts
        anybody now. We're all very tired. Nothing
        else I can do. Just wait. R. J. MacReady,
        helicopter pilot, US outpost number 31.
```
(Lancaster, transcribed from the film)

Lancaster's screenplay questions the prudence of trust, and character-

The Screenplay Adaptation

izes an age in which suspicion is rampant and trust is rare, as MacReady
explains to Blair.

```
    Blair's droopy-eyed, heavily drugged features loom up
    at MacReady through the window.

                        MAC READY
              How you doin', old boy?

                         BLAIR
                        (softly)
              I don't know who to trust.

                        MAC READY
                       (humoring)
              Know what you mean, Blair. Trust is a tough
              thing to come by these days.
    (53-54)
```

The implication is that trust is illusory. The scene echoes the existen-
tialist principle that you can never actually know what goes on inside
someone else's psyche; therefore, to trust someone else is to delude
yourself. Furthermore, because the will to power is the primary force
in everyone, everyone possesses a drive to overwhelm everyone else.
Thus, everyone is potentially a threat. This is the paranoid existential
atmosphere that Lancaster creates in his screenplay, and Carpenter
skillfully renders to film.

In Lederer's script for Hawks, trust is assumed, and the characters
work communally against the Thing. Each man is merely part of the
collective. In Lancaster's script the possibility of successful communal
effort is thwarted. The individual characters fail to establish effective
bonds with one another, as indicated by Palmer's refusal to form a
search party with Sanchez.

```
    He [MacReady] tosses torches to Sanchez and Palmer.

                        MAC READY
                      (continuing)
              Sanchez, you and Palmer search the inside.
              . . .

                         PALMER
              I ain't going with Sanchez.
```

181

Sanchez snaps his head toward Palmer. Palmer looks at
the others.

                        PALMER
                     (continuing)
        I ain't going with him. I'll go with Childs.
        . . .

                        SANCHEZ
        Well, screw you, man!

                        PALMER
        I ain't going with you!

                        CHILDS
        Well, who says I want you going with me?!

                        MAC READY
        Cut the bullshit . . . Okay, Sanchez, you
        come with us. Norris . . . you stay here.
        . . . (Lancaster 82)

You cannot work as a team if you cannot trust the men next to you, and
if you can never truly know them, you can never trust them.

Unlike Henry's status as a hero, MacReady's heroic stature is not
contingent on him winning the battle with the Thing, but on his refusal
to abnegate his self regardless of how inevitable failure may be. Lancaster sets this up in the scene that introduces MacReady's character.

INT. MAC READY'S SHACK—CLOSE ON ICE CUBES

being dumped into a glass, followed by the pouring of
whiskey. An electronic Voice is heard.

                        VOICE
        Bishop to knight four.

MacReady takes a sip of his drink; makes his way over
to his electronic chess game. A large Mexican sombrero
hangs on his back. He is tall; about thirty-five. His
shack is sparse but unkempt. A few centerfolds on the
wall are interspersed by an occasional poster of some
Mediterranean or South American paradise.

The chess game is of larger than normal size. The
pieces move automatically with the press of a button.

182

He sits down and chuckles over his opponent's bad move.

                    MAC READY
          Poor little son of a bitch. You're starting
          to lose it, aren't you?

He confidently taps out his move. His companion's response is immediate.

                    VOICE
          Pawn takes queen at knight four.

MacReady's grin slowly fades as he examines the board.
There is a pounding at his door. MacReady broods for a
bit, heedless of his visitor and makes his next move.

                    VOICE
                  (continuing)
          Rook to knight six. Check.

More impatient pounding. MacReady glares at his opponent for a beat. He bends forward, opens up a flap
containing the chess game's circuitry and pours in his
drink. There ensues a snapping, popping sound as smoke
and sparks rise from the machine; followed by a flush
of chess gibberish.

MacReady gets up from his seat, mumbling on his way to
the door.

                    MAC READY
          . . . Cheating bastard. . . .
          (9-10)

MacReady may lose the game, but he would rather destroy the machine than concede that victory. This is the unfailing strength of will
that shapes his character. The scene with the chess game foreshadows
the climax of the film. It helps us to understand that MacReady does
not destroy the entire camp in a last ditch effort to save humanity. He
does it because death is preferable to concession. What the Thing
threatens to take from him is the one thing that holds value: his self-
determination. MacReady would rather die than lose that. What is left
of the camp is a ruin that resembles the charred insides of MacReady's
chess machine.

Fig. 11. R. J. MacReady (Kurt Russell) embodies the existential hero
in Bill Lancaster's screenplay for John Carpenter's *The Thing* (1982).

```
INT. CAMP

A ruin. One half of it burnt almost to the ground. Mac-
Ready wears a thick blanket which covers him like a
shroud, from his shoulders to the floor.

He walks bent over and in much pain, trying to blunt
patches of fire with an extinguisher. It is futile. He
gives up. (118-19)
```

When faced with a battle he cannot win, he has only two possible options—total destruction or surrender—and MacReady will not surrender his individuality. It is the only thing on which he can rely.

MacReady has no lofty notions about saving the world. He is involved in a struggle for his own survival. Significantly, he is characterized as the most levelheaded member of the expedition. Blair, in contrast, is obsessed with saving the world. He sees himself as the savior of mankind, and he is driven insane by his loyalty to the herd. Lancaster's script is consistently clear on this point: You are the only one you can trust. No one else.

Campbell's novella takes lack of trust to terrifying dimensions. Like the twelve characters in Lancaster's screenplay, the thirty-seven men in Campbell's story are infiltrated by a Thing that appropriates their physical and mental identities. The Antarctic team has difficulty locating the Thing, because it could be in any one or more of them,

The Screenplay Adaptation

could, in fact, *be* any one of them. The result is the same pervasive lack of trust we find in Lancaster's script. Campbell writes, "The group tensed abruptly. An air of crushing menace entered into every man's body, sharply they looked at each other. More keenly that ever before— *is that man next to me an inhuman monster?*" (343). But Campbell points out that the threat is even closer than the man next to you. The threat in his novella and Lancaster's screenplay is invasive. In both, victims are not merely transformed into vampires or zombies; they are taken over *completely.* They are *wholly* appropriated. This forces the characters to confront serious ontological questions. Kinner, the company's cook, articulates the problem when he asks MacReady the following question: "Kinner shuddered violently. 'Hey. Hey, Mac. Mac, would I know if I was a monster? Would I know if the monster had already got me? Oh Lord, I may be a monster already'" (Campbell 331). Kinner's question helps us understand how MacReady in Lancaster's script differs from the other men. If the Thing assimilates all characteristics of a person, including his consciousness, then a person cannot subjectively know he has not already been taken over. If the Thing takes him over completely—adopts his physical appearance, his mannerisms, and his thoughts—what criteria can he use to determine if he has already been assimilated? This conundrum is laid out most fully in Campbell's story. When the Thing takes over someone in the novella, it thinks and makes decisions as that person would. It manages to fool so thoroughly because there is no observable behavioral difference. This same characteristic of the Thing is implied in Lancaster's screenplay in the scene where Garry offers his command to Norris.

> GARRY
> I don't know about Copper, but I give you my word, I did not go near that blood. I guess you'll all feel a little easier if somebody else was in charge. Norris, I can't see anybody objecting to you.
>
> NORRIS
> I'm sorry fellas, but I'm not up to it.
> (Lancaster, transcribed from the film)

We learn later that Norris had already been taken over. Nevertheless, he refuses command, even though he could accomplish the Thing's objectives more efficaciously if he were in charge. This is because, when it took him over, the Thing assumed all of Norris's emotional reservations. It makes decisions that Norris would have made, leaving us to wonder how the Thing differs from Norris. What essential characteristic of Norris has been lost? In *Invasion of the Body Snatchers* (1956) that essential human characteristic is the ability to experience emotion, but Lancaster's script is subtler than that. Lancaster avoids an obvious explanation, leaving open the possibility that there is nothing unique to distinguish us from an exact copy. Nothing except the force of our individual will. Thus, not only is the primary threat in the screenplay internal, but the characters only defense against it is also internal.

Stephen King claims that there are only two types of monsters: those that pose an external threat and those that pose an internal threat. The first type is found in films such as *Mimic* (1997), *Them!* (1954), and *Independence Day* (1996), in which the threat is "out there" lurking, stalking the characters. The primary motivation for the characters is physical survival. If the creature gets them, they die. If they get it, it dies. It's a simple equation, and one that is duplicated in film after film. It employs the most basic principle of scripting conflict—place your character in a life-threatening position from which there is no apparent escape, then, after a series of failures, have him extract himself from the situation through the use of his physical or mental prowess. The threat embodied in Lederer's *Thing* is external. Hawks and the studio even intensified the externality of the creature by keeping photos of the creature out of publicity stills and posters, and by keeping the creature out of frame throughout most of the film. Their motivation was to clearly establish the Thing's otherness.

Like all science fiction and horror films in which the threat is external, the resolution in Lederer's *Thing* involves a standoff between human and other. The humans represent good; the Thing represents evil. When the human side emerges victorious, human superiority in the universe is reaffirmed, and the expectations of the audience are satisfied.

An external threat simplifies all elements of a story. To survive the creature, one stays alive. To locate it, one finds its lair or hiding place. To defeat it, one merely figures out how to kill it. But an internal threat, such as we find in Lancaster's *Thing,* is much more insidious and complicated. A heartbeat is no longer indicative of survival. An internal change may have occurred, one that is not even accessible to human consciousness. Therefore, it is difficult for a character to determine if he has escaped the threat, and virtually impossible for him to locate it. To locate the threat, he must first be able to separate himself from its source. But how do you determine where Mr. Hyde ends and Dr. Jekyll begins? How do you separate David Banner from the Hulk?

You cannot destroy what you cannot locate, and an internal threat is hard to locate. It haunts the unfathomed shadows of the unconscious. Furthermore, when the threat is internal, there is no place to run, no place to hide, and no way to get away from it. You carry it with you wherever you go, and any attempt to destroy it also threatens to destroy self.

Because the threat is primarily internal in Campbell's original story, the novella, as Lancaster notes, contains "mostly talk." One of the problems confronting Lancaster when he was writing the screenplay was how "to turn it [the story] into physical action as well as verbal action."[6] He solves this problem by inserting actions scenes that present the threat as other, as in the kennel sequence.

```
INT. TUNNEL

Clark, sleepy, irritated, makes his way down the freez-
ing corridor. The wind soughing loudly overhead.

CLARK

Reaches the kennel door. The savage outpouring of noise
from within baffles and angers him. He unlatches the
door.

                    CLARK
              What's got into. . . .

Smack! Just as he opens the door, two dogs, as if jet-
tisoned from a cannon, knock him off his feet. Growls,
barks, snarls. And a screeching from within.

INT. KITCHEN

MacReady is fetching himself a beer. The sound of the
```

6. From an interview with Bill Lancaster appearing in *Starlog* (May 1982).

far-off screeching. He freezes. A Beat. He turns and
sprints.

HIS BEER CAN

as it smashes the glass of the fire alarm. He pulls the
lever.

INT. TUNNEL
The alarm is blaring throughout the camp. MacReady,
Garry, Norris run through the narrow tunnel led by
Clark. MacReady carries a shotgun. Garry, half-dressed,
has his .44. Clark, a fire ax.

                    CLARK
          I don't know what the hell's in there, but
          it's weird and pissed off, whatever it is.

INT. HALLWAY

Chaos. Men, half-naked, bounce from their cubicles.
Pulling on their pants, digging into shoes.

INT. CHILDS' CUBICLE

Childs is grappling with his belt buckle.

                    CHILDS
          Mac wants the what??

                    BENNINGS
             (at the doorway)
          That's what he said. Now! Move!

Bennings is off.

INT. TUNNEL

as the men approach the locked kennel door. The two
dogs, thrown into Clark, bark ferociously and scratch
at the door trying to get back in. One is badly blood-
ied.

The fight inside rages on. MacReady and Clark brace
themselves by the narrow door. Norris and Garry hold
back the two hysterical dogs. Clark undoes the latch
and he and MacReady enter the kennel.

188

The Screenplay Adaptation

The light has been broken and it is pitch black. Mac-
Ready snaps on his flashlight. Norris and Garry can't
contain their animals and the dogs burst into the room.
They smash into MacReady and send him sprawling. Total confusion: the dogs; the men; the screeching; the
blackness.

                    CLARK
          Mac, where are you?

MacReady gropes for his flashlight and rights himself.
He finds Clark. Then shines it around the cramped room
trying to get his bearings.

The light finds a mass of dogs in a wild melee in the
corner.

Barking mixed with hissing, a gurgling, a screeching.
Dogs being hurled about and then charging back into the
fray with a vengeance.

The flashlight illuminates parts of some "thing." A
dog. But not quite. Impossible to tell. It struggles
powerfully. Garry pokes his head into the blackness.

                    GARRY
          What's going on, damn it?

MacReady aims his shotgun at the entire pack.

                    MAC READY
          I'm going to shoot.

                    CLARK
          No! Wait!!

Clark wades into the pack, grabs at dogs' hides and
throws them back. He then wields his ax into the fray,
chopping and hacking away at the gurgling, hissing sil-
houette.

From out of nowhere, a large, bristly, arachnid-like
leg springs up and wraps around Clark's ax. It sends
Clark smashing violently into the wall.
(Lancaster 31-33)

The Thing's assimilation of the dogs in the kennel is set in opposition
to the men, thus establishing a visual metaphor for what we later learn

is primarily an internal conflict. What occurs physically to the dogs, occurs psychologically to the men.

Lancaster, to his credit, does not abandon or subvert the internal threat. He sets up chaotic battle sequences in order to generate motion on the screen, but the real threat of the Thing is still the threat to the individual. The further we get into the screenplay, the more frequently the dialogue contains questions of identity. People disappear and reappear, and throughout, Lancaster seasons the dialogue with double entendres that throw identity into question. All the following, for example, occur in a span of only four pages.

```
"What's taking you?!" (Childs asks Nauls)
"Where are you Garry?" (Childs)
"Where's . . . Where's Garry?" (Childs)
"Garry's missing!" (Childs)
"MacReady, that you?" (Norris)
"Where's Sanchez?" (MacReady)
"Who . . . Who is that?" and "Hey, who. . . ."
   (MacReady)
"Where the hell were you?" (MacReady to Sanchez)
"Anybody see Fuchs . . . or hear him? . . . Huh?"
   (MacReady)
"We've got to find Fuchs." (MacReady) (76-80)
```

As the story accelerates toward its climax, Lancaster establishes a psychological sense of misplaced identities, precisely what the Thing threatens.

An internal threat jeopardizes identity itself. Not just life, but the essential value of life—an individual's ability to be the one living it. Lancaster's script in Carpenter's able hands succeeds, without kowtowing to narrative clichés, to map the paranoia of self-doubt. The film doesn't promote communal values, and doesn't contain the starry-eyed optimism of movies such as *Independence Day* and *Star Wars*. It recounts the story of a man's struggle to maintain his individualism and hold on to the one quality that separates him from the herd—the strength of his will, and in doing so, compels us to question ourselves.

The Thing, like all good tragedies, forces us to question sacrosanct beliefs; therefore, it makes us uncomfortable. Unlike films such as *Scream, Friday the 13th,* and *Alien, The Thing* does not let us off the hook at the end. It does not validate our expectation that everything will turn out for the best. It shows us that order is not always restored and the monster is not always vanquished. But what is particularly brilliant about Lancaster's version of *The Thing* is that it drags us into the nightmare, raising in us the same questions that its characters confront.

Who am I? Who are you? Whom can I trust?

Lancaster's and Lederer's variant adaptations of Campbell's short story expose creative contributions rendered during adaptation. Working from the same source material, Lancaster and Lederer produce significantly different screenplays, indicating that screenplay adaptation is often more than simple redaction and can be considerably more involved than translation. The finest adaptations (e.g., Kubrick's *Shining*, Kaufman's *Adaptation*, Nunnally Johnson's *The Three Faces of Eve*, Richard Brooks's *In Cold Blood*, and so on) can stand alone as original creative works, having equaled or surpassed their source material.

7

The Original Screenplay
and Aesthetic Commerce

Natural Born Killers

Original screenplays can be traced back to the beginning of the twentieth century when Edwin Porter wrote the scenario for *The Great Train
Robbery* in 1903 (Ramsaye 416–22). However, Frank J. Marion's *The Sub-
urbanite* was the first scenario to be copyrighted as a "dramatic composition." The Biograph Company and American Mutoscope copyrighted
the scenario on November 25, 1904, technically making it the first legally recognized original work written for the screen. Some debate over
the scenario ensued between the U.S. Copyright Office and attorneys
representing Biograph and Mutoscope over whether the scenario quali-
fied as a dramatic composition (see Loughney). The scenario for *Sub-
urbanite* is little more than a scene list, of the type Georges Méliès used
years earlier, coupled with a summary of the story, like those found in
the Edison catalogue. Nevertheless, the copyright was issued and the
original scenario legally acquired the status of a dramatic composition.
Thus, the origin of the screenplay proper is primarily a legal issue. The
distinction between an original screenplay and a screenplay adaptation
is also primarily legal in nature.

Many of the questions raised in adaptation studies are deemed
moot when considering an original screenplay. Thomas Leitch provides
a back door into these issues by asking questions regarding screenplay
adaptation that still remain to be explored and answered.

Several fundamental questions in adaptation theory remain unasked, let alone unanswered. Everyone knows, for example, that movies are a collaborative medium, but is adaptation similarly collaborative, or is it the work of a single agent—the screenwriter or director—with the cast and crew behaving the same way as if their film were based on an original screenplay? Since virtually all feature films work from a pre-existing written text, the screenplay, how is a film's relation to its literary source different from its relation to its screenplay? Why has the novel, rather than the stage play or the short story, come to serve as the paradigm for cinematic adaptations of every kind? Given the myriad differences, not only between literary and cinematic texts, but between successive cinematic adaptations of a given literary text, or for that matter between different versions of a given story in the same medium, what exactly is it that film adaptations adapt, or are supposed to adapt? Finally, how does the relation between an adaptation and the text it is explicitly adapting compare to its intertextual relationships with scores of other precursor texts? (Leitch 150)

Questions about screenplay adaptation are also questions about the original screenplay. Unlike adaptations, an original screenplay has no *easily identifiable* textual precedent; yet, this distinction has more to do with legal issues of ownership than with creative issues. Screenplay adaptations based on novels, short stories, poems, stage plays, songs, newspaper articles, and so on, have varying legal obligations to the copyright owners of source materials. Screenplays such as Charlie Kaufman's *Adaptation* (2002), based on Susan Orlean's *The Orchid Thief* and Woody Allen's *Everything You Ever Wanted to Know about Sex but Were Afraid to Ask* (1972), based on David Reuben's book of the same title, owe no more to their source material than Paul Schrader's *Taxi Driver* (1976) owes to Harry Chapin's song "Taxi," Arthur Bremer's diaries, and Dostoyevsky's *Notes from the Underground*; *Taxi Driver*, however, is marked as an original screenplay while the others are considered adaptations. On the flip side, screenplays such as Stewart Raffill and Stanford Sherman's *Ice Pirates* (1984) and Tim Curnen, R. J. Robertson, and Jim Wynorski's *Forbidden World* (1982) are considered original screenplays despite their almost total reliance on George Lucas's *Star Wars* (1977) and Dan O'Bannon and Ronald Shusett's *Alien* (1979), respectively.

The point where derivation becomes adaptation is nebulous when we approach the boundaries between the two. At the extremes, determinations are relatively simple, though never absolute. We can, for example, map the relationship between Dashiell Hammett's novel *The Maltese Falcon* and John Huston's screenplay adaptation of the novel with a great deal of certainty. Authorial determination is not as simple for Kaufman's *Adaptation*. In the end, the quest for origins, though enlightening, may never be definitive except as a matter of legal ownership. Kaufman's *Adaptation* is an adaptation by legislative mandate; its debt to Orlean's book is a legal issue, not a creative one. Curnen and collaborators' *Forbidden World* is an original screenplay, not because of its autonomy from extant texts, but because no legal link has been established between it and other, extant works.

Even when a screenplay is written for the screen, issues of authorship can be complicated. Consider, for example, *Natural Born Killers*, for which Oliver Stone (along with David Veloz and Richard Rutowski) received a writing credit, but which was originally written by Quentin Tarantino. Tarantino's work, according to the Writers Guild of America guidelines, only merits a "story by" credit, a meager designation that shrouds Tarantino's contribution to the film and discounts the amount of Tarantino's original screenplay that survived Stone's revision. As a result, reviewers and critics have given little credit to Tarantino. Richard Corliss, for example, in his review for *Time*, attributes *Natural Born Killers'* origin to Tarantino, but claims that Tarantino's script "got spun and spindled" by "Stone and his collaborators" (Veloz and Rutowski), implying that Oliver Stone's film bears little resemblance to Tarantino's original vision. Edward Guthman in the *San Francisco Chronicle* argues that *Natural Born Killers* is "bolder than anything he's [Stone] done on screen before," but fails to adequately recognize Tarantino's contribution. When I first examined copies of Tarantino's third draft (March 12, 1991) and Stone and collaborators' reworking of that script (draft five, May 11, 1993), I expected to find what colleagues and film aficionados assured me I would find: a severe and comprehensive revisioning of a Tarantino "story." I expected to find only a kernel of the final product in Tarantino's script. After all, virtually no one, when discussing *Natural Born Killers*, was saying much about Tarantino. And Tarantino, in a media blitz for *Pulp Fiction*, wasn't saying much about *Natural Born*

Killers. What Tarantino did say wasn't favorable. He openly censured Stone's adaptation and disassociated himself from the project. Nonetheless, Tarantino's contribution to the film is significant, even though Stone's *Natural Born Killers* is not the film Tarantino would have made. *Natural Born Killers* is a Tarantino script in a Stone frame.

The heart of Stone's *Natural Born Killers* is in Tarantino's screenplay: a razor-sharp critique of the media's culpability with the violence it feeds on, skillfully and stylishly rendered in a self-reflexive cinematic roller coaster ride. *Natural Born Killers* outlines the relationship between the media and violence. Like Mickey and Mallory's marriage of blood at the Rio Grande Gorge (Stone's addition), the media depends on "natural born killers" as much as "natural born killers" depend on the media. The media provides killers with infamy while killers provide the media with sound bites and images. This union of murderers and media gives birth to contemporary culture. Mickey is Mickey Mouse with a .9 mm, loveable and deadly. Mickey and Mallory are the M&Ms of violence, providing the media one tasty tidbit after another.

Tarantino continues the gritty, street-level violence found in films such as Martin Scorsese's *Taxi Driver* (1973, one of Tarantino's favorite films), Gus Van Sant's *Drugstore Cowboy* (1989), and Brian De Palma's *Blow Out* (1981, another of Tarantino's favorite films). His heroes are brutal, dishonest men striking out at a universe gone mad with meaninglessness. But Tarantino's vision is focused; Stone, in contrast, struggles to put the "big picture" on the page, literally and metaphorically. Stone wants answers. When he screams "why?" he expects a reply—Tarantino does not. This difference in perspectives represents the primary difference between Tarantino's and Stone's visions and, we can presume, the motivation behind Stone's (re)vision of Tarantino's *Natural Born Killers.*

Technically, Stone gave Tarantino's script unity, added coherence, and sought to suture Tarantino's fragmented style. For those who love the dynamically disjointed style of *Reservoir Dogs* (1992), *True Romance* (1993), and *Pulp Fiction* (1994), Stone's version is sacrilege; for those who prefer the clear messages and unity of *Wall Street* (1987), *Born on the Fourth of July* (1989), and *JFK* (1991), Stone's version is an improvement. Those who find value in both can appreciate Stone's changes while remaining sympathetic with Tarantino's original vision.

Fig. 12. Mickey (Woody Harrelson) and Mallory (Juliette Lewis)
take on symbolic proportions in Oliver Stone's revision
of Quentin Tarantino's *Natural Born Killers* (1994).

From the first sequence of *Natural Born Killers*, Stone's vision is at work. Tarantino begins his script in a New Mexico coffee shop/diner with Mickey ordering a piece of key lime pie, quickly establishing Mickey Knox as a man with a taste for something different. Mickey passes on "apple" pie (an obvious symbol of the American mainstream) to try something that the waitress tells us is "an acquired taste." Stone enlarges Tarantino's scene and darkens the foreshadowing by adding the following image to the opening of the script.

> A black scorpion crawls towards us on hot tarmac. The sound of an approaching PICKUP. A tire crushes the life from the scorpion, CAMERA rising from it to reveal a desolate DINER in the middle of nowhere. (1)

This short but effective establishing shot serves three purposes. First, it offers the image of the crushed scorpion as a symbol for the violence that takes place throughout the film. The scorpion, like all of Mickey and Mallory's victims, was merely in the wrong place at the wrong time and paid for this with its life. Second, the opening introduces the approaching pickup that will shortly deliver Sonny, Otis, and Earl, "three tough-looking rednecks," three *scorpions*, to the diner—their hot tarmac. Third, it starts the screenplay on an active rather than a static image.

Stone builds on the "acquired taste" Tarantino scripts for Mickey. Toward the end of Stone's script, during the prison riot and Mickey and Mallory's bloody escape, Wayne Gale, a narcissistic Geraldo Riveraesque television journalist, acquires "the taste" when he is seduced by the violence:

```
. . . [Wayne] reaches down inside himself and grabs the
gun off a dead Deputy—and fires a blast into an oncom-
ing DEPUTY who drops. He fires another, and another!

                    WAYNE
    YOU BASTARDS! YOU FUCKSHITEATIN BLOODY BASTARDS!!!
(117)
```

Although melodramatic, this shift in Wayne's character (absent from Tarantino's script) helps to unify Stone's message—violence is infectious. Furthermore, Stone holds the media just as responsible as the criminals for the carnage, equating the shooting of a camera with the shooting of a gun; both, when mishandled, can be deadly. Stone places Wayne's shift to violence immediately after Mickey's line:

```
                    MICKEY
    Get the camera! Get the fucking camera!
```

Instead of the camera, Wayne picks up a gun and "shoots," inviting us to question whether or not there is much of a difference between the two means of perpetuating violence. Afterward, Stone drives the point home.

```
Wayne is pumped, yelling.

                    WAYNE
    It was great! It was fuckin' great!

Mickey patches his shoulder up.
```

MICKEY
I'm proud of ya! (gives him a high five) Got the
feeling now?

WAYNE
I'm alive! For the first fucking time I'm alive!
Thank you Mickey. Let's kill all these motherfuck-
ers!

*Mallory takes the gun away from him, gives him the
video.*

WAYNE
No! No!

MALLORY
Sorry Wayne, you're not centered. You keep shooting
with that. (119)

This camaraderie among Wayne and Mickey and Mallory is absent
from Tarantino's script, in which Wayne tries but is unable to bond
with his captors:

WAYNE
Mickey, can I talk to you alone?

MICKEY
No.

WAYNE
This is crazy. You can't escape like this.

MICKEY
Probably not, but we're gonna give it the old college try.

WAYNE
We'll all be killed.

MALLORY
Exciting, isn't it? (112)

From this point forward, through the escape and Wayne's eventual execution, Wayne is an order taker. Mickey and Mallory have all the real
power. Media is the captive of the violent criminal.

199

Tarantino's strength is character. He is a master at crafting faces from the underbelly of life. But, in an attempt to provide the script an overarching message, Stone makes quite a few alterations to the characters. Stone's changes to Mickey and Mallory are few but significant. Mickey and Mallory become, for Stone, "angels" of death. Mallory, in particular, becomes a dancer and a poet. For example, Stone extends Tarantino's "outrageous PROCESS SHOT" at the beginning of the film, adding directions that betray his desire to instill some higher truth in the characters:

> The CAR crashes off the road, through a barbed wire fence, fishtails—races on, mowing through brush. Mickey floors it and howls to get 400 horses under control. MALLORY yells. Can you believe? Can you see Life in Death? (5)

None of this moralizing is present in Tarantino's version. Furthermore, Stone adds a scene after the process shot in which Mickey and Mallory seem to muse over their higher purpose:

> EXT. NIGHT—STARS
>
> A Vault of Southwest Stars, clean as milk, pouring down on the TWO LOVERS in the middle of nowhere. Mickey peeing in the dark. Softer Music (Cowboy Junkies' "Sweet Jane" style).
>
> MICKEY
> Goddamn! Looks like the world's comin' to an end, Mall.
>
> Mallory is dancing barefoot on the hood of the car. As she sings/talks, the stars become light-moving explosions into the earth.
>
> MALLORY
> (dreamy, looking up)
> I see angels Mickey . . . comin' down for us from heaven. I feel their feathered wings . . . I see you ridin' a red horse, drivin' the horses, whippin' 'em—they're spittin,' frothin' all over the mouth—comin' right at us . . . I see the future . . . and there's no death Mickey . . . cause you and I are angels.

```
She gets out of the car. Mickey, buttoning up, turns to
look at her for a moment.

                        MICKEY
        That's goddamn poetry . . . damn I love you Mall.
(6)
```

Here, as throughout the script, Stone shapes Mallory as a poet for an age of violence. Mickey and Mallory become more than the "natural born killers" in Tarantino's script; they become agents of some higher truth—harbingers of the new violence, representatives of a culture in decay. Later, Stone places Mickey and Mallory, full of snake venom, at a drive-in movie, seemingly for no other reasons than to establish the link between visual representation and Mickey and Mallory's violent cultural behavior (a connection Tarantino subtly implies but does not aggrandize) and to place Mickey and Mallory near the site where Scagnetti dumps his victim's body. At the drive-in, Stone has Mickey and Mallory redisplay their spiritual sensitivity (in case we missed it the first time):

```
                        MALLORY
        Angels Mickey . . . I see angels.

                        MICKEY
        Ya, I see em.

                        MALLORY
        They're guarding us. Each step we're together . . .
        Oh God . . . it's perfect. We're gonna make it
        Mickey . . . we're gonna . . .

                        MICKEY
        Goddamn Mall, that's poetry. (23-24)
```

Stone takes every opportunity to expand the subtleties of Tarantino's script into metaphysical issues and imply that transcendental forces are exerting influence over human behavior. For example, in a courtroom sequence, Tarantino describes "Mickey's *demonic* glare" [my emphasis] right before he kills a witness on the stand. Stone builds this look into a thread that runs through the entire script, an axis around which he constructs his moral point.

Stone's Mickey is not merely demonesque, he is possessed of a demon. The stereotypical wise, old Indian (perhaps Stone's most glaring addition), sees Mickey's demon. After Mickey shoots the Indian, the only murder for which Mickey and Mallory show any remorse, a "DEMON FACE" is superimposed over Mickey's reflection. It is the same demon face Mickey sees during his peyote dream sequence.

The prison riot is not the unleashing of pent-up aggressions by angry men caught in civilization's trap that Tarantino envisioned; rather, it becomes the tool of supernatural forces. McClusky, from the control room, watching the violence on *monitors* (as the clerk at the Drug Zone watches *American Maniacs*, as we watch the film), "sees mayhem":

> Cons fighting cons, fires, yelling, water flowing from
> broken toilets and sinks. Cons are pounding out steel
> mesh windows with pipes. Rape and murder. In the Psych
> Unit: Violence, sexual perversion, people dancing, cry-
> ing, climbing. Everyone feels the demon's arrival.
> (Stone 112)

Stone, by firmly summoning supernatural causes, actually removes responsibility from the characters. The prisoners are "possessed" by the demon, Mickey's demon; they have no choice in their actions—a vivid contrast to Tarantino's characters who choose to commit violence, characters for whom responsibility is never at issue. Note Stone's revisions of the following statements made during Mickey's interview with Wayne Gale:

TARANTINO	STONE
MICKEY	MICKEY
You'll never understand. Me and you, Wayne, we're not even the same species. I used to be you . . . then I evolved. From where you're standing, you're a man. From where I'm standing, you're an ape. I'm here . . . I'm right here . . . and you . . . you're somewhere else, man. You say why? I say why not?	You'll never understand. Me and you, Wayne, we're not even the same species. I used to be you . . . then I evolved. From where you're standing, you're a man. From where I'm standing, you're an ape . . . I'm here . . . I'm still evolving . . . and you, you're stuck somewhere

(later . . .)

else man. You're pre-
senting a reflection of
yourself. You buy and
sell the Fear. You say
why? I say why not?
(later . . .)

MICKEY
Everybody thought I'd
gone crazy. The cops,
my mom, everybody.
But you see, they all
missed the point of the
story. I wasn't crazy.
But when I was hold-
ing the shotgun, it all
became clear. I real-
ized for the first time
my one true calling in
life. I'm a natural
born killer.

(92-95)

MICKEY
. . . I guess . . .
Wayne . . . you just
gotta hold that ol'
shotgun in your hand
and it all 'comes clear
to you like it was for
me that first time.
That's when I knew my
one true calling in
life . . .

. . . Shit, I'm a natu-
ral born killer.

(97)

Stone apparently cannot resist an opportunity to moralize; his Mickey condemns Wayne as a "reflection," a ghost who "buy[s] and sell[s] the Fear" (97), to, in effect, indict the entire television industry for capitalizing on violence. Not surprisingly, Stone, on *Politically Incorrect*, stated that he didn't see himself as a "media person" and blamed the media for "sensationalizing violence for dollars." He said of his efforts on *Natural Born Killers:* "I'm trying to interpret a culture going to hell in a hand basket." By distancing himself from the media, Stone frees himself to criticize it.

Tarantino's Mickey feels no such moral compunction and remains focused on himself without the need to address issues outside his unique universe. Tarantino's dialogue is more definite, more direct. Mickey is not mulling things over and "guessing" what drives him to kill—he knows.

Mickey's murder of the Indian becomes the equivalent of murdering a priest in films of the 1940s and 1950s—justice must be paid. The murder is a key plot point in Stone's script; no longer are the "angels"

Fig. 13. A culpable media surrounds serial killer Mickey Knox
(Woody Harrelson) in *Natural Born Killers* (1994).

on Mickey and Mallory's side. The murder of an Indian medicine man cannot go unpunished. Thus, shortly after the killing, Mickey and Mallory are captured at the Drug Zone. On the television, Gale's *American Maniacs* is playing surveillance footage from one of Mickey and Mallory's convenience store robberies. In the footage, Mickey and Mallory leave behind "one OLD INDIAN," and escape. At the Drug Zone, police subdue Mickey and Mallory. This time they failed to leave one old Indian behind. The spree is apparently over.

Again, to make sure we get the *message*, Stone inserts a couple of reminders:

> Mickey tearing past vitamin displays, knocking down a rack of stuffed animals. His strength is fading. Snake juice coursing through his veins.
>
> FLASH—THE DEAD INDIAN
>
> FLASH—THE SUN. BUDDHA . . . some sign of spiritual hope.
>
> He gets to the door, swings out through the glass. (29)

In killing the wise, old Indian, Mickey violated some higher law. Divine justice is served when Mickey and Mallory are apprehended, convicted, and separated. Although Stone's point is "preachy," he does do a skillful job of integrating it into the story. Mickey's "demon" was passed on to him, presumably by his father (whom he refuses to discuss) just as Mallory's violence is a result of sexual abuse at the hands of her father, just as McClusky's violent nature was passed on from his father:

```
                    MCCLUSKY
      Yeah. My old man beat the tar out of me—but I
      didn't kill him.
```

And Scagnetti's violent nature is a result of watching his mother get gunned down by Charles Whitman at the University of Texas. Violence begets violence; the abused become the abusers. At times Stone's script almost becomes a public service announcement touting the evils of the fast food generation. Stone's characters have a tendency to launch into sermons. Note the following exchange between Scagnetti and Mc-Clusky:

```
                    SCAGNETTI
      Ever since [the day his mom was shot] I've had a
      strong opinion about the psychopathic fringe that
      thrives today in America's fast food culture. I
      tend not to exhibit self-discipline becoming of a
      peace officer.
                    MCCLUSKY
      You got a right Jack. Say, you don't mind d'you, if
      I call you Jack—?

                    SCAGNETTI
                 (ignores the question)
      Not at all. But I tell you what it is. These fucks
      think they're special—Daddy yanked their dicks,
      Momma never gave 'em a hug—so they have carte
      blanche to take innocent life. They think they're
      invincible. I never caught a killer yet who ever
      dreamed he might get caught. And they all look the
      same when I catch 'em—like little kids with their
      hands in the cookie jar.

                    MCCLUSKY
      That's my observation as well. We have an army of
      shrinks who talk about mania and schizophrenia and
```

```
multiphrenia and obsessions. But it's all bullshit.
It's Pride! Arrogance! Somewhere, somehow they get
the idea they're better than everyone else—it makes
me sick. And Mickey and Mallory Knox are the sick-
est I've ever seen. (36-36A)
```

In addition to making Mickey and Mallory "angels" of a higher truth, symbols of a culture gone "to hell in a hand basket," Stone builds Wayne Gale's character into a caricature—a violence-mongering media pimp. Wayne, we learn, not only perpetuates violence through his ratings-hungry broadcasts, but also through his personal life. On the phone with his son, Wayne takes the same aggressive attitude that Mickey does:

```
                        WAYNE
            (pause, his son comes on)
Hi Jimmy, it's your Pop! Yeah so, you going to
Judo? When . . . oh I thought that was today . . .
how was school? . . . Oh next time, you kick his
ass. Daddy'll show you . . . Daddy loves you very
much. (gooing and kissing sounds) (71)
```

Like Mallory's father, McClusky's father, and Mickey's father, Wayne passes violence on to his son. Wayne, like Mickey, is part of the problem. For some, Stone's agenda may be stressed too strongly, his script may be too neat, too tidy, with too many dopplegängers, too overplotted; however, in fairness to Stone, no one criticized Shakespeare because *Hamlet* had too many sons avenging the deaths of their fathers. If we must criticize Stone, we should criticize him for not making his moral issues problematic enough (a trap Shakespeare does not fall into). Wayne, for example, prior to acquiring the "taste" for murder, attempts to keep his family together even though he's pathologically self-interested and involved in an affair with an Asian woman:

```
                        WAYNE
. . . look honey, nothing happened! I swear! I've
been faithful . . . since that incident . . . I
don't know what you think you found. Look we'll
talk about it when I get home . . . about two hours
. . . is Jimmy okay? . . . Of course I'm not okay
. . . this is worse than Baghdad . . . listen if I
```

```
get through this Delores, it's all straight sailing
from now on . . . I love you. (114)
```

Wayne is lying, of course, in accord with his character, but he's still holding the family unit together, as dysfunctional as that family may be. After he kills, his tone changes dramatically:

```
                    WAYNE
Blow it off bitch! You hear me . . . I ain't never
comin' home. I'm free of you. I'm alive! For the
first fucking time I'm ALIVE. So guess what—You
Piss Right Off! (122)
```

Wayne's family, once tenuously held together by deceit, completely disintegrates when Wayne's moral prohibition against murder disappears. Violence begets violence and dissolves the family unit, thus, presumably, the fabric of America. The decay of morality is linear and causally linked to a lust for violence.

The only solution Stone offers for the moral decay of society is banal, at best, and presented as a trite sound bite:

```
                    MICKEY
You know the only thing that kills the Demon? . . .
Love. That's why Mallory is my salvation. She was
teaching me how to love. It's like being in the
Garden of Eden.

                    WAYNE
"Only love can kill the demon." Hold that thought.
(93)
```

However, even with his sermonizing, Stone is a master scriptwriter. Whether or not we agree with the moral positions he so forcibly thrusts upon us, we should not overlook his dramatic skill. Stone knows the screenplay genre well and evidence of his skill abounds. One of his most impressive alterations to Tarantino's script is his reshaping of the character of McClusky. Tarantino's McClusky is part of a group of characters who represent prison authority. In Tarantino's version, McClusky (chairman of the prison board) and Wurlitzer (jail superintendent) are divided symbols of authority. Stone, wisely, reduces Wurlitzer to a deputy warden and transfers all Wurlitzer's significant dramatic actions to McClusky's character (the "Warden" in Stone's script). Mc-Clusky thus becomes a major player in the drama. McClusky brings Scagnetti in to "write the script" of Mickey and Mallory's death; Mc-Clusky negotiates with Wayne Gale over Mickey's interview; and Mc-Clusky takes Wurlitzer's place in the "nose to nose" confrontation with Mickey immediately before Mickey and other's escape. By using one character instead of two, Stone heightens the drama. McClusky and Mickey become polar opposites, moral gunslingers facing off at high noon. McClusky is rounder and larger in Stone's version.

Stone also develops and enlarges the character of Scagnetti, the hard-boiled street-wise cop/writer. Tarantino's Scagnetti is a stereotyp-ical tough cop. The character, as presented in Tarantino's draft, lacks depth. Note how typical Scagnetti's entrance in Tarantino's script is:

Over black screen, we hear:

> CAPTAIN SQUERI
> Send Scagnetti in here.

INT. POLICE STATION (SQUERI'S OFFICE)—DAY

CAMERA is position in the middle of the office. The door is in the middle of the frame.

JACK SCAGNETTI flings the door open and steps inside Squeri's office. Squeri's never seen.

> SCAGNETTI
> You wanted to see me, Capt'n?

> CAPTAIN SQUERI (O.S.)
> Scagnetti, go up to interrogation room C. Dewight McClusky, chairman of the prison board, is waiting to meet you. You're gonna deliver two prisoners from the county jail to Nystrom Insane Asylum in Bakersfield.

> SCAGNETTI
> This is bullshit. I'm a detective. You want an errand boy, call Jerry Lewis.

Scagnetti spins around and leaves the room, SLAMMING the door shut behind him. Captain Squeri shouts after him.

CAPTAIN SQUERI (O.S.)
Jack! (6)

This exchange between the controlling captain and the rebel cop is a cliché, common to virtually every police drama in the last twenty years. Such literary renderings are certainly beneath a writer with Quentin Tarantino's gift for clever, dramatic scenes, a writer who constructed the riveting overdose sequence in *Pulp Fiction* and the intense interrogation scene between Dennis Hopper and Christopher Walken in *True Romance*.

Stone revises Scagnetti into a man with a "sexual obsession with murder." In Stone's script, Scagnetti assumes an ominous visage. Mickey and Scagnetti stand on opposite sides of the law, but they are driven by similar passions. Scagnetti's first entrance in Stone's script is far from cliché:

INT. GAS STATION—DAY

Peering at Mallory's underwear, JACK SCAGNETTI expresses reverence, moving his attention to the hood of the Corvette, dusted with crime powder. He's a cop, one of the best. He consults a LOCAL COWBOY SHERIFF.

SCAGNETTI
Jesus, a perfect ass . . . you can even see the crack . . . that's the back . . . arm . . . her head . . . fuckin' dry saliva drops still on the fender.

He drops down to examine the DEAD ATTENDANT.

SCAGNETTI
. . . poor bastard was eatin' her when she did 'im.

He looks in the attendant's mouth, pulling out a small pocket knife. Using the tweezers, he removes a pubic hair from the dead man's mouth. He holds it to the light, looking at it intensely.

SCAGNETTI
Mallory Knox . . . meet Jack Scagnetti. (11)

209

Scagnetti is a man sexually aroused by a crime scene, concisely framed here by Stone. He is a depraved man with a "taste" for new experiences. Later, when Scagnetti matter-of-factly strangles Pinky, a hooker, and then disposes of her dismembered body at a garbage dump on the edge of town, we learn the depths to which his depravity sinks. Scagnetti is another Mickey, only he does not have Mallory. Not surprisingly then, Mallory becomes the object of his fascination. By the time Scagnetti and Mallory meet alone in Mallory's cell, Stone's Scagnetti is substantially more threatening than Tarantino's Scagnetti.

TARANTINO	STONE
SCAGNETTI Who are you supposed to be? Squeaky Fromme? Is that it? Is Mickey your Charles Manson? Is Mickey Jesus? Is that the attraction? Or does he just got a big dick? *Scagnetti changes to Mallory's other ear.* That's it, isn't it? Mickey's got a big donkey dick. (83)	SCAGNETTI Who are you supposed to be? Squeaky Fromme? Is Mickey your Charles Manson? Or does he just got a big dick? That's it, isn't it? Mickey's got a big donkey dick. But you ain't seen mine. You never been fucked by the real Prince Charming. *Scagnetti changes to Mallory's other ear. He's playing with a cobra here, and he knows it. It turns him on, deeper into sexual obsession with murder.* (94)

Tarantino's Scagnetti is vicious, but he's not in competition with Mickey; Stone's Scagnetti is. Mallory's commitment to Mickey is a challenge to Scagnetti's masculinity, and Scagnetti's need to prove his manhood makes him vulnerable to Mallory and ultimately leads to his downfall:

INT. MALLORY'S CELL—DAY

SCAGNETTI
OK, spread um! . . . I'll show ya I'm the bad motherfucker here!

MALLORY smiles and suddenly starts to dance. Spreading her arms, undulating her belly. She's a natural born dancer.

SCAGNETTI watches her, fascinated, misunderstanding. He peels off his shirt.

> SCAGNETTI
> (changing tone, intimate)
> I know you . . . I saw what you did to that kid at the gas station . . . I know what you like.

> MALLORY
> Yeah? . . . what do you think about . . . right now?

Mallory is weaving like a cobra around him, getting close but never touching him, making him sweat. Pulling his pants down half-way, he takes her seat.

> MALLORY
> Tell me what you want . . .

Scagnetti is screaming with lust and murder. His head revolving 360 degrees around the back of the chair to watch her. He can't help himself. He's not thinking straight. He's lost it.

She gets in his face, very close. About to kiss him first with her belly, then with her lips.

We even think she might be going along with him. He's moving his lips closer to hers. She smiles—that long slow orgasm of a smile.

Then she nails him. Smashing into his face with a head-butt. Breaking his nose in an explosion of blood and pain. Scagnetti lets out a horrible SCREAM. She tears into him. (Stone 104)

Stone has reshaped the scene into an intense seduction. Just as Scagnetti is seduced by Mallory, we are seduced by the scene—coaxed in, half-suspecting that violence lurks beneath the surface. Again, Stone's message is clear: those who find violence sexy and are seduced by it are destined to violent ends: Wayne, Scagnetti, McClusky, and even, in Stone's script (though changed in the film), Mickey and Mallory.

We may agree or disagree with Stone's vision, but we cannot argue against his craft. The only technical sore thumb in the script is the character of Owen. During Mickey and Mallory's escape, when the situation seems hopeless, Owen pops up mysteriously to lead them to safety. Stone offers no setup for Owen's arrival; he plants no seeds earlier in the film to make Owen's arrival seem plausible; he has him appear out of nowhere like a supernatural force, a deus ex machina that literally emerges from the smoke to lead Mickey and Mallory to safety.

Owen wants no more than Wayne wants—to go with Mickey and Mallory. Both ask to be taken along. Neither request is granted. Wayne is killed, because, as Mickey sermonizes, Wayne is self-interested:

```
                      MICKEY
      You're scum Wayne. You did it for ratings. You
      poured gasoline on the fire. You didn't give a shit
      about us or about anything Wayne except yourself.
      That's why nobody really gives a shit about you
      Wayne . . .

      . . . You gonna feed on your own misery.
(130)
```

Wisely, Owen's character was downplayed in the film, reduced to a brief cameo. However, Stone's original vision for him demonstrates Stone's commitment to *message* films. Tarantino ends his script after Wayne's execution, at the point when the camera runs out of film. Tarantino's conclusion is open-ended, but forceful and reflexive; it leaves us to wonder if the story is ever really over. The last scene in Stone's script is trite. Mickey and Mallory refuse to take Owen to Mexico with them because, presumably, Mickey and Mallory are a nation of two, and, in a nation of two, there is no room for another citizen. Owen is disappointed because, as he puts it, he'd "really like a *taste* of old Mallory" (my emphasis). Like Mickey and Scagnetti, Owen is interested in the "wild kind." When Owen realizes that Mickey is standing between Mallory and him, he shoots Mickey. But Owen's murder of Mickey is more than a simple execution; it is an evil rite of passage:

```
                      MALLORY
      You better pull over and dump this prick before I
      really get mad, Mickey.
```

212

```
Mickey pulls to a sever stop, turns.

                    MICKEY
     All right Owen . . .

He is staring down the barrel of Owen's gun. Owen has a
crazy grin on his face.

SPECIAL EFFECT: Owen now has the face of the DEMON!

Mickey understands. He laughs.

Owen pulls the trigger, a BLAST fills the screen.

Mallory turns in STOP MOTION, looking at Owen with
vengeance in her eyes. She SCREAMS at what she sees.
ANOTHER BLAST fills the screen.

                    CUT TO BLACK: (134)
```

The demon has been transferred to Owen. The cycle continues. Ironically, Stone, in an attempt to point to the ills of society, to affix blame on the media for perpetuating violence in American culture, actually removes the onus of responsibility for violence from the people who commit violence. Mickey and Mallory, the prisoners in the riot, and Owen at the end, are all pawns of the demon, unable to command their own destiny. We are repeatedly told that what happens to Mickey and Mallory, and Wayne, and Owen, is *fate*. Thus, the real battle rages in the abstract—between demons and love, between reality and representation, and *not* between men.

Stone is a master at his craft, but his materials are the materials of moral allegory. Tarantino, an equally competent craftsman, is a writer of human drama. Both visions collide in *Natural Born Killers*. Stone produced a critique of media and its culpability in the violence it (re)presents; however, Tarantino deserves credit for the screenplay's acerbic drama and violently sharp edges.

The loss of authority Tarantino sacrificed to Stone is indicative of a situation Morris E. Cohn pointed out in 1947, that for a screenwriter "to get his work done, . . . he must very often give up his ownership" (184). This is a problem inherent in aesthetic commerce. When art becomes product, commercial forces exert influence over the art. The original screenplay is arguably the most likely candidate to reshape

213

aesthetics in the film industry, yet, because of its unpredictability as a salable product, it is also less likely to be produced.

What is needed is more close examination of the screenplay (both those written for the screen and adaptations of previously existing works), more interrogation of the screenplay's function within the larger disciplines of film and literature, and further critique of the screenplay's role within the broader cultural landscape. Only when scriptwriting ceases to be, as Frank Capra has noted, "the least understood and the least noticed" (iv) part of the filmmaking process can we begin to understand Orson Welles's opinion that the writer should "have the first and last word in film-making, the only better alternative being the writer-director, but with the stress on the first word" (qtd. in Thomas 9). Only by turning our attention to the screenplay can we hope to map the territory occupied by this important American literary form.

Works Cited

Abrams, Brett L. "Latitude in Mass-Produced Culture's Capital." *Frontiers: A Journal of Women Studies* 25.2 (2004): 65–95.

Adams, Hazard, ed. *Critical Theory since Plato*. New York: Harcourt Brace Jovanovich, 1971.

"AFI's 100 Years . . . 100 Movies." *American Film Institute*. 1998. 26 Sept. 2004. http://www.afi.com/tvevents/100years/movies.aspx.

Allen, Michael Patrick, and Anne E. Lincoln. "Critical Discourse and the Cultural Consecration of American Films." *Social Forces* 82.3 (2004): 871–94.

Allen, Woody. *Four Films of Woody Allen*. New York: Random House, 1982.

"All-Time USA Box Office Leaders." Filmsite.org. Created by Tim Dirks. 1996–2004. 26 Sept. 2004. http://www.filmsite.org/boxoffice.html.

Ansen, David. "Review of *The Thing*." *Newsweek* 28 June 1982.

Aristotle. *On Rhetoric*. Trans. George A. Kennedy. New York: Oxford UP, 1991.

———. *Poetics*. Trans. S. H. Butcher. Dramabook. Vol. [D27]. New York: Hill and Wang, 1961.

Armer, Alan A. *Writing the Screenplay: TV and Film*. 2nd ed. Belmont: Wadsworth, 1993.

Axelrod, Mark. *Aspects of the Screenplay*. Portsmouth: Heinemann, 2001.

Baker, Carlos. *Ernest Hemingway: A Life Story*. New York: Scribner, 1969.

Balázs, Béla. *Theory of the Film*. New York: Dover, 1970.

Baudry, Jean-Louis. "Ideological Effects of the Basic Cinematographic Apparatus." *Film Quarterly* 28.2 (1974–75): 39–47.

Bazin, André. "De la politique des auteurs." *Cahiers du Cinéma* 70 (April 1957): 2–11.

———, and Hugh Gray. *What Is Cinema?* Berkeley: U of California P, 1967.

Beauchamp, Cari. *Without Lying Down: Frances Marion and the Powerful Women of Early Hollywood*. New York: Scribner, 1997.

Bell, Derrick. "The Sexual Diversion: The Black Man/Black Woman Debate in Context." *Speak My Name: Black Men on Masculinity and the American Dream*. Ed. Don Belton. Boston: Beacon P, 1995. 144–54.

Belton, Don. "Introduction: Speak My Name." *Speak My Name: Black Men on Masculinity and the American Dream*. Ed. Don Belton. Boston: Beacon P, 1995. 1–5.

Bevington, David, ed. *The Complete Works of Shakespeare*. 3rd ed. London:

Scott, Foresman, 1980.

Bielby, Denise D., and William T. Bielby. "Women and Men in Film: Gender Inequality among Writers in a Culture Industry." *Gender and Society* 74.2 (1996): 248–70.

Bigsby, C. W. E. *David Mamet*. London: Routledge and Kegan Paul, 1985.

Billson, Anne. *The Thing*. London: BFI, 1997.

Blesh, Rudi. *They All Played Ragtime*. New York: Knopf, 1950.

Bogle, Donald. *Toms, Coons, Mulattoes, Mammies, and Bucks: An Interpretive History of Blacks in American Films*. 4th ed. New York: Continuum, 2002.

Boon, Kevin Alexander. *Chaos Theory and the Interpretation of Literary Texts: The Case of Kurt Vonnegut*. Lewiston: Edwin Mellen P, 1997.

Browning, Todd, and Garrett Fort. *Dracula*. Screenplay, 4th draft—final, 26 Sept. 1930. Vol. 13 of *Universal Filmscripts Series—Classic Horror Films*. *Dracula: The Original Shooting Script*. New York: MagicImage Filmbooks, 1990.

Brunette, Peter, and David Wills. *Screen/Play: Derrida and Film Theory*. Princeton: Princeton UP, 1989.

Buckland, Warren. "A Close Encounter with *Raiders of the Lost Ark*: Notes on Narrative Aspects of the New Hollywood Blockbuster." *Contemporary Hollywood Cinema*. Ed. Steve Neale and Murray Smith. London: Routledge, 1998. 166–77.

Burnett, Charles. Interview. *African-American Screenwriters Now*. Erich Leon Harris. Beverly Hills: Silman-James P, 1996. 19–35.

Cain, James M. *Double Indemnity*. New York: Vintage, 1992.

Callahan, George, and George Wallace Sayre. *The Shanghai Cobra*. Dir. Phil Karlson. 1945.

Cannistraro, Philip V. "Fascism and Italian-Americans in Detroit, 1933–1935." *International Migration Review* 9.1 (1975): 29–40.

Campbell, John Wood. "Who Goes There?" *The Best of John W. Campbell*. Ed. Lester del Rey. New York: Ballantine, 1976.

Capra, Frank. "Preface." *Best American Screenplays*. Ed. Sam Thomas. New York: Crown, 1986. iv.

Carpenter, Frederic I. "Hemingway Achieves the Fifth Dimension." *PMLA* 69.4 (1954): 711–18.

Chopra-Gant, Mike. *Hollywood Genres and Postwar America: Masculinity, Family, and Nation in Popular Movies and Film Noir*. London: Tauris, 2006.

Coen, Ethan, and Joel Coen. *Barton Fink*. Screenplay, 19 Feb. 1990.

———. *Fargo*. Screenplay, n.d.

———. *Miller's Crossing*. Screenplay, n.d.

Cohn, Alfred Abraham, and Samson Raphaelson. *The Jazz Singer*. Wisconsin/Warner Bros. Screenplay series. Ed. Robert L. Carringer. Madison: Published for the Wisconsin Center for Film and Theater Research by the U of Wisconsin P, 1979.

Cohn, Morris E. "Literary Works: A Question of Ownership." *Hollywood Quarterly* 2.2 (1947): 184–90.

Comolli, Jean-Louis, and Jean Narboni. "Cinema/Ideology/Criticism." *Contemporary Film Theory.* Trans. Susan Bennett. Ed. Antony Easthope. London: Longman, 1983.

Conrich, Ian. "Killing Time . . . and Time Again: The Popular Appeal of Carpenter's Horrors and the Impact of *The Thing* and *Halloween.*" *The Cinema of John Carpenter: The Technique of Terror.* Ed. Ian Conrich and David Woods. New York: Wallflower P, 2004. 91–106.

Corliss, Richard. *Talking Pictures: Screenwriters in the American Cinema, 1927–1973.* Woodstock: Overlook P, 1974.

Cowgill, Linda J. *Secrets of Screenplay Structure.* Los Angeles: Lone Eagle, 1999.

Culler, Jonathan. *Structuralist Poetics: Structuralism, Linguistics, and the Study of Literature.* Ithaca: Cornell UP, 1975.

Cuvier, Georges. Recherches sur les ossements fossiles de quadrupèdes [microform]; Ou, l'on rétablit les caractères de plusieurs espèces d'animaux que les révolutions du globe paraissent avoir détruites, 1812.

De Abreu, Carlos, and Howard Jay Smith. *Opening the Doors to Hollywood.* Beverly Hills: Custos Morum, 1995.

Dean, Ann. *David Mamet: Language as Dramatic Action.* Rutherford: Fairleigh Dickinson UP, 1990.

Dillard, Annie. "Contemporary Prose Styles." *Twentieth Century Literature* 27.3 (1981): 207–22.

Divine, Christian. "Paddy Chayefsky and the Golden Age of Words." *Creative Screenwriting* 10.3 (2003): 55–59.

Dreyer, Carl Theodor. *Four Screenplays.* Trans. Oliver Stallybrass. Bloomington: Indiana UP, 1970.

Eagleton, Terry. "Introduction: What Is Literature?" http://www.dartmouth.edu/~english/Eagle1.html.

Egri, Lajos. *The Art of Dramatic Writing.* New York: Simon, 1960.

Eisenstein, Sergei. "The Dramaturgy of Film Form." *Film Theory and Criticism: Introductory Readings.* Ed. Leo Braudy and Marshall Cohen. 5th ed. New York: Oxford UP, 1999. 25–42.

———. *Potemkin, a Film.* Trans. Gillon R. Aitken. Classic Film Scripts. New York: Simon, 1968.

Eliot, T. S. *The Waste Land. Anthology of American Literature.* Vol. 2. 4th ed. Ed. George McMichael. New York: Macmillan, 1989. 1166–77.

Ellis, Trey. "How Does It Feel to Be a Problem?" *Speak My Name: Black Men on Masculinity and the American Dream.* Ed. Don Belton. Boston: Beacon P, 1995. 9–11.

Ellison, Harlan. "With the Eyes of a Demon: Seeing the Fantastic as a Visual Image." *Creative Screenwriting* 20 (July/August 1998): 23–29, 59.

Epstein, Julius J., Philip G. Epstein, and Howard Koch. "*Casablanca.*" *Best American Screenplays, Complete Screenplays.* Ed. Sam Thomas. New York: Crown, 1986.

Fell, John L. *Film before Griffith.* Berkeley: U of California P, 1983.

Fergusson, Frances. "Introduction." *Aristotle's Poetics.* Trans. S. H. Butcher. New York: Hill and Wang, 1985.

Field, Syd. *Four Screenplays: Studies in the American Screenplay.* New York: Dell, 1994.

———. *Screenplay: The Foundations of Screenwriting.* New York: Delacorte, 1982.

———. *The Screenwriter's Workbook.* New York: Dell, 1984.

Finler, Joel. *The Movie Director's Story.* London: Octopus, 1985.

Foreman, Carl. "*High Noon.*" *Film Scripts.* Vol. 2. Ed. George P. Garrett, O. B. Hardison Jr., and Jane R. Gelfman. New York: Appleton, 1971. Screenplay, 1952.

Francke, Lizzie. *Script Girls: Women Screenwriters in Hollywood.* London: BFI, 1994.

Freud, Sigmund. *The Standard Edition of the Complete Psychological Works of Sigmund Freud.* Vol. 17. Ed. and Trans. James Strachey. London: Hogarth, 1953.

Frost, Robert. "Home Burial." *Anthology of American Literature.* Vol. 2. 4th ed. Ed. George McMichael. New York: Macmillan, 1989. 984–87.

Froug, William. *The Screenwriter Looks at the Screenwriter.* New York: Macmillan, 1972.

Frye, Northrup. *The Anatomy of Criticism.* Princeton: Princeton UP, 1957.

Gates, Tudor. *Scenario: The Craft of Screenwriting.* London: Wallflower P, 2002.

Geuens, Jean-Pierre. *Film Production Theory.* Albany: State U of New York P, 2000.

Glazer, Benjamin. "The Photoplay with Sound and Voice." *Introduction to the Photoplay.* Los Angeles: University of Southern California and the Academy of Motion Picture Arts and Sciences, 1929. 44–57.

Goodman, Michael. Pacific Film Archive. Qtd. in The Thing from Another World (Das Ding aus einer anderen Welt). Celtoslavica. 5 July 2003. http://www.celtoslavica.de/chiaroscuro/films/thing/the_thing.html.

Gross, Linda. "Review of *The Thing.*" *Los Angeles Times* 25 June 1982.

Hammett, Dashiell. *The Maltese Falcon.* Vintage Books ed. New York: Vintage, 1989.

Hampton, Benjamin Bowles. *History of the American Film Industry from Its Beginnings to 1931.* New York: Dover, 1970.

Hemingway, Ernest. *A Farewell to Arms.* New York: Scribner, 1969.

———. *The Sun Also Rises.* New York: Scribner, 2003.

Hillier, Jim. *Cahiers du Cinéma: 1960–1968—New Wave, New Cinema, Reevaluating Hollywood.* Harvard Film Studies. Cambridge: Harvard UP, 1986.

Hinden, Michael. "'Intimate Voices': *Lakeboat* and Mamet's Quest for Community." *David Mamet: A Casebook*. Ed. Leslie Kane. New York: Garland, 1992. 33–48.

Holmer, Paul. *C. S. Lewis*. New York: Harper, 1976.

Horne, William. "See Shooting Script: Reflections on the Ontology of the Screenplay." *Literature Film Quarterly* 20.1 (1992): 48–54.

Horton, Andrew. *Laughing Out Loud: Writing the Comedy-Centered Screenplay*. Berkeley: U of California P, 2000.

———. *Screenwriting for a Global Market*. Berkeley: U of California P, 2004.

———, and Joan Magretta, eds. *Modern European Filmmakers and the Art of Adaptation*. New York: Frederick Ungar, 1981.

Humm, Maggie. *Feminism and Film*. Edinburgh: Edinburgh UP, 1997.

Huston, John. *The Maltese Falcon*. Screenplay, final version, 1941.

Jacobs, Lewis. *The Rise of the American Film*. New York: Harcourt Brace, 1939.

Jenkins, Steve. "*The Thing*." *Monthly Film Bulletin* 49 (August 1982): 158–60.

Kaminsky, Stuart M. *American Film Genres: Approaches to a Critical Theory of Popular Film*. Dayton: Pflaum, 1974.

Kaufman, Charlie. *Adaptation*. Screenplay, rev., 21 Nov. 2000.

Keane, Christopher. *How to Write a Selling Screenplay*. New York: Broadway, 1999.

Keneas, Alex. "Review of *The Thing*." *Newsday* 25 June 1982.

Kuleshov, L. V. *Kuleshov on Film: Writings*. Berkeley: U of California P, 1974.

Laferriere, Dany. "Why Must a Black Writer Write about Sex?" Excerpt. Trans. David Homel. *Speak My Name: Black Men on Masculinity and the American Dream*. Ed. Don Belton. Boston: Beacon P, 1995. 35–41.

Lancaster, Bill. "Interview." *Starlog* (May 1982).

———. *The Thing*. Screenplay, second draft, n.d.

Lane, Christina. *Feminist Hollywood: From* Born in Flames *to* Point Break. Detroit: Wayne State UP, 2000.

Langley, Noel, Florence Ryerson, and Edgar Allen Woolf. *The Wizard of Oz*. Screenplay, 15 March 1939.

Lawrence, Carol Munday. Interview. *African-American Screenwriters Now*. Erich Leon Harris. Beverly Hills: Silman-James P, 1996. 65–81.

Lederer, Charles. *The Thing*. Screenplay.

Lee, Lance. *A Poetics for Screenwriters*. Austin: U of Texas P, 2001.

Leitch, Thomas. "Twelve Fallacies in Contemporary Adaptation Theory." *Criticism* 45.2 (2003): 149–71.

Lerch, Jennifer. *500 Ways to Beat the Hollywood Script Reader*. New York: Fireside/Simon, 1999.

Lindsay, Vachel. *The Art of the Moving Picture: Being the 1922 Revision of the Book First Issued in 1915*. New York: Liveright, 1970.

Logan, John. *The Aviator*. Excerpt. *Vanity Fair* (January 2005): 3–20.

Loughney, Patrick G. "In the Beginning Was the Word: Six Pre-Griffith Motion Picture Scenarios," *Elsaesser* (1990): 211–19. Originally published in *Iris* 2.1 (1984).

Mamet, David. *Glengarry Glen Ross.* Screenplay, first draft, n.d.

Marling, William. *The American Roman Noir: Hammett, Cain, and Chandler.* Athens: U of Georgia P, 1995.

Marx, Karl. *Capital: A Critique of Political Economy.* Vol. 1. Trans. Ben Fowkes. New York: Vintage, 1976.

Mast, Gerald, and Bruce F. Kawin. *A Short History of the Movies.* 5th ed. New York: Macmillan; Toronto: Maxwell Macmillan Canada, 1992.

McCollum, Kelly. "Shaft—The Beginning." Shaft official Web site, 1995. http://www.shaft-themovie.com/thelegend.html. 4 Nov. 2001.

McCreadie, Marsha. *The Women Who Write the Movies: From Frances Marion to Nora Ephron.* New York: Birch Lane, 1994.

McKee, Robert. *Story: Substance, Structure, Style, and the Principles of Screenwriting.* New York: Harper, 1997.

Mellen, Joan. *Big Bad Wolves: Masculinity in the American Film.* New York: Pantheon, 1977.

Mencken, H. L. "A Soul's Adventures." *Smart Set* 49.2 (1916): 150–56.

Micheaux, Oscar. *Lying Lips.* Screenplay, 1939.

Milne, Peter. *Motion Picture Directing: The Facts and Theories of the Newest Art.* New York: Falk, 1922.

Mitchell, Wendy. "William H. Macy Makes Losing Hot with "The Cooler." 2003. IndieWire. 16 Dec. 2005. http://www.indiewire.com/people/people_031219macy.html.

Mulvey, Laura. "Visual Pleasure and Narrative Cinema." *Visual and Other Pleasures.* Bloomington: Indiana UP, 1989.

Münsterberg, Hugo. "From the Film: A Psychological Study: The Means of the Photoplay." *Film Theory and Criticism: Introductory Readings.* Ed. Leo Braudy and Marshall Cohen. 5th ed. New York: Oxford UP, 1999. 401–7.

Nietzsche, Friedrich Wilhelm. "Assorted Opinions and Maxims." 1879.

———. *The Will to Power.* Trans. Walter Arnold Kaufmann and R. J. Hollingdale. Vintage Books ed. New York: Vintage, 1968.

Nyswaner, Ron. *Philadelphia.* Screenplay, 21 Sept. 1992.

Ouellette, Laurie. "Reel Women: Feminism and Narrative Pleasure in New Women's Cinema." *Independent Film and Video Monthly* (April 1995): 28–34.

The Oxford English Dictionary Online (OED). Pennsylvania State University, University Park: Oxford UP.

Palmer, Frederick, and Eric Howard. *Photoplay Plot Encyclopedia: An Analysis of the Use in Photoplays of the Thirty-Six Dramatic Situations and Their Subdivisions. Containing a List of All the Fundamental Dramatic Material to Be Found in Human Experience, Including the Synopses of One Hundred Produced*

Representative Photoplays, with a Detailed Analysis of the Situations Used in Each. Practical Suggestions for Combining Situations, for Testing the Strength and Novelty of Plots, and for Building Plots; and an Index Referring to Each Producer, Author, Star, Story, and Situation Mentioned in the Text. Los Angeles: Palmer Photoplay Corporation Department of Education, 1920.

Patterson, Frances Taylor. *Cinema Craftsmanship: A Book for Photoplaywrights.* New York: Harcourt Brace and Howe, 1920.

———. *Scenario and Screen.* New York: Harcourt Brace, 1928.

Petrie, Graham. "Auteurism: More Aftermath." *Film Quarterly* 27.3 (1974): 61–63.

Pound, Ezra. *Cantos.* New York: New Directions, 1948.

———. "A Retrospect." *Literary Essays of Ezra Pound.* Ed. T. S. Eliot. New York: New Directions, 1935. 3–14.

Preston, John. "Review of *The Thing.*" *New Statesman* 27 Aug. 1982.

Pudovkin, Vsevolod Illarionovich. *Film Technique, and Film Acting.* 1st Evergreen ed. New York: Grove P, 1976.

Rafferty, Terrence. "Now Playing: Auteur vs. Auteur." *New York Times* 22 Oct. 2006, late ed., final, sec. 2.

Ramsaye, Terry. *A Million and One Nights: A History of the Motion Picture.* London: Frank Cass, 1964.

Rank, Otto. *The Double.* Trans. and Ed. Harry Tucker Jr. Chapel Hill: U of North Carolina P, 1971.

Raynauld, Isabelle. "L'importance du scénario dans le cinéma Québécois: Développements d'une pratique d'écriture, de 1896 a 1996." *Études Canadiennes* (June 2002): 209–24.

Rickey, Carrie. "Review of *The Thing.*" *Village Voice* 6 July 1982.

Ruark, Jennifer K. "Professor Seeks to Make Film about Lawyer Who Defended Racist Murderers; Scholarly Press Publishes Screenplays of 3 Novels by Doctorow." *Chronicle of Higher Education* 30 May 2003, A16.

Russin, Robin U., and William Missouri Downs. *Screenplay: Writing the Picture.* Los Angeles: Silman-James P, 2003.

Salt, Barry. "The Early Development of Film Form." *Film before Griffith.* Ed. John L. Fell. Berkeley: U of California P, 1983. 284–98.

Seger, Linda. *The Art of Adaptation: Turning Fact and Fiction into Film.* New York: Owl Books, 1992.

———. *Making a Good Script Great.* New York: Samuel French, 1994.

———, and Edward Jay Whetmore. *From Script to Screen: The Collaborative Art of Filmmaking.* New York: Henry Holt, 1994.

Self, Robert T. *Robert Altman's Subliminal Reality.* Minneapolis: U of Minnesota P, 2002.

———. "Robert Altman and the Theory of Authorship." *Cinema Journal* 25.1 (1985): 3–11.

Selznick, David O. Memo to B. P. Schulberg, General Manager, Paramount

Studios. 8 Oct. 1930.

Shagan, Steven, and Steven Zaillian. *Primal Fear.* Screenplay, 26 Feb. 1995.

Shyamalan, M. Night. *The Sixth Sense.* Screenplay, n.d.

Siodmak, Curt, and Ardel Wray. *I Walked with a Zombie.* Screenplay, n.d.

Slater, Thomas J. "June Mathis: A Woman Who Spoke through Silents." *American Silent Film: Discovering Marginalized Voices.* Carbondale: Southern Illinois UP, 2002. 201–16.

Smyth, J. E. "Anita Loos Rediscovered: Film Treatments and Fiction by Anita Loos. Edited and annotated by Cari Beauchamp and Mary Anita Loos. University of California Press, 2003." *The Moving Image* 5.1 (2005): 161–64.

Stack, Tim. "'X'-Man." Entertainment Weekly's EW.com. 17 Dec. 2006. http://www.ew.com/ew/report/0,6115,1169530_1_0_,00.html.

Stamp, Shelley. "Lois Weber, Progressive Cinema, and the Fate of 'The Work-a-Day Girl' in Shoes." *Camera Obscura* 19.2 (2004): 140–69.

Staples, Donald E. "The Auteur Theory Reexamined." *Cinema Journal* 6 (1966): 1–7.

Sterritt, David. "Fantasy and Sci-Fi: Mixed Signals from Today's Filmmakers." *Christian Science Monitor* 24 June 1982.

Stone, Oliver, David Veloz, and Richard Rutowski. *Natural Born Killers.* Screenplay, fifth draft, 11 May 1993.

Stone, Peter. *Charade.* Screenplay, 1 Oct. 1962.

Storm, Ole. "Introduction." *Four Screenplays.* Bloomington: Indiana UP, 1970. 9–24.

Shusett, Ronald, Dan O'Bannon, and Steven Pressfield. *Total Recall.* Screenplay, fifth draft, n.d.

————, and Gary Goldman. *Total Recall.* Screenplay, final draft, 22 Aug. 1989.

Tarantino, Quentin. *Natural Born Killers.* Screenplay, third draft—rev., 12 Mar. 1991.

————. *Pulp Fiction.* Screenplay, n.d.

————. *Reservoir Dogs.* Screenplay, 22 Oct. 1990.

————. *True Romance.* Screenplay, rev., 1 Aug. 1991.

Thomas, Sam, ed. *Best American Screenplays.* New York: Crown, 1986.

Thompson, Kristen. *Storytelling in the New Hollywood: Understanding Classical Narrative Technique.* Cambridge: Harvard UP, 1999.

Thomson, Desson. "Behind the Screen: Hollywood and the Indie Offerings." WashingtonPost.com. Live online discussion, 29 Oct. 2004. Accessed 11 Sept. 2005. http://www.washingtonpost.com/wp-dyn/content/discussion/2004/10/22/DI2005040307765.html.

Thornton, Billy Bob. *Sling Blade.* Screenplay, n.d.

Tidyman, Ernest. *Shaft.* Screenplay, final draft, 16 Aug. 1970.

Todorov, Tzvetan. *The Fantastic: A Structural Approach to a Literary Genre.* Trans.

Richard Howard. Cleveland: P of Case Western Reserve U, 1973.

Towne, Robert. *Chinatown.* Screenplay, second draft, 7 Sept. 1973.

———. *Chinatown.* Screenplay, third draft, 9 Oct. 1973.

Trottier, David. *A Complete Guide to Writing, Formatting, and Selling Your Script.* Los Angeles: Silman-James P, 1995.

———. *The Screenwriter's Bible.* 4th ed., expanded and updated. Los Angeles: Silman-James P, 2005.

Truffaut, François. "Une certaine tendance du cinéma français." *Cahiers du Cinéma* 31 (January 1954): 15–29.

Turnbull, Margaret (scenario), and Robert Ralston Reed (story). "Witchcraft." *Cinema Craftsmanship.* Ed. Frances Taylor Patterson. New York: Harcourt Brace, 1920.

Uhls, Jim. *Fight Club.* Screenplay, shooting script, n.d.

Wellek, René. *A History of Modern Criticism: 1750–1950, Vol. 5: English Criticism, 1900–1950.* New Haven: Yale UP, 1986.

Wiegman, Robyn. "Race, Ethnicity, and Film." *The Oxford Guide to Film Studies.* Ed. John Hill and Pamela Church Gibson. New York: Oxford UP, 1998. 158–68.

Winsten, Archer. Review of *The Thing. New York Post* 25 June 1982.

Wolfe, Bernard. "Ecstatic in Blackface: The Negro as Song-and-Dance Man." *The Scene before You: A New Approach to American Culture.* Ed. Chandler Brossard. New York: Rinehart, 1955. 51–70.

Worland, Rick. "Before and After the Fact: Writing and Reading Hitchcock's *Suspicion." Cinema Journal* 41 (Summer 2002): 3–26.

Index